India

Loti's idea in going to India was to discover if in the Buddhist faith he could find anything to replace the Catholic religion in which he could no longer believe. He visits the ruined temples of the ancient gods, listens to the languorous Oriental music on the moonlight nights; he experiences nameless dreads, indescribable terrors.

Pierre Loti, perhaps the world's most prolific, romantic and exotic travel writer and novelist, was born as Julien Marie Viaud in Rochefort in Western France in 1850. A childhood fascination with exotic lands across the seas led him to embark on a naval career that enabled him to seek love and adventure in many latitudes. He drew on these real life experiences when writing the romantic novels and travel books that made him one of the most popular authors of his day. Although his prolific output brought him both fame and fortune he remained a romantic escapist and never gave up his beloved naval career. He retired from the French navy in 1910 and died in 1923.

The Pierre Loti Library

Siam

Aziyadé

Egypt

Japan
Madame Chrysanthemum

Morocco

India

Japan and Corea

The Sahara to Senegal

Jerusalem and the Holy Land

Tahiti
The Marriage of Loti

The Iceland Fisherman

A Tale of the Pyrenees

A Tale of Brittany

Pierre Loti: Romance of A Great Writer
Edward B. D'Auvergne

India

Pierre Loti

Routledge
Taylor & Francis Group

LONDON AND NEW YORK

First published in 2002 by Kegan Paul International Ltd

This edition published in 2013
by Routledge
2 Park Square, Milton Park, Abingdon, Oxfordshire OX14 4RN

Simultaneously published in the USA and Canada
by Routledge
711 Third Avenue, New York, NY 10017

First issued in paperback 2016

*Routledge is an imprint of the Taylor & Francis Group,
an informa business*

British Library Cataloguing in Publication Data
A catalogue record for this book is available from the British Library.

Library of Congress Cataloging-in-Publication Data
Applied for.

ISBN 13: 978-1-138-97253-7 (pbk)
ISBN 13: 978-0-7103-0814-6 (hbk)

CONTENTS

INDIA

INTRODUCTION

It is midday on the Red Sea. There is light, light everywhere, so much light that cries of admiration and astonishment are forced from us ; it is as if we issue from gloom into a clear air of boundless space. The passage from our Northern Autumn to the perpetual Summer that reigns here, is made almost imperceptibly by our modern ships that do not heed the wind. Silvery crested waves dance on the blue waters, and the sky seems more distant from the earth ; the clouds, too, have more definite form and are further off ; new depths of space become apparent, and our horizon is extended.

It seems as though our eyes could appreciate new forms and colours in the increasing brightness which we had been unable to perceive before. From what a land of shadows we must have come, and what can this festival of light be that has sprung on us suddenly and unbidden ?

A melancholy brightness pours relentlessly on this land of tombs, this country thick with dust of bygone races ; but we forget it when we reach our northern clime, and are surprised to find it there once more on our return. Its rays shine constantly on the hot and languid gulfs, and on their sand or granite shores ; it bathes the ruins and that world of dead stones which guard the ancestral faith and the secrets of those the Bible tells us of. This melancholy light is ever present, just as it must have been in the old, sacred times, and these things give our narrow imagination a sense of infinity, and tell of a time without beginning or end. The biblical times, however, whose antiquity inspires our trust, are but of yesterday when we look back on the history of the world, fearful in the immensity of the past. This superb and intoxicating brightness is but the passing effect of our slowly decaying little sun upon a favoured zone of our still smaller earth, an earth that nestles close to him, as if frightened by the vast and chill orbits of the other planets.

The blue sky too, enwoven with the phantasy of passing clouds, that looks so deep, is but a thin, deceptive veil that serves to screen the yawning space behind. No, this is all nothing, only the space behind is real.

This empty space, this black abyss into which worlds ceaselessly fall, this kingdom that knows neither commencement nor decay, is the one eternal reality.

I must yet spend some seven or eight days amidst the shining blue of heaven and sky before I reach my journey's end. I make my way to India, the cradle of human faith and thought, with nameless dread, fearing that I may find nothing but a cruel and final deception.

I have not come here to make a trifling call, but to ask or beg the keepers of the Aryan wisdom to give me their belief in the lasting duration of the soul in place of the ineffable Christian faith which has vanished from my soul.

The day declines in wondrous splendour. The sun that draws us with him in the madness of his eternal wandering will soon have passed from our view. Our side of the world will turn towards that deep space, towards that land of shadow which the transparencies of the night air will let us see more clearly. But now the magic of the evening, with the burning rays of coppery rose, steals on us. In the east a chain of desolate mountains, whose granite slopes glow like a furnace, rise from the sea. They are Sinai, Serbal, and Horeb, and the feeling of religious respect, which centuries have impressed upon our race, invades us once more.

The burning summits do not linger long, for the sun has sunk beneath the waters and the evening enchantment is over. Sinai, Serbal, and Horeb fade in the twilight, and are no longer distinguishable. Were they other than crests of jagged rock, idealized in our minds by the superb poetry of Exodus ? Vast and calm night will soon restore all things to their true proportions, for space is already filled by legions of wandering suns which make me think of the black emptiness into which they and we are falling. I dream, too, of the miserable fate of our little planets chained to a sun that they can never hope to reach, ever attempting to narrow the orbits of their mad circlings, instead of plunging into space as do the more glorious suns.

A cloudless limpidity spreads from the zenith to the horizon, and the limitless void into which myriads of worlds fall (like sparks from a rain of fire) is unbared before our eyes.

A sense of alleviation comes from the starry night, like some breath of tenderness or pity that is poured into a pardoned soul.

My God ! If the Indian sages that I seek could but convince me that I might find pardon and pity too.

THE BURIED CITY

CHAPTER I

THE BURIED CITY ·

INDIA at last, with its forests and its jungles. The sun dawns on a forest of vegetation, an ocean of eternal greenery; whilst a boundless plain of mystery and silence stretches from my feet to the extreme horizon.

I watch the light dawning on this silent wilderness of green from the summit of a hill that rises like an island out of the plains. It is India of the forests and the jungles, though veiled in mist. In the centre of Ceylon, sheltered by interlacing trees, there is a spot of profoundest peace: it is the place where the marvellous Anuradhapura stood—the city which was buried in a night of leaves more than two thousand years ago. The day breaks slowly through a leaden sky, thick with storm and gloom. The midnight hour is striking now in France, but here the earth presents this region of crumbling ruins to the sun once more.

Where can the wonderful town be? I look round, like a sailor searching from the mast across the sea, but nothing of human origin is visible. Nothing but trees, trees everywhere, trees in serried ranks, a rolling forest which loses itself in illimitable distance. Lower down there are lakes, inhabited by crocodiles, where herds of wild elephants come at dusk to drink. From the forest and the jungles the morning call of birds is heard. But are there no traces of the marvellous city left?

Here and there, however, are some curious green and wooded hills, which rise in a strangely regular fashion above the leafy plains. They are the towers of old temples and giant dagabas, built two centuries before the reign of Christ; the forest has been unable

[1] This is the literal translation of the Indian name. Anuradhapura was destroyed at the commencement of our era by the great Malabar invasion.

to destroy them, but has wrapped them in its green winding-sheet, covering them gradually with its soil, its roots, its monkeys, and its trailing growths. The place where men worshipped in the earliest times of Buddha is still nobly marked, and the sacred city which slumbers under all these overhanging branches is still here.

Even this hill on which I stand was once a sacred dagaba—built by myriads of the faithful in honour of their prophet, the forerunner and brother of Jesus.

The pediment is guarded by a row of elephants carved in stone, and by gods whose features time has now obliterated. What a delirium of prayer and adoration, and what a din of crashing music must have daily filled this temple in the olden times !

" The Temples and the Palaces of Anuradhapura are numberless, and their golden cupolas and pavilions shimmer in the sun. In the streets are crowds of soldiers armed with bows and arrows. Elephants, horses, chariots, and countless multitudes pass in a continual turmoil. There are jugglers, dancers, and musicians from many lands, whose timbals gleam with golden ornaments."

Now there is silence, shadow, and green night; men have passed away and the forest has closed on everything. The wakening morning shines on all these buried ruins as calmly as it shone on the virgin forest in the first dawnings of creation.

Before visiting the mainland, I must wait some days in Ceylon for the reply of a noble Maharajah whose guest I am to be, and I have preferred to seek shelter here, rather than in the vulgar towns of the coast.

I had to leave Kandy (the home of the old Cingalese kings) before daybreak, travelling through the region of the great palms, where all the magnificence of the equatorial land is unfurled. After midday the appearance of the country changes, it thered palms and areca trees gradually disappear. Doubtless we have entered into a colder zone, for the forests resemble our own more closely. The little coach travels through an incessant, warm, and scented rain, drawn by horses which are changed every few miles. Sometimes we gallop along the streaming road, or fall into an obstinate trot, broken by ugly rushes.

More than once we have to jump down, because some half-trained brute threatens to destroy everything. Two Indians drive our ever-changing team; one holds the reins, whilst the other is ready to jump down should danger threaten. A third blows a horn as we pass through villages scattered amongst tree palms, or warns the slowly-moving zebu carts. We should have reached our destination at eight o'clock, but the storms constantly increase our delay.

Towards evening villages become rarer, and the forest is more dense. There are no more of those cleared spaces which looked so small and so lost by the side of the all-conquering forest; and our trumpeter has no longer need to play for any one.

The palms have altogether disappeared, and now that the day has declined I should have said that we were in some lonely European land where a perpetual summer reigns. It is true that the tangle of climbing plants is more luxuriant, and from time to time we pass a flowering cactus, or some great red lily with twisted petals, or gorgeous butterfly chased by a more gorgeous bird, which tell us that this is not our home. But the illusion of our country and our woods ever returns.

Since sunset we have passed neither village nor trace of man; silence reigns in the green depths through which our road takes its interminable course, and we are travelling much faster now in the warm caressing rain that still beats on us.

As darkness comes on, an insect humming gradually rises from the ground and makes the silence more perceptible. On the damp forest soil myriads of wings keep up a noisy music; such music as has been heard nightly since the birth of the world.

The sky is covered, and the night quite dark. For hours we have trotted rapidly between two great rows of trees, which resemble overgrown and fantastic hedges in some boundless park. Sometimes great

black animals loom out of the shadows and bar our
further progress, harmless and stupid buffaloes which
we must drive aside with whips and cries.   The road
once more resumes its dull monotony, and silence is
only broken by joyous insect rustlings.

One thinks of the forest denizens sheltered by the
calm of night, large and small wild creatures on the
watch or on the prowl, so many pricked ears, and so
many dilated eyes watching the least movement in
the shadowy wood.

The clearing through the mysterious trees extends
ceaselessly in front of us, a pale gray streak hemmed
in by high black walls ; in front, behind, and on all
sides the impenetrable jungles cast their terrifying
shadows on us.

When our eyes have grown accustomed to the
night, we can see, as if in a dream, the vague forms of
velvet-footed prowlers flitting amongst the thickets.

Towards eleven o'clock some little lights are seen,
and the roadsides are strewn with the long stones of
crumbling ruins, and above the trees the silhouette of
giant dagabas stand darkly forth against the gloomy
sky.   I had been warned, so I knew that these were
not hills, but only the temples of the buried city.

We found our night's lodging at an Indian inn,
standing in an exquisite garden, whose flowers
beamed in the light of our passing lamps.

Now the day dawns, and in the forest beneath me
I can hear the birds awakening ; bushes and weeds
like those of the jungles surround me as I stand on
the temple's tower.   Gray-winged bats, whose slumbers I have disturbed, flit in the morning air, and tiny
leaping squirrels, full of vitality and grace, peer at
me from out their leafy hiding-places.

At my feet some of the trees which form the winding street of the dead city are decked as for a spring
pageant with red, rose, and yellow flowers.   Suddenly a storm breaks over their heads, passes on,
and disappears like a mist in the dim distance.

Now the sun quickly rises from the rain-clouds and

beats down upon my head; it is time to seek some shady cover, so I descend the sacred tower by a ladder of branches to the green night where the men of this country dwell.

Amongst the monstrous roots which twist like serpents over the red earth, lie confused heaps of ruins and fallen stones. Hundreds of broken gods, stone elephants, altars, and chimeras are scattered about, giving proof of the fearful havoc wrought by the Malabar conquerors nearly two thousand years ago.

Pious Buddhists of our times have collected the most precious relics from the precincts of the indestructible dagabas, and have ranged the decapitated heads of the old gods in rows along the steps of prostrate temples. Some shapeless and broken altars still stand upright. These they decorate each morning with beautiful flowers and ever-burning lamps.

Anuradhapura in their eyes is still the sacred city where pilgrims from afar come to meditate and pray in the shadow of the great trees.

The dimensions and outlines of the great temples are still marked by sequences of columns, stones, and marbles starting from the towers and losing themselves in the woods. The most sacred spot was only reached after threading an interminable series of passages, which were guarded by inferior gods and monsters, a world of stone images now lying scattered and broken on the ground.

Besides these temples which rise above the swelling jungle, there are hundreds more which have fallen down, also the ruins of countless palaces. There are as many columns hidden in the forest as there are tree trunks, and all mingle in the eternal green twilight.

Towards the beginning of our era, the Princess Sanghamitta, who was a great believer, had a branch of the tree which sheltered Buddha, when the true faith was first revealed to him, brought here from the north of India; that branch still lives and has become a great and complex tree, for after the manner of the banyan the branches have rooted too; it is surrounded by

venerable altars, daily strewn with fresh sweet-smelling
flowers, on whose stones the ever-lighted sacred lamps
keep constant vigil amidst the dim green twilight.

A gloom of sadness is thrown over the forest by the
beautifully sculptured marble porches, whose steps
are guarded by smiling gods, which lead to no house.
Time has left no further trace of these dwellings,
which were of wood, but the steps and paving stones,
and the gorgeous entrances which open on to weeds
and roots and earth.

In one corner of Anuradhapura a village has existed
for several years, a pastoral village which does not
disturb the melancholy of the place, for it is concealed,
like the ruins themselves, under overhanging branches.

The Indians who have returned to the buried city
do not cut down the forest trees, but merely clear away
the brambles and trailing growths, unbaring the fine
sward where their goats and zebus can pasture at their
pleasure, happy in wandering through the sacred groves.

Those who dwell among the sacred ruins, who
bathe in the ponds of the old palaces, think that the
spirits of the princes and the kings of old return.
So they shun the shadows of the great dagabas on
moonlit nights. All conspires to make the spot a
shady refuge for prayer and meditation. A church-
like calm hovers over the woody glens and the fine
carpeting of grass, on which tall trees rain down
showers of blossoms like large azaleas.

How touching it is to see little lamps placed before
the statues broken two thousand years ago, and fresh
flowers that deck these old stones !

It is not usual to offer bouquets to the Indian gods,
but rather to strew the altars with flowers ; jasmines
in large quantities—nothing but the flowers snatched
from their stalks—gardenias and waxy blooms of
heavy odour that form a scented ground on which
Bengal roses and red hibiscus flowers are placed ; and
there are many such scattered over the stones of these
crumbling temples, whose mouldering remains daily
sink deeper into the earth.

THE ROCK TEMPLE

CHAPTER II

THE ROCK TEMPLE

At the edge of the forest which shelters the ruins, and close by the jungle, stands the Rock Temple in which the ancient images of the gods are still preserved intact.

Scattered about in various parts of the wild plain we perceive rocks similar to those of the temple.

Some ancient cataclysm must have hurled these smooth, round masses here. The swollen, brown shapes that look like enormous beasts crouched amongst the grasses, bear no resemblance to the surrounding soil.

Those which shelter the temple look like a collection of reposing monsters, and the largest ones support the upright dagaba (the Buddhist steeple), just as an elephant carries its tower; an old whitewashed tower rising from a sombre base. As I approach the solitary wastes of the jungle, sketched out silently in the hot evening sun, there is no one near the temple. The heaps of scented flowers lying on the ground, jasmines and gardenias, and the faded wreaths of former days tell one that the gods are not forgotten.

The monster-like rocks are bathed on one side by a lagoon in which crocodiles dwell under the lotus leaves. On drawing closer, faint lines can be seen etched on the sides of the polished stones, vague bas-reliefs so faintly traced as to resemble mere reflections, but drawn with such skill as to give a semblance of life; trunks, feet, ears, and the general outlines of elephants are here. The mysterious characteristics of the stones, which naturally resemble the skin of

15

the royal animals in texture and colour, have been utilized, too, with the strangest art.

Plants have grown here and there in the hollows of the rounded stones, plants whose sharp outlines and vivid colourings contrast in an unreal fashion with the surrounding tones of old, dull leather, for the hue of the periwinkles is too rosy and the hibiscus flowers are much too red, whilst the young areca trees, whose tufted plumes droop from their thin stalks, are too magnificently green.

Behind the group of rocks is concealed an old house which shelters the priestly guardians of the temple, one of whom now advances to meet me. He is young, and, like all Buddhist priests, clothed in a single, saffron-coloured garment which leaves one arm and shoulder exposed. He brings a highly ornamented key, over a foot in length, to open the sanctuary for me. As he advances, key in hand, his beautiful grave face and mystic eyes give him the look of some bronze-coloured St. Peter, clothed in raiment of coppery yellow that the sun has gilded.

We ascend a stairway cut in the rock out of whose rugged sides periwinkles grow; the dreary wastes of the jungles extending around us. The sanctuary is hollowed out of the heart of the principal stone, and we first enter a little cavern, a sort of atrium containing a table covered with white gardenias on which the offerings for the gods are placed. At the back is the entry to the sacred place, an entry guarded by bronze doors and a huge chased lock.

When the doors are thrown open with a grating crash, the huge painted idols confront us, and it seems as if some great cavern of precious perfumes had been unsealed, for freshly sprinkled essences of roses and sandal, masses of gardenias and tuberose make a thick white carpet on the ground, and embalm the air with intoxicating odours. Thus are the gods, who live in an almost perpetual gloom, ever bathed in the most exquisite scents.

There is hardly room for four or five persons in the

narrow temple, which is shut in like a dungeon and almost filled by the statues. Goddesses twelve feet in height, cut from the solid rock, decorate the walls with their closely serried forms; their faces have the same yellow tint as the priest's robe, and their head-dresses touch the ceiling. A Buddha of super-human size is seated in the middle, in the pose of one sunk in a perpetual dream, and smaller gods of the size of dolls are gathered round his knees, whilst the circle of staring goddesses seems to be gathered round in an air of anxious expectation. In spite of the brilliance of their golden ornaments and the freshness of the blue and red colouring of their stony robes, these long-eyed divinities give one the instant impression of fearful antiquity.

My unexpected visit has allowed a little daylight to filter into their grotto and permitted them to see, through the open vestibule, the confines of the jungle, where their crowds of worshippers lived in bygone ages. I look at them for a moment, almost em-barrassed at finding myself so close in front of them, and I soon allow the priest to close the holy closet, so that the inmates of the rock may be plunged once more in silence and scented shades.

I take my leave, for I cannot understand these symbols, and this Buddhist peace is as yet hidden from me; the guardian in the yellow robe goes calmly back to his hermitage—priest of a strange temple, having no other care than the arrangement of his flowers, living a joyless life in this deserted place where sorrow never comes, living only in the hope that he may prolong his ego—after this present incarnation has ended—in an impersonal and sad eternity.

The sun is sinking as I leave the Rock Temple to return to the lofty forest under which Anuradhapura slumbers, and as I am leaving to-morrow at daybreak, I will wander amongst the ruins till night comes.

" The largest streets are those of The Moon, The King, The Sand-Covered Street and a fourth. In the

Street of The Moon there are eleven thousand houses. The distance from the principal door to the door of the South is sixteen miles; and from the door of the North to the door of the South is sixteen miles also."

In reality, these fallen stones, these ruins and sculptures of the olden times, seem never-ending; gods crowned with tiaras, heraldic monsters with the bodies of crocodiles, elephants' trunks, and birds' tails. Columns everywhere, some standing, others fallen and broken; the thresholds of the fallen houses, guarded on each side by a smiling goddess, seem to invite us to enter, amidst thickets of roots and ferns—the houses of the inhabitants of the olden times, people who were hospitable no doubt, but whose dust has ceased to exist centuries ago.

The evening hour, with its harmonies of ruddy gold, finds me far from the house where I have my lodging. I am in the quarter of the King's Palaces, of which nothing remains but the monstrous foundation, the steps and the sculptured pavement. A death-like silence reigns, unbroken by the cry of insect or of bird. Here I rest at the edge of the gigantic tank, walled in with thick granite blocks, that was the bath of the royal elephants.

This lily-covered expanse of slumbering water makes a clearing amongst the high trees, and lightens the feeling of oppression caused by the overhanging branches; nevertheless the air is still heavy and motionless. Bubbles of air continually make eddies on the surface of the treacherous water—bubbles breathed out by crocodiles who bask in the warm mud, in which silent worlds of tortoises and snakes reside.

There are no climbing plants here, and as no bushes mask the view, it is possible to see the boundaries of this kingdom of ruins which extends around us. Towards the west a fire seems to spring from the level of the ground and scatters its dazzling rays among the trees. It is the setting of the sun, which in these latitudes is immediately succeeded by night-fall.

I must hasten further whilst there is light, and as this is my last evening, make my walk as long as possible.

The secret charm of the new land that I tread in the growing dimness lies in the delicate, dry, and sandy soil covered by short, fine grasses as were the woods my childhood knew, and the impression of my native land is heightened by the tracks traced by the shepherds and their flocks. There are trees, too, which have a sober little foliage, netted with gray veins like our evergreen oaks, and were it not for the great red lilies and bouvardias which now and then take me by surprise, it would indeed be like home, for the same pastoral calm and gentle melancholy reign here as there.

But these great stones and ruins are always here to disturb my dream, and statues with mysterious faces haunt the place. The dimness increases, and in the dusk the outlines of lonely Buddhas, sitting and smiling in vacancy, are almost terrifying.

I make my way back in the dusk by another road which has an even sweeter sadness, and a more marked resemblance to my native land. Though still conscious, in a latent manner, perhaps, of the Indian forest which surrounded me on all sides, I felt myself back among the oak woods of Saintonge or of Aunis, and walked forward confidently. Believing myself quite alone, a sudden tremor ran through me when I saw a huge, black man, whose head was bent sideways, and whose hands were on his hips, near by my side—a granite Buddha who had been there for two thousand years.

Drawing closer, one can see, even in the fading light, his lowered eyelids and his eternal smile.

A spiritual and holy calm seems to diffuse itself now that the moon is shining and the towers of the great temple train their black shadows over the jungle.

The moonbeams have a bluish tinge, and the light
of Eden seems to illuminate the first and only night
that I shall spend amongst these woods.

The splendour of the clearness of our warm July
nights comes back to me, but here there is something
different, something more lasting, something that tells
of a perpetual and never-ending summer.

Between the trees the sky is visible, and the fine
lawns, traversed by little paths, are illuminated with
a strange radiance. Silence seems gradually to
deepen as I penetrate the woods, in spite of the night
music of the insects, which vibrates madly around me.

Alone I wend my way towards the shadows cast
by the great dagabas of which the Indians are afraid ;
whither my guide, thinking of the spectres of kings
and priests, has not chosen to follow me.

On nearing one of the temples I instinctively choose
the side lit by the moon, in order to reach the gigantic
dagaba. No doubt this open space, which served as a
peristyle, is haunted by spectres. Suddenly my footsteps resound on hollowed pavements and I am in the
midst of broken altars and mutilated images bathed
in a bluish glow. The vast stillness of Anuradhapura
seems yet more strange, and I stop short like some
frightened native ; indeed, I dare not walk round the
dagaba, or cross that patch of noisome shadow.

Where are the kings and priests who built this
monstrous temple ? Do they dwell in Nirvana or in
nothingness, and how can their spirits ever return
from such far-distant realms ?

Their Buddhist faith, too, seems a dead and perished
thing, buried under these ruins and covered by the
dust of the ancient idols.

THE HOME OF THE MAHARAJAH OF TRAVANCORE

CHAPTER III

THE HOME OF THE MAHARAJAH OF TRAVANCORE

20th December

IT is the evening hour, and a period of calm and freshness follows the hasty sunset. It is but a few moments since I reached Palancota, an unknown village where I am to pass the night. Here, for the first time, I feel how far from home I am, amidst these trees and the silence that spreads over the declining day.

I made halt for a week in the damp, green island of Ceylon, to which the French steamer had brought me; then last night I crossed the ever-raging Gulf of Manar in a poor coasting vessel; since then I have travelled all day to this village, where I am met by an envoy of His Highness the Maharajah of Travancore, who quarters me in a little white house standing amidst shady trees.

To-morrow I set out on my journey in an Indian zebu cart for the land of Travancore, where my wanderings are to commence. This land is also styled "The Land of Charity," and is, I am told, a place of blissful peace, cut off from the mad turmoil of our age, an isolated country sheltered by spreading palms.

It is quite night now, an exquisite summer night; but there is no moon. A carriage takes me to see a Brahmin temple, one of the largest in the south, that has been illuminated for me. This temple is situated in a neighbouring town named Tinnevelli.

We trot easily along a flat road, under the mys-

terious interlacings of overhanging trees; trailing
roots hang from the extended branches, myriads of
trailing roots which look like tresses of long hair.
Thousands of stars sparkle through the smallest gap
among the branches, whilst under the leaves crowds
of fireflies flit like sparks of flame. All these scintilla-
tions intermingle, so that in our rapid course we do
not know which are stars and which are fireflies.

It is a joy to breathe the dry and healthful air after
the everlasting dampness of Ceylon; it seems a
summer night of France, and crickets sing everywhere
as they do in June with us. Strange wayfarers pass
along the roads, bronze figures draped in white muslin,
whose naked feet pass noiselessly over the ground.
Occasionally the sound of a distant tom-tom is heard,
or a few groaning notes of the bagpipes tell us of
India, and of Brahma, and how far we are from home.
White houses with verandas commence to loom
among the shady trees that line both sides of the road.
They are the houses of Tinnevelli, the town towards
which we journey. At last, at the end of an avenue
of palms, whose black heads are balanced on their
frail stalks, a strange and striking outline is visible,
the great temple. A stranger might recognize it, for
its shape has been vaguely impressed on us by many
pictures, but I did not expect to see it so large, nor
that tower so high in the evening sky. It is a monstrous pylone, in all probability graven with images
of intertwining forms of gods, whose roof, bristling
with monsters, casts its dark profile on the starry
firmament.

Our carriage soon passes under a granite archway
framed by square columns of primitive style. Five
ramparts once passed, we find ourselves in a square
inclosure open to the shining stars. This I am not
allowed to cross. The pylone, however, rises quite
closely before us; its extraordinary proportions seem
to overhang and dwarf the doorway which I may not
tread, although it stands widely open. With my
eyes I seek to penetrate the dim obscurities of the

sacred temple whose infinite recesses are outlined by many twinkling and mysterious lamps.

I am allowed to look from here, but I must not approach or gaze too long. Under the columns of the peristyle that adjoins each side of the yawning entry, vendors of flowers, wreaths, and sacred cakes made for the gods are stationed, their stalls illuminated by little, flickering lamps. These dancing flames only light up the groups of men and the worn bases of the columns, which were once carved with monsters and with fantastic groups. The motionless nude forms of tawny merchants which rest against the ruddy granites might be taken for those of the gods themselves; their eyes glitter in the dim light, whilst their long hair falls in a black flood upon their shoulders. Above them gloom reigns supreme amongst the dim outlines of columns and vaulted arches.

The temple seems to my stealthy gaze to be of infinite extent. Endless rows of columns rise from an obscurity which the many-lighted lamps are powerless to dispel. The air is filled with sounds of prayer and chanted psalms, while white-robed forms flit dimly across the dark background.

The framework of the doorway through which I look, but through which I must not pass, is of a strange and unknown order of architecture. Notwithstanding that its proportions are those of a cathedral door, it has a low and furtive look, as if crushed by the weight of the monstrous pylone that overhangs it; and the colossal pyramid of gods towering to the stars makes it seem the entrance of a mysterious subterranean cavern.

This is my first visit to a Brahmin temple, but I immediately receive a hostile impression, a dismal feeling of dread and heathenish idolatry. I had not expected this, nor yet that I should have been refused admission. How childish were the hopes that I had cherished, I who had hoped to find some ray of light in the religion of our Indian ancestors!

Oh! for the sweet, deceptive peace of our Christian

3

churches which are open to all, and kind even to those who can believe no longer. . . .

They tell me that there are temples in other parts of India which are less sullen, and into which I may be allowed to enter, but it is hinted that I had better retire now, if I do not wish to be indiscreet. Should I desire it, our carriage may drive round the huge temple.

The inclosure is square and large enough to contain a town. In the middle of each of the four blank walls a huge pylone rises, under which a door has been hollowed out, but, except for this, these walls are as gloomy as those of a citadel.

Our carriage pursues its lonely road through the dim silence; even the place we are in is sacred and must not be trod by common men. We pass dark masses, which look like pedestals of idols supported on gigantic wheels and which seem to have been cast up here by chance. These are the chariots in which the gods are placed on feast days, when thousands of frenzied arms push them along the ground; but to-night they slumber with their wheels embedded in the ruts like dead things.

As we retrace our way under the avenues of palms whose dark heads are bent in all directions, a clamour of religious frenzy breaks over us, and the hollow sound of tom-toms fills the serene night air; horns bray like monsters, and barbarous noises fill us with a sense of terror.

I

21st *December*

I am still in the village of Palancota. During the whole night bronzed serving-men have waved great fans in the air to drive mosquitoes and winged night-moths away. The doors and windows of the little native house have remained open during the night, so that the first gay beams of the dawning day find ready access, and I awake amidst the splendour of the rising sun.

The veranda, still fresh with dew, offers an exquisite shelter, for it is snowy with whitewash, and the thick-set irregular pillars are covered with jasmines.

A calm, pastoral country extends around me, bathed in a blissful morning charm ; the gentle glow of one of our September mornings shines on a land that has been parched by autumn droughts. There are no great palms here, nor any of the rank vegetation of Ceylon, nothing but small trees with modest leaves, like those of our woods. Fields that have been reaped, orchards, pleasant, well-kept lanes wandering through the short grass, and further off, amidst the branches, little walls and carefully whitewashed houses. I look with astonishment on sights almost like those familiar to my childhood.

There are even sparrows, common sparrows just like those which nest among our roofs ; but they are bolder, for, like all Indian living things, they have a confidence in man to which I am not accustomed.

Parts of this land closely resemble my own, and call back the charm of summer's declining days, though it is winter here.

A gentle sense of melancholy steals over me, and without, however, being wholly able to forget that I am in this far-off land of India, I dream that I am once more in my native land. These flat plains, whitewashed walls, and ripening harvests call to my mind the countrysides of Aunis and Saintonge, and the peaceful dwellings of the Isle of Oberon nestled amid the glories of their ripening vines.

There are, however, many things to dispel my dreams : a naked wayfarer brushes silently through the grass, turning his dusky countenance to me ; a humming bird that has the changing hues of a precious stone settles among the sparrows ; and a little girl of six, who has been sent with a message to me from the village, has strangely lengthened eyes, and pins threaded with blood-coloured rubies are passed through her quivering nostrils.

Something strange and unhomely is seen in the distance among the trees, the angle of a pylone, the corner of a pyramid of gods and monsters springing from a temple of Vishnu hidden in the woods.

In spite of the shade afforded by the trees, the mid-day sun beats fiercely on the little whitewashed houses. A brightness, which eclipses that of our most gorgeous September day, hovers over the neighbouring orchards and the drooping grass. No one passes along the lanes, and everything is still. The great fans slumber too, for their attendants have gone to rest. All is silent and motionless, only the crows keep wakeful. They enter the room and wander round me. Their hopping noises and the silky swish of their wings are the only sounds that break the torpor that reigns everywhere.

The thought comes to me that our Christmas is close at hand, and this never-changing summer seems to fill me with an indescribable sadness.

The carriages which are to take us on our two days' journey to the wished-for land of Travancore make their appearance one after the other: two native chariots drawn by trotting bulls of the shape of long sarcophagi, into which one slides from the back, and in which it is impossible to sit upright. The one pro-vided for me is drawn by a pair of white cattle, whose horns are painted blue; that of my servants has brown animals with copper-encircled horns. Mean-while, till the sun is less powerful, the four peaceful, indolent, and gentle zebus lie on the grass and wait.

II

We start at three, under the still fierce rays of the sun. My chariot is provided with mats and carpets, but is too low to allow me to sit upon them, so that I have to lie down, like a sick man in an ambulance, whilst my zebus at once fall into the hobbling trot which must be the accompaniment of my slumbers for the next two days.

We change our teams of men and cattle frequently, for relays are placed along this road, which is the sole means of communication in the south between eastern India and Travancore. Up till now the happy " Land of Charity " has no railroad to draw away its riches ; on the northern side the communication with the little State of Cochin is by means of boats, which thread a series of canals and lakes, but intercourse from other sources is barred by the natural defences of this fortunate land.

There are no ports on the western coast, nothing but inaccessible shores on which great breakers beat. The Great Central Chain of the Ghauts keeps watch on the east, with its rugged peaks and tiger-swarming forests.

My good cattle trot or gallop merrily along. Now that we have passed the village, the long, endless road extends before us, stretching its long, blood-coloured monotony between two rows of great trees that look like ash or walnut. The walnuts are young banyan trees, which in time will grow to be giants ; hair-like roots have already commenced to grow here and there, and drooping from the branches to the ground, seek the earth so that they may form new stems. Vast lonely plains, thinly scattered with palms, appear between the trees.

Some holes are made in the sides of the cart to give air and light ; and at the back there is that tiny round door through which I had to crawl with lowered head.

The chariot for the luggage and the servants follows closely in the wake, and the zebus with their good-natured long faces are my nearest neighbours ; these gentle, ambling cattle, driven by a single rein threaded through their nostrils, almost touch my feet as I lie extended on my back, and their horns are bent backwards as if they feared to do any one an un-willing injury. The bronze-hued driver is quite naked, and balances himself on the pole with a marvellous alertness, sitting cross-legged, with his hands placed upon his knees; he lashes his cattle with a thin reed or urges them on by making a noise like that of an angry monkey.

The desert wastes extend on either hand, becoming more awe-inspiring as we proceed further. Sometimes there are a few poor rice or cotton fields in the sad rays of the setting sun.

The outlines of the Ghauts are seen on the horizon, walling in the land of Travancore. We must cross them to-night by their only pass.

I am astonished to see these arid plains, on which grass even will not grow, after the luxuriant vegetation and the damp atmosphere of Ceylon. Some gray stalked palms which hardly seem to belong to the plant kingdom are dotted here and there, smooth and straight as tall masts. Swollen at the base, they taper towards the summit, which bears a little bunch of rigid fans posed on the stem whose length is out of all proportion to it. These stiff outlines are repeated endlessly on both sides of the road as far as the eye can reach.

There are no passengers on the well-kept road, with its bordered sides of banyan trees, and it might be thought to lead to nowhere. Gradually the exhausting heat and the rhythmic sequence of repeated jolts causes a vague drowsiness in which my thoughts commence to wander.

Towards five o'clock we pass four grotesque wayfarers, an important event to sleep-laden eyes that have become accustomed to the deserted road; four tall, scantily-clothed men, who march along with rapid footsteps. They wear large, red turbans, and their loins are swathed by red and white striped cloths.

Where can these gorgeously-apparelled men be going in such haste, and what may they seek in the midst of the desert?

Gradually I lose consciousness, and slumber rivets me to my stifling couch.

I awake an hour later; twilight has come and I can but catch one last impression from the dying day.

The mountain chain has suddenly come closer, as if it had made a leap of some three miles, and now shuts out the eastern plains. Its deep, purple contours are outlined with incredible clearness against the rosy background that the setting sun has left; the granite peaks are truly Indian in character, and take shapes that are unseen elsewhere, apeing the forms of pyramids, towers, and pagoda roofs. Thin, reedy palms, and fierce-looking aloes are the only plants that grow here; their erect forms stand out sharply against the declining light, and the pale clearness of the sky is pierced by the outlines of their black leaves.

Suddenly darkness comes, and I feel a shade of melancholy, for the night will be moonless.

Till morning dawns I am jolted in my narrow sarcophagus, and I only receive a whirl of confused impressions. Furious cries, the jangling of bells as we pass other zebu wagons that unwillingly give place to us; stoppages to change our cattle and our men in dimly seen roadside villages; villages inhabited by sleeping Brahmins, who have placed little lighted lamps filled with coco-nut oil in the niches of the walls to frighten away the evil spirit of the night.

22nd December

Next morning at daybreak I am aroused with many salutes, for we have reached the village of Nagercoïl, where I am to repose till sunset. The mountain chain that I had seen before me yesterday outlined on the evening red, is now behind me, bathed in the rosy pallor of the dawning day; we have crossed it during the night, and are now in Travancore. The little veranda-fronted house at which my zebus stop is the hotel, and the white-robed Indian who salutes with both his hands pressed on his forehead is the hotel-keeper who has had orders to await me and to reserve the whole house for me.

Like those of every Indian village, this " Travellers' Rest " consists of three or four whitewashed rooms on the ground floor, very clean, almost bare, with couches of rattan cane on which to sleep.

The roof, which is upheld by thick columns, over-laps the sides of the house, so as to give shelter from the rays of the burning sun.

I bathe and then breakfast under fans waved by listless serving-men. Then I am only conscious of the melancholy sadness of a darkened room, the suave silence and the visits of the crows, who come and hop about the floor of my room.

At two o'clock a dispatch comes from the Dewan (the minister of the Maharajah), stating that a carriage drawn by horses has been sent for me to a village called Neyzetavaray, in readiness to start at eleven o'clock at night.

So I decide to set out at once, instead of waiting as usual for sunset, in order that I may reach Neyzet-avaray to-night, and spend the rest of the night in the carriage.

Our departure takes place under a dazzling white light and the repeated two-handed salutes of the inn-keeper; the bronzed waiting-men stand round my carriage in attitudes of silent appeal, nor does the nearly naked old woman, whose function is to fill the bath, allow her presence to be forgotten. I give some little coins of Travancore silver money to all these people, little thick coins like shining grains of silver, and then our zebus trot out briskly into the stifling heat.

The land gradually becomes more leafy, soon equal-ling the magnificence of Ceylon, and the jungle is full of flowering shrubs. The tall tufted palms that but yesterday looked so yellow and dried up, are now luxuriant bouquets of fans ; coco-nuts with their great green feathers reappear in clumps, and from the banyans of the roadside, that form an archway over our heads, trailing roots descend in hairy masses to the ground. The country seems to be but a wilder-

ness of trees, an inextricable green entanglement.
Just now we meet many people travelling along the
shady road; folk in zebu carts like our own, and
shepherds leading their flocks; processions of women
too, countless groups of women carrying burdens on
their heads in grass-woven baskets.

Here and there we pass little granite temples, roofed
with flat stones, and temples of uncertain age that
look like miniature replicas of those of ancient Egypt;
or, maybe, under some huge banyan, which has
become sacred in virtue of its great age, the tomb of
a holy fakir, garlanded with fresh flowers, or a statue
of the elephant-headed god Ganesa, that some pious
hand has adorned with a necklace made of interwoven
pinks and roses.

It is a somewhat unexpected surprise that though
most of the men are handsome, the women we meet in
such numbers are not beautiful; the bronze colour
seems to harmonize better with the faces of the men,
whose moustaches, too, hide the lips, which in the
women are somewhat noticeably thick. With the ex-
ception of a few very young ones, who have the pure
outlines of a Tanagra figure, nearly all have prematurely deformed busts, not even hid by drapery.
They wear a golden ring in each nostril, and the ear
lobes are so much lengthened by weighty rings, that
they hang down to the shoulders of the old people.
It is true that these are but the wives of pariahs, for
those of the higher caste, that we have not yet seen,
do not travel along the roads carrying burdens.

From time to time we pass tall, solid tables of
granite, which have been thoughtfully provided so
that these women may relieve themselves of their
burdens, and replace them on their heads without the
trouble of stooping down.

A charming tranquillity hovers over the land, and
the scattered villages embowered in greenery are
sunk in a calm like that of paradise.

Under a shady banyan tree, near which an old idol
of Siva stands, I see a white-bearded man of Hebraic

cast of countenance, dressed in a violet-coloured robe, peacefully reclining with a book in his hands ; it is a bishop—a Syrian bishop ; surely a strange and unexpected encounter in this country of the mysterious rites of Brahma.

On reflection, however, there is nothing unusual in it. I knew that the Maharajah of Travancore had about five hundred thousand Christians among his subjects, Christians whose ancestors had churches here when Europe was still under pagan rule. These claim that they are the descendants of St. Thomas, who came to India about the middle of the first century. More probably they are Nestorians who arrived later from Syria, a land that still continues to send them priests. In any case, they come of an old and venerable stock, of that there can be no question. Jews, who emigrated after the second destruction of the temple of Jerusalem, are also found in the more northern parts of the kingdom. As in the case of the Christians, no one has ever disturbed them, for religious tolerance has always existed here, and in no instance has human blood been shed in this " Land of Charity."

Our zebus still maintain their constant trot. Towards evening the sun becomes overcast, and, as in Ceylon, a tropical dampness fills the air. Cocoa palms—those denizens of the lands of hot rains—become more predominant now that we have entered the infinite expanse of feathered palms which extends from the western shores to the coast of Malabar, plunging hundreds of miles in an everlasting green light. As we pass at the foot of the spurs of the Ghaut Chain our outlook is hemmed in by rocky peaks, overhanging forests, and masses of black cloud.

The journey had already lasted some four hours when the sense of weariness, aggravated by the cadenced jolting of our zebus, became so intolerable that I had to slip through the little opening at the front of my sarcophagus, and sit for a while on the pole in the pose of a crouching monkey by the side of my driver. The daylight has waned considerably, and under the black clouds and overhanging palms it is almost twilight. The green tunnel of banyans extends as ever in front of us, but here and there fantastic objects are seen looming from the woods through the evening shadows. They resemble huge, shapeless animals ; sometimes they are scattered and sometimes in flocks, or even piled on one another. These strange objects consist of granite blocks— blocks which have the soft roundness of elephants and the bronze colour of their skin ; there is no connection between them, and they look as if they had come here separately, or as if they had been rolled or thrown here, like corpses heaped up after a massacre. Now the larger roots and branches of the trees take the shape of elephants' trunks ; indeed, it looks as if nature had had some vague idea of this particular animal shape in all her creation, as if the first thought of the elephantine form had existed here from the remotest antiquity, even from the date when the first unconscious thought had fashioned matter with stone. At present it looks as if elephants or the embryos of elephants were crowded round us, and the resemblances are even more striking now that it is quite dim in the woods which lie about us.

It is eight o'clock, and the heavy clouds which threatened us have cleared off without leaving a trace ; the sky is pure, and the night starry. Crickets and grasshoppers chirp madly, and all the branches of the trees vibrate with insect joy.

A confused waving of torches is seen in front of us, and we behold a crowd advancing through the dusky foliage. We can hear the sound of drums and cymbals, and a chorus of human voices which accompanies the merry procession on their way through the avenues of palm and banyan.

In the flickering light of torches we see some twenty bare-chested young men, who carry an ornamented and flower-decorated palanquin on their shoulders, in which reposes one of their fellows, like a rajah or some god, in golden crown and long gilt robe.

It is a marriage procession, and this is the bridegroom who is being carried by his friends with such
religious ceremony.

Towards eleven o'clock, as I was lying asleep at
the bottom of the cart, one of the little loopholes was
opened, and a letter, sealed with the arms of Travancore—two elephants and a seashell—was handed to
me by the light from the lantern. We have reached
the village of Neyzetavaray, and the letter is from
the Dewan, bidding me welcome in the name of the
sovereign, and telling me that the carriage awaits me.

It is a great pleasure to leave the Indian cart, to
step into this elegant and well-hung carriage, and to
set forth at a brisk trot with these two splendid
horses. A coachman in the livery of the Maharajah
—a long robe and a gilt turban that shines hazily
through the gloom—is on the box, whilst two active
footmen are stationed on the step. They almost
seem to have wings as they run forward, uttering
fearful cries in order to clear the way of the zebu
carts which are now far more plentiful. It gives me
an intoxicating sense of joy to move along so easily
and so quickly through the calm starry night past
the flying palms, after having endured so many jolts
in my narrow box. We cleave the delicious night
air, laden with the perfume of flowers, as if our road
lay through some never-ending fairy garden.

Again we see the red light of torches and hear
strains of music ; it is another marriage procession
wandering along in spite of the late and silent hour.
This time the bridegroom is on horseback, and looks,
with his golden robe hanging over his horse's crupper,
like some king of the Magi.

Towards one o'clock in the morning, great dark
palm feathers suddenly cease to interlace above our
heads ; there is a clearing in the forest and we reach
a street. But this street, bathed in the clear, ashy
gray light that falls in tropical regions from the stars
on moonless nights, seems to be plunged in profound
slumber. Houses, which must be white in the day-

light, now have a bluish tinge. All have a story rising above their verandas, from which little pointed festoons or lace-worked windows look through complicated columns. Lower down, on either side of the closed doors, little lamps shine like glow-worms; these tiny flames are placed in niches to keep watch against the intrusion of evil spirits. Many animals crouch motionlessly on the steps, as closely as possible to the human habitation, as if they, too, sought shelter from some unknown spell; zebus, sheep, and goats, who do not even wake as we pass by. There is no other sound than that of our light wheels upon the sanded road, and all these houses, slumbering cattle, and vague shapes of things unseen, are bathed in an uncertain bluish light, that looks like the reflection of some far-off Bengal fire.

In front of us there is a vast inclosure with a monumental door surmounted by miradores and columns opening on to an avenue which rows of lanterns show to be large and wide. Tops of palm trees and palace roofs rise above this wall, and quite at the back in the direction of the straight avenue the gigantic towers of Brahmin temples are seen. We are evidently going to enter the inclosure, for this must be the capital of Travancore, the true Trivandrum, the residence of the Maharajah, and the bluish street, peopled by slumbering animals, can only have been a suburb.

I was not aware that only Indians of high caste are permitted to inhabit this privileged inclosure till my carriage turned sharply to the right from the face of the great door which I thought we should enter. Plunging once more into long shady roads resembling park avenues, we stopped at length before a splendid dwelling standing in a garden, which, alas! was built in European style.

An apartment has been prepared here for me, and the gracious hospitality of the Maharajah awaits me in a European dwelling that seems like a kindly anomaly in the midst of old and marvellous Hindustan.

III

23rd December

Towards the close of the first night I spent in Trivandrum a terrible noise was heard on my roof; rushes were succeeded by sounds of battle, and in my half-waking starts I thought I could recognize (not without some dread, seeing that my rooms were open), the springs and yells of some members of the tiger tribe; but the calm of the night and the wood-work of the roof must have exaggerated the noise, for these were only the tiger-cats of the neighbourhood, which sleep by day in the garden trees and disport themselves during the night, boldly invading the dwellings of men.

The early morning at Trivandrum is a period of unspeakable sadness. A murmur of human voices is heard before the wild and sad dawn breaks through the pallor of the sky, sounds that seemed to come from a distance, from the inclosure sacred to Brahma; a cry that is like that of humanity itself waking to new tortures, and ever oppressed by thoughts of death. The birds then make their homage to the returning sun, but their morning serenade has not the charming gaiety of those that sing in our meadows in the springtime. Here the twitterings of the smaller birds are drowned by the mocking voices of parakeets, and the funereal croakings of the crows. First, one or two isolated croaks are given as a signal, then a hundred and a thousand join in fearful concert to celebrate the glories of death and putre-faction. Crows are everywhere; the whole of India is infested with them, and even here, in Travancore, the land of peace and enchantment, their cries are heard directly the day breaks; their voices fill the vaulted arches of the palms, and serve to dim the joy of all that lives and wakes under the glorious foliage. They say " Here we watch, we who wait for the death of all that lives. Our prey is certain and everything will belong to us."

After a while the cawing ceases, and the birds disperse. Once more the far-off rumour of men's voices is heard, so deep and powerful that one feels that there are thousands of these Brahmins assembled in the great sanctuary calling on their God. A confused noise of tambourines, cymbals, and sacred shells comes from all points of the forest of palms in which Trivandrum is situated, telling of the morning adoration in little temples scattered amongst the woods.

At last the sun appears, and the dwelling-houses, which are either entirely open, or but shut off from the darkness by light blinds, are at once flooded with its rays. Now all the melancholy of daybreak vanishes in this exquisite hour of splendid brightness. I descend to the garden, a sort of clearing in the midst of the palm forest, where there are lawns and trees covered with rose-coloured flowers ; ferns and plants loving a moist heat grow in great luxuriance, and those wonderous-foliaged Indian plant, that are tinged like flowers with dull red, violets pale carmine, or striped with white, like the veinings of a reptile's back, or spotted with eyes like those of a butterfly's wings.

Contrary to the custom which obtains with us, seven o'clock in the morning, the time when a trace of freshness still lingers among the green avenues, is the ceremonial visiting hour of Trivandrum ; and I am informed that to-morrow morning at that hour I shall be conducted through the sacred precincts and presented to the Prince. As midday approaches all signs of life cease ; for in spite of the shade afforded by the palms, the vertical rays of the sun plunge everything into somnolence and torpor ; even the crows are silently seated on the ground under the shelter of the shady trees.

The road that I can see from my veranda, disappearing into the green twilight, becomes deserted. There are still a few passers-by, men and women dressed in scarlet loin-cloths, whose deeply bronzed chests shine with coppery-coloured reflections ; these reddish figures move noiselessly on naked feet along the blood-coloured road, whose tone is heightened by the vividly contrasting green of the surrounding palms. Sometimes the earth trembles under the heavy and almost noiseless footsteps of the Maharajah's elephants as they return from some work in the fields to the stables of the palace where they sleep. After that nothing more is heard, and, emboldened by the silence, little leaping squirrels possessed with mad activity enter my room.

Towards evening human activity begins again, and I leave my retreat in one of the Maharajah's carriages, the fleet horses of which give me an illusion of freshness.

I am quartered in the nearer parts of Trivandrum, where the trees are no longer masters, and lawns interspersed with beautifully sanded avenues have been laid out. Scattered among the gardens are all the buildings necessary to the life of a modern capital—ministries, hospitals, banks, and schools. All these things would have been less out of place had they been built in the Indian style, but in these modern days we have to be content to find the same errors of taste in all the countries of the world. Churches and chapels are found here too, Protestant, Catholic, and Syrian ; the latter are the oldest and have façades of childish simplicity. I, however, did not come to Travancore to see these things, and I begin to perceive how difficult it will be to come into real touch with the India of the Brahmins, that deeper India which I feel surrounding me ever here, ever living and unchangeable, ever haunting me with mystery.

Outside the new quarters the palms extend their sovereignty over the immense Trivandrum of the low-caste Indians. All the movement and the bustle of the somewhat silent town is concentrated in the " Street of the Merchants." At this hour it is filled with people, and my horses must move slowly through the crowds. I might call them a race of gods, so beautiful are their faces, and their attitudes so noble. The expression on their countenances is profound and unfathomable.

The perfection and grace of an antique bas-relief are realized by these crowds whose arms and chests seem hewn from bronze.

These superb and refined Brahmins look on costumes and ornaments with disdain, and are less clothed than the natives of middle caste or even than pariahs. A cloth of grayish white is girded round the loins, and across the naked chest nothing but a little linen cord worn round their shoulders, the outward sign of rank, that the priest has knotted around them when they were born and which is never removed ; a sacred cord with which one lives and dies. On their foreheads, between the dark grave eyes, the monogram of their god is inscribed ; but this must be piously repainted each day after the morning ablution : a red disc with three white lines for the followers of Siva, and for those of Vishnu a sort of red and white trident, which starts between their eyebrows, and whose points reach the hair, adding a strangely puzzling look to their expression.

There are few or no women, though at the first glance the long tresses of polished ebony hair, sometimes knotted and sometimes hanging over their shoulders, would give the impression that these were of the other sex. Those who show themselves are of the lower castes, and have common features like the carrier-women we met upon the road. The wives and daughters of the Brahmins, who walk by thousands in the evening air, are doubtless in the reserved inclosure.

All the houses which I saw last night, closed and sleeping in the bluish light, now form an animated bazaar, where fruits, grain, and lightly printed stuffs of antique design are sold ; there are also wares of yellow copper, bright as those of gold, many-branched slender lamps mounted on tall feet like those of

4

Pompeii, plates and vases for religious usage, and gods and goddesses mounted on elephants.

My guide takes me to visit the factories founded by the ruling sovereign, where pottery is made after the beautiful ancient fashion ; there are others where carpets are woven of long wools whose colours are copied from those of Rajputana or Cashmere, and finally the workshops where patient workers chisel ivory obtained from the elephants of the neighbouring forests, making little Brahmin gods or the handles of fly-fans and parasols.

But this was not what I had come to India to see, and the only thing that interested me was the real Indian life of the closed palaces and the forbidden Temple.

Trivandrum has a zoological garden too, with parks of gazelles and ponds of crocodiles, as well kept up as those of Europe ; one of the few places where it is possible to escape from the stifling shade of the palms, and to overlook the distant prospect of forests and jungles. Lawns have been laid out with rows of exotic flowers and other matchless plants ; and one can wander in confidence through this artificial forest where all the branches are carefully trimmed, and where the tigers and serpents which inhabit the neighbouring jungles are kept in cages.

A band of natives executes European airs with great precision in a kiosk situated in the garden during that short and fleeting hour between the cool evening and the sudden fall of darkness. Among the rare listeners stationed in the sanded avenues are a few slim, nude forms, and one or two white babies (the only ones living in Trivandrum) looking very pale in their Indian nurses' arms, and some children of native princes who, alas ! no longer wear the national costume, but are disfigured into the odd forms of Western dolls, dolls still beautiful in spite of their coppery tinge and great black velvety eyes. As this garden is situated on an eminence, it is possible to see the Indian Ocean in the distance ; an ocean that has no ships, and which, unlike that of other countries, has no communication with the outer world; here it is but a useless and hostile element sequestrating one from other lands, since there are no ports along the coast, not even barques or fishermen—nothing but a girdle of insuperable breakers. The apparition of the far-off sea adds a feeling of melancholy to the sad thoughts of exile that steal over me during this fashionable evening hour, when the band plays for the few lonely babies of Trivandrum.

Now the sun sets quickly in a moment of glorious splendour, the red earth seems lit up with a rose-coloured Bengal fire, and the inextricable tangle of branches that extends as far as the eye can reach assumes a more vivid tone, as if illuminated by green Bengal flames. Now the night falls without any intervening twilight, prematurely and almost suddenly, though its time is invariable and, unlike our own, uninfluenced by the season. There is still light in the garden, but under the trees and in the leafy lanes it is quite dark. Now an outcry rises from the great Temple of Brahma, and from the other temples, scattered round, the sound of the cymbals and sacred shells is heard once more. Thousands of little lamps filled with coconut oil twinkle amongst the woods, tracing the dim roads in lines of tiny red flames.

IV

24th December

It is seven o'clock in the morning; the hour of official visits and princely receptions. As I take my carriage and set out for the Maharajah's palace where I am to be presented to my host, the bright, warm rays of the eternally summer-like sun of Travancore strike slantingly under the palms, and bespatter the stem of the arecas and coco-nuts with tones of rosy gold. We trot through the avenues of green palms and soon reach the huge door which I had expected to pass through on the night of my arrival; this door gives access to a square space which incloses a town within the town, and into which people of low caste are never allowed to enter.

This time my carriage crosses the threshold guarded by a picket of armed cavalry. The sacred character of the place is at once apparent, for we pass an immense tank in which a thousand Brahmins, plunged to their waists in water, are making ablutions and praying according to rites that are as old as the world. With their dripping hair, and wetted breasts that shine in the sun like new bronze, they look like water gods, but so absorbed are they in their dreams that not a single one turns to look at the carriage brushing past them, in whose honour the military guard plays fife and tambour.

The walled-off space contains residences of princes, schools, and the huge temple whose four colossal towers dominate all else, four obelisks of sculptured gods pointing to the sky. The fronts and external walls of the palaces are somewhat sad and commonplace; above the doors, however, the usual monsters rear their fierce heads and tell of India, just as in the extreme East dragons are characteristic of China.

A glowing red pervades the whole, for the dust, red as the roads themselves, has for centuries covered all these buildings with tones of blood and of burnt sienna.

Another squad of cavalry is drawn up before the Maharajah's door, superbly accoutred men in red turbans, who handle their repeating rifles with truly modern precision.

The Maharajah himself appears on the threshold. I had feared to see the Prince dressed in a European frock coat, but no, he has had the good taste to prefer the Indian dress, a turban of white silk and a velvet robe with large diamond buttons.

The first reception-room is paved with earthenware, and crystal chandeliers hang from the ceiling. In the middle stands a throne of chiselled silver, whilst

the other furniture is carved from massive black ebony
in that Indian style of lace-like decoration in which
the Asiatic workman excels all others.

I have been commanded to convey a French decoration to His Highness, and when my simple mission
has been fulfilled, we speak of that Europe which the
Prince will never see, for the unswerving rules of his
caste do not allow him to leave India. We speak, too,
of literary matters, for the Prince has a cultivated
and refined taste. Then he takes me into a high
gallery to show me the marvellous ivories and other
treasures which he is pleased to collect, and soon it
is time for me to withdraw.

As I return through the green shade of the palms,
I regret that I have been unable to converse on more
serious subjects with this amiable prince, whose soul
must be so different from our own. We shall meet
again during my stay here, but my first interview has
taught me that the mysteries of his inmost thoughts
will be as impenetrable to me as the great temple.
There is a radical difference of race, ancestry, and religion between us ; then we do not speak the same
language, and the necessity of conversing through a
third person forms (in spite of the affability of my
interpreter) a barrier which isolates us from all
communion.

I am to be presented to the Maharanee (the Queen),
who lives in a separate palace, in two or three days,
though she is not the Maharajah's wife, but his
maternal aunt. The principal families of Travancore
belong to an ancient race that has almost disappeared
from the rest of India, in which the transmission of
name, title, and fortune is solely through the female
side, who in addition have the right to repudiate their
husbands at will.

In the royal family the Maharanee is the eldest of
the daughters, and the Maharajah the oldest son of
the first princess of royal blood. As neither the
actual Queen nor her sisters have any female descendants, the dynasty is shortly bound to expire.

The children of the Maharajah have no right to reign, and they do not even bear the title of Prince.

The women of this caste, whose family name is Nayer, nearly all have features of an especial delicacy. They wear plain bands of hair on each side of their foreheads, but the rest of the hair, which is very black and smooth, is piled into a mass on the top of their heads. This falls forward on to one side like a soldier's cap, giving a somewhat rakish expression, which contrasts strongly with their grave and formal manner.

V

25th December

Towards five o'clock in the evening, as the burning sun has commenced to sink, quantities of musicians in zebu chariots arrive, almost stealthily. The Maharajah has lent me the orchestra from his palace for several hours.

They come barefooted and noiselessly, entering my room with the velvety step of a cat ; then these artists, who have fine and delicate profiles, make ceremonious bows and seat themselves on the ground. They wear little gilt turbans on their heads and diamonds in their ears, and are draped in the antique fashion with a piece of silk barred with gold, which is thrown over one shoulder so as to leave part of the chest and a metal-encircled arm free. Aromatic odours and scents of rose waters escape from their light clothing.

They carry huge instruments with copper strings, like gigantic guitars or mandolines, whose curved handles end in monsters' heads. These guitars, which give out different tones, vary much amongst themselves, but they all have large bodies, whilst here and there along the neck hollow balloons, looking like fruits clustered round a stalk, are placed to increase their resonance ; they are very old and

precious, so withered, that they have acquired great
sonority; they are painted or gilt, or inlaid with
ivory, and even their quaint appearance fills me with
a sense of mystery, the mystery of India. The
musicians smilingly show them to me; some are
made to be stroked by the fingers; others to be played
with a bow; others again are struck with a stick of
pearl; and there is even one that is played by rolling
a little ebony thing looking like a black egg over the
strings. What refinements unknown to our Western
musicians! There are tom-toms tuned to different
pitches, and boy singers whose robes are of especial
richness. A printed programme prepared for this sole
purpose is placed before me, in which the strange but
melodious names of the musicians are all in twelve
syllables.

It is five o'clock, and all, to the number of about
twenty-five, are seated in readiness on the carpet;
the room is already filled with shadow, and punkhas
keep the air in motion with their slow and wearied
movement. All the monster-headed guitars are in
readiness, and the musicians are about to commence.
What agonizing sounds most instruments of such a
size produce, and what a clamour such tom-toms.
I am all attention, prepared for much noise. Behind
the musicians an arched door, leading to a white
vestibule, remains open, and a golden ray from the
setting sun falls on a group of red-turbaned soldiers
of the Maharajah's army standing in the reddish
glow, but the musicians themselves are plunged in
vague shadow.

Can the concert have commenced? From their
grave and attentive attitudes, and the way in which
they watch one another, it would appear so. But
there is nothing to be heard. But yes; a hardly
audible high note, like that of the prelude to " Lohen-
grin," which is then doubled, complicated, and transformed into a murmured rhythm, without growing
any louder. . . . What a total surprise, this almost
toneless music coming from such powerful instru-

ments! One might have said the buzzing of a fly
held within the hollow of one's hand, or the brushing
of the wings of a night-moth against the glass, or
the death agony of a dragon-fly. Then a musician
places a little steel thing in his mouth and rubs his
cheek over it, so as to produce the murmurings of a
fountain. One of the largest and most complicated
guitars, that the player caresses with his hand as if
he feared it, says " hou, hou " all the time on nearly
the same notes, like the veiled cry of the screech owl ;
another instrument, which is muted, makes a sound
like that of the sea breaking on the shore ; and there
are hardly audible drummings played by fingers on
the edge of the tom-toms. Then suddenly come
unexpected violences, furies that last for a couple of
seconds, when the strings vibrate with full force,
and the tom-toms struck in another way give out
dull and heavy sounds like elephants walking over
hollow ground, or mimic the rumblings of subterranean
water, or a torrent that falls into an abyss. But this
subsides quickly, and the nearly silent music continues.

A young Brahmin with beautiful eyes is seated
cross-legged on the ground holding an instrument
whose rude shape contrasts with the delicate refinement of the others ; it is made of common pottery,
and has pebbles inside a sort of jar with a large opening in one of its smooth and swollen sides.

The sound which he draws from it varies according
as he leaves the jar open, or stops the opening by
pressing its mouth close to his body. He plays on it
with marvellously nimble fingers and sometimes the
sound is light, at others deep, occasionally hard and
dry like a crackling of hail ; then the pebbles are
heard moving at the bottom.

When the voice of one of the guitars rises above the
whispered silence, it is always in a melody of training
sounds, a passionate and full-voiced song that plunges
into agony ; and the tom-toms, without drowning
the trembling and plaintive notes, beat an accompaniment of mysterious import which expresses the

exaltation of human suffering far more poignantly than our most supreme music.

" The elephants are here." Some one utters this phrase, thus breaking the charm that holds me a listener. What elephants ? Oh, yes ! I had forgotten—I had expressed a desire this morning to see the elephants caparisoned with palanquins on their backs in the Indian manner, and the order for their equipment had been graciously given to the Palace stables.

The music ceases, for I must go outside to see the elephants. When I reach the threshold I find myself in the presence of three enormous beasts, awaiting me and standing by the door, sharply defined in the brightness of the setting sun. Their heads face me, and at first I can only distinguish amongst their trappings the threatening ivory tusks, and the huge trunks of rose colour veined with black, and the striped ears which keep up a continual and fan-like motion. Long green and red robes, colonnaded palanquins, necklaces of bells and head ornaments of gold embroidery that fall over their huge foreheads. Three superb animals in their prime of seventy years so gentle and tractable ; they turn their intelligent little eyes towards me as they kneel down in order to allow me to mount if I should wish.

A gracious twilight fills the room as I return to the music of beating wings and rustling insects.

Each of the guitars chants its despair in turn by intervals of almost voiceless harmony, the one that is struck by the hand or bow, the one that is beaten with the pearl rod, and that strangest one of all which weeps when the little egg-shaped ebony ball is rolled over its strings.

Their songs have not the bewildering echoes of some far-removed sadness, as those of Mongolia or China have, for they are almost comprehensible to our senses ; they betray the sad brooding of a race that is not different from our own, though long centuries have parted us ; they and our gipsies use the same fevered phrases, though in a somewhat coarser way.

Human voices were only introduced towards the end. One after the other great-eyed, slender youths, clothed in gorgeous draperies, executed trills with wonderful rapidity, but their childish voices are already broken and worn ; the man in a golden turban, who conducts, first plays a weird prelude and then with lowered head looks into their eyes in the manner of a serpent fascinating a bird. I feel that he cast a spell on them, and that he could, if he wished, break the whole mechanism of their feeble throats. It seems the words which they chant to these sad rhythms are prayers to an offended goddess whom they wish to appease.

Finally, it is the turn of the great master, a man of about twenty-five to thirty, who has a beautiful face and an expression of energy. He is going to represent, with action and song, the plaints of a young girl whose lover loves her no longer.

Seated on the ground he seems plunged in meditation whilst his face becomes sombre. Then, all at once, the voice bursts forth with the cutting tone of Eastern bagpipes, though the upper notes are possessed by a hoarse, manly quality, and an infinity of sorrow is expressed in a poignant and, to me, novel manner. The sorrow expressed in his face and the contractions of the delicate hands, is rendered with highest art.

This orchestra and these singers belong to the Maharajah, and their music resounds daily in the silence of his guarded palace, where ever-bowing servants, whose hands are joined in a perpetual salute, walk with cat-like steps. How far away the thoughts of this prince must be from ours, and how different his conceptions of the sadnesses of life and love and death! But this strange and rare music, which is part of his being, reveals a portion of his soul to me that I should never see in our short and formal interviews, so burdened with ceremony and foreign words.

VI

26th December

Three thousand Brahmins, who live in the sacred inclosure, and bathe in the holy pond, are at present the guests of the Maharajah. They have come from the surrounding countries, and from those forests where they live on fruit and grain, absorbed in mystic dreams and disdainful of the things of this world. They have assembled to celebrate a religious festivity that lasts for fifty days, and is held every six years. They offer long prayers of expiation for blood that was shed many years ago in a neighbouring country during a war of conquest ; it matters little that it was countless years ago ; the spilt blood still calls for supplicating cries, still demands religious music, and the bellowings of sacred shells like those graven on the arms of Trivandrum. The ray-crowned idols of Pandavas, which are thirty feet high, and have hideous faces, and fierce downcast eyes, have been drawn for this occasion from their secret sanctuaries. Muscular efforts aided by ropes have rolled them into the open air and sunlight of the temple courtyard, where they may strike terror into the minds of the simple— whilst the initiated pray to the invisible and ineffable Brahma from the depths of their souls. During these celebrations, the entire Brahmin inclosure palpitates with the intense life of ancient rites, of burning prayers of terror, and of ecstasy. I can hear the far-off murmurings which have an irresistible attraction for me, but I am rigidly excluded, and neither the influence of the Maharajah nor that of any one else can help me.

The festival of the initiated has found an echo among the believers of the middle and lower castes who live under the immense palms that cover the rest of the town, and who, like myself, are excluded from communion with the Brahmins. Prayers and supplications are heard there too, in the whitening dawn, and at the time of sunset.

Imploring cries are heard in all the cemeteries and at the foot of the sacred trees under which warriors have been buried. The little sacred lamps have been lit all along the shady roads and at those places where monumental stones arise ; and music offerings and flowers are here too. The smallest temples and even the simple altars consecrated to the divinities of the jungles shine with a thousand trembling flames. Here I am welcome to wander as I choose, under the gloom of the interlacing palms, in search of the music and the lights that lure me to them.

I reach a very old and humble temple, with broken granite columns, standing at the foot of huge trees which lose themselves in the gloom. Tiny lamps filled with coco-nut oil, which look like glow-worms, cast their light about the temple, which is garlanded with flowers and ornaments of pleated reeds. The horrible parrot-faced god is stationed in the furthermost of two or three little rooms, where he crouches, many-armed, with his green face overshadowed by a high headdress. Here young, white kids disport themselves in these sacred precincts, of which they are the familiar and venerated occupants. Half-nude worshippers, decked in necklets of flowers, throng round the door, but the noise of the tambourines and bagpipes is almost drowned by the constant and plaintive bellowings of the sacred shells.

Smiles of welcome greet me, and after having placed wreaths of jasmine flowers, which have intoxicating odours like that of incense, round my neck, the people stand on one side that I may see.

Now I reach a place where a monstrous fig tree of great age stands. Men are assembled round a granite platform, supported on pillars which must have belonged to some ancient funeral monument, revelling in the sound of maddening music. The customary lights, the garlands of roses or jasmine, and the offerings of fruit and grain are here too. A kind of officiating priest, a man of low caste, whose face is quite black, recites ritual phrases in a frenzied manner, broken by the din of the tom-toms. Women stand behind the tree, almost hidden in shadow, and utter constant and long-protracted cries. Children tend a fire of grass which has been lighted on the ground, and into whose flames the tom-toms are constantly thrust so that they may retain their dry, sonorous tones. The officiating priest is seized with increasing excitement, and soon seems possessed of an evil spirit. He gives vent to terrible howls and seeks to dash his head against stones or trunks of trees. A hedge of naked arms is formed round to keep him from harm, till at length he falls on the ground exhausted and motionless with a horrible rattling in his throat.

Yet it would seem that this incomprehensible god, whom they worship under the palms to the sound of the tambours and the savage music, is the same deity in different shape that the mysterious Brahmins worship in spirit in the secret recesses of the great temple.

Indeed, this god is but another form of the God we adore. For there are no false gods, and the wisdom of sages who profess that theirs is the true God, and that they alone know his name, is but childish folly. For the rest, the conception of a God seated amidst the unmeasurable and inaccessible, be he one or many, be he named Brahma, Jehovah, or Allah, so far exceeds our comprehension, that a little less or greater error can hardly matter in our ideas of Him. No doubt, too, that He listens just as attentively to the prayer of the simple, uneducated native, who wanders through the forest pouring forth his agony of life and death at the foot of some green-faced fetish.

VII

26th December

The cry of the crows is so much intermingled with all the other sounds of India, that one ends by ceasing to heed it. I have already almost ceased to notice the hideous morning *aubade* that immediately succeeds the murmurings that rise from the temple. A great tree that stands before my terrace is one of their favourite nightly resting-places ; a tree covered with large branches which bend under the weight of their black burden.

As I take my seat in the carriage this morning, the first rays of the sun, which rises at a fixed hour each day, just commence to penetrate through the leaves and under the vaulted palms ; once more I cross the forbidden inclosure in order that I may present myself before the Maharanee (the Queen).

Directly we have passed the entrance, I see the sacred ponds again in which Brahmins plunged to their waists in water are making their customary morning ablutions.

This walled town, which I am visiting at a much earlier hour than on the last occasion, contains not only the dwellings of the princes standing amidst gardens of palms, but streets bordered by humble houses built of clay that are inhabited by Hindoos of high caste. This charming hour of daybreak is the one chosen by the long-eyed housewives for the decoration of the earth that lies in front of their dwellings. They trace wonderful patterns in white powder upon the red soil, which has previously been well swept and beaten. Their designs are but fleeting, and are carried away by the lightest wind or by the feet of men, goats, dogs, and crows. They do their work very quickly, guiding themselves in the tracing of these designs by marks which have been placed there beforehand, and are visible to them alone. Bending forward in a graceful attitude, they move the little box which contains a powder that escapes in a white trail like an endless ribbon over the surface of the ground. Complicated arabesques and geometrical figures grow marvellously under their hands. Often, too, they place a hibiscus flower, an Indian pink, and a yellow marigold at the chief junction of their network of lines after the design is completed. The little street, decorated from one end to the other in this manner, seems to be momentarily covered by a fairy carpet.

The whole of this quarter has retained its character of old-world elegance, honest peace, and simple dignity.

In front of the door of the Maharanee's garden red-turbaned soldiers are drawn up, who salute and present arms to the sound of fife and drum, in faultless manner. The Queen's husband descends from the steps in front of the house to welcome me, with truly distinguished courtesy. Like the Maharajah, he has had the good taste to retain his Indian dress of velvet with diamond buttons, and his turban of white silk. Notwithstanding this, he is a scholar and a man of refined literary taste. The Queen holds her receptions in a room on the first floor which is, I am sorry to say, decorated with European furniture, but she herself, in national costume, looks like a charming personification of India. She has a regular profile, pure features, and magnificent large eyes, in fact, all the beauty of her race. In accordance with the tradition of the Nayer family, her jet-black hair is wound round her forehead. Enormous rings of diamonds and rubies hang from her ear-lobes, and her naked arms, which are much bejewelled, are unconcealed by her velvet bodice. For the rest, a piece of silk figured with exquisite designs in gold covers her statuesque form. Oh ! it is easy to imagine the degree of refinement to which a noble lady of sovereign race may attain in a country where even the lower classes are cultured, but the especial charm of this Maharanee lies in her benevolence and in a reserved and gentle sweetness.

There is a charm of sadness, too, which is apparent behind her smiles. I know one of the griefs which has darkened the almost cloistered life of the Queen. Brahma has given her no daughter, nor any niece that she might adopt, so her dynasty is doomed to expire, and doubtless there will be great changes in Travancore, a land hitherto sheltered from the march of centuries.

We speak of Europe, which has a charm for her imagination, and I see that one of her dreams has been to know this strange and far-off country, as inaccessible to her as the planet Mars or the moon, for no Indian lady of noble birth, not to mention a queen, may undertake such a voyage without incurring so great a loss of caste that she would at once fall to the rank of a pariah.

During the few remaining days which I shall spend here I may sometimes have the honour to see the Maharajah, but never again the gracious Maharanee, so before leaving I seek to impress her image on my mind, for her face does not seem to belong to our times, and it is only in old Indian miniatures that I have had a glimpse of such princesses.

After my visit to the Maharanee has terminated, I go, without leaving the Brahmin inclosure, and see the sons of one of her sisters, who are heirs presumptive to the throne, after whose death the dynasty will terminate.

They bear the title of first and second prince, and live in separate dwellings standing in the midst of gardens. Though these young men wear plumes of diamonds in their turbans, hunt the tiger and follow the rites of Brahma, they are none the less conversant with the trend of modern thought, and occupy themselves with literature or natural philosophy. One of them, who had in accordance with my request taken me to see the trappings of his elephants, showed me some remarkable photographs which he had taken and developed himself, and which he had afterwards sent to an exhibition in Europe, having the wish to gain a medal.

I felt a desire this evening, as the sun was setting, to see the Indian Ocean, whose waves break on the barren shores about a mile from Trivandrum.

I had to cross the whole extent of the walled town, but the livery of the Maharajah's carriage insured me safe conduct. I passed peaceful little streets bordered by Brahmin houses, the red walls of palaces and gardens, and skirted the precincts of the great temple to which I had never been so close.

The town once crossed, I found myself in a sandy waste amongst the dunes, where the last red rays of the setting sun still lingered. A few broken and twisted palms were scattered here and there, all leaning in the same direction, having yielded like the trees of our own coasts to the force of the sea winds. Heaps of sand which must have taken centuries to accumulate, crumbled remains of madrepore shells and stones, the pulverization of myriads of existences, announced the near presence of the great destroyer, whose terrible voice commenced to make itself heard. Suddenly the road made a turn among the dunes, and the ever restless ocean was spread out before me.

In other regions of the world it seems as if human life flocked instinctively towards the sea. Men construct their dwellings by its shores, and their towns as nearly as possible to its waters ; they are jealous of the smallest bay that can contain ships, and even the smallest strip of coast.

Here, on the contrary, it is shunned as something dead or void. This sea is but an abyss that cannot be crossed, that serves no purpose, and but inspires terror. It is almost inaccessible, and no one ventures on it. Before the endless line of breakers, and along the endless extent of sand, the only human trace that I can see is an old granite temple, lowly and rude, with worn columns, half eaten away by salt and spray. It is placed here to appease and exorcise the restless devourer which imprisons Travancore, and which, calm as it is this evening, will shortly, when the summer monsoon commences, rage furiously during an entire season.

VIII

Friday, 29th December

Among the many graceful favours which the Dewan, in accordance with the instructions of his

5

Serene Highness the Maharajah, showered on me, one of the most charming and unforgettable was my reception of to-day at the college for young ladies of noble race.

I set out on my way directly the sun had risen, not, indeed, without some misgivings, for I dreaded some tedious display of learning. In the forest palms, however, where we allowed our horses to walk, fearing that we might arrive too early, I saw first one, then two, three pretty little girls, sparkling with magnificent ornaments ; naked-footed children of about twelve years with white flowers in their hair, whose gold-embroidered silks and the jewels which covered their arms and neck shone in the first rays of the early morning sun. Their steps, like mine, were directed towards the Brahmin inclosure, but when they saw my carriage they commenced to hasten, running as fast as the bands of precious silks encasing their legs would allow them. Was it possible that these toilettes of Peris or Apsaras were assumed in my honour ?

I found all the little Indian fairies assembled at the college in their dazzling array. It was holiday time, it seems, but they consented to give up a morning for me. A little one advances and presents me with one of those highly scented and formal bouquets in which flowers and gold thread are mingled.

It is the Maharajah's pleasure to diffuse education in his kingdom, education which has but proved a scourge to us, but which will be beneficent at Travancore, since faith has not ceased to irradiate all earthly things. His Highness had also wished to show me a rare and unexpected spectacle in connection with this college of noble ladies which quite equals or even excels our own ; and the word of command had been issued to the parents that the little ones should be decked in the heavy jewels of their mothers and grandmothers. Youthful arms and swelling bosoms glittered with ancient jewellery, set in matchless archaic mountings, such as the goddesses of the temples wear.

The class-rooms were like those of our European colleges, light and simply furnished, with geographical charts and instructive models hanging on the white-washed walls. But the strange scholars all looked like idols, from the little ones whose great black eyes glittered, and whose dark bronze skins were seen between their loin-cloths and their golden corselets, up to the older ones, who wore a veil of white Indian muslin over their dark coiled hair, and who already wore the grave and anxious expression of approaching womanhood.

Essays of style and historical compositions are shown me, also pretty drawings after European models that the little goddesses had made, quite in the manner of our own children; they were signed with names many syllables in length—melodious names that read like a phrase of music.

A little one of five or six had copied an eagle of complicated plumage standing on a branch; but she had commenced in the middle of the paper without taking measurement, yet, though there was no room left for the head, she had sketched it all the same flattened and widened out, extending to the edges of the paper, and not a detail or a feather was omitted, and she had bravely signed her beautiful name—Apsara.

I see gold-embroidered velvets and veils diaphanous as mists; diamonds, rubies, emeralds, and transparent enamels; many bracelets, some so large that they must be held on to the little arms by thread; necklets made from scarce Portuguese coins, which dated from Goa's times of splendour, and which have slept for centuries in coffers of sandal wood.

Finally, there are songs, pieces of music for violins, and then dances—slow and complicated dances that have a religious tinge, consisting of a series of rhythmic steps and a waving of jewel-laden arms.

These pupils, belonging to castes never seen by strangers, are all beautiful, refined, and graceful, and have eyes such as one can but see in India. Oh!

how can I describe the impression of chaste and transcendent beauty that these mysterious little flowers have given me ?

IX

Saturday, 30th December

I leave Travancore to-morrow morning, where many more favours have been showered on me than I deserve, seeing that I have simply acquitted myself of the agreeable duty of offering a cross to the prince. I shall go northward in one of the great decked boats belonging to the Maharajah, by way of the chain of lakes, and it will take me about two days and two nights to reach the little kingdom of Cochin, where I shall stop for a while. After that there will be a journey of thirty to forty hours outside Cochin, then I shall come to the more frequented regions, where the railroads run, and I shall rejoin the main line from Calicut to Madras.

As this is my last evening in Trivandrum, I linger longer than usual in the groves which run through the town, where feeble lamps burn dimly under the shade of the dense palms whose conquering night they are powerless to dispel.

The subjugating yoke of plant life is even more apparent now, when everything is wrapped in a magnificent fall of green, than it is in the daytime.

I am leaving to-morrow morning, though I have seen hardly anything, and have in no way penetrated the secret heart of India ; I have divined nothing of the Brahminism of which this country is one of the centres, for everything seems barred to Europeans, even though the most gracious hospitality be extended to them.

My chance wanderings finally bring me to the street of the merchants, the great straight street that leads to the inclosure which guards the palaces and temples ; the sky is clear and the night starry. Crowds of long-haired men wander under the light of antique lamps which are supported by tall thin stalks. These are buyers and sellers of hammered copper-printed muslins, idols, and Brahmin images—everywhere a press of naked chests, black heads of hair, and sparkling dark eyes. Stalls where roots, grain, and cakes, the frugal nourishment of the Brahmins, are displayed; myriads of little shops, always lit by the same kind of ancient lamps, whose double or triple flames are supported by figures of monsters or of gods.

The porch of the sacred inclosure is seen at the end of the street in the same direction, but much farther on the great temple, through whose open door the inner depths, outlined by thousands of little flames, are visible; there is the sanctuary of Brahma, the soul of this land of dreams and meditation.

The whole building is illuminated, even to the depths where the priests alone may venture; the nave is outlined by points of flame that cluster towards the centre into a geometrical pattern; this must be a gigantic chamber, but it is too far off for me to distinguish. As ever, people are playing within, for the sound of music and the braying of trumpets reaches me, mingled with the long murmurs of human voices. The door that I may not cross stands ever open, and above it the huge pyramid, which I know to be composed of a mass of stone-carved gods, raised its head through the thin mists till its jagged summit seems to mingle with the stars. It is usual in times of solemnity, such as the present one, when prayers and supplications are unending, to light a trail of little flame on each of the four pyramids; these little fires commence above the doors and climb up amongst the black masses of the sculpture till they seem to trace a road to heaven through the ranks of stone-carved gods.

At length the street becomes deserted, and the shopkeepers commence to close their wooden shutters and to kindle the little lamps that stand in niches in the walls, and which serve to keep evil spirits from the houses. I watch the merchants finishing their daily reckoning. The tiny round silver or copper coins of Travancore are collected in a bag, then they take handfuls of them on a counting-board, which consists of a plank furnished with holes ; a little piece of money drops into each hole, and when the board is quite full one knows the exact number ; then these are shaken into a chest and the reckoning recommences. Others write down figures and make calculations on bands of dried palm-leaf, which look like ancient papyri, and I fancy that I am back in olden times.

At length the hour has come when all signs of life cease, save the little lights on the walls and the more distant illuminations of the temples ; all is plunged in gloom and silence. No women are visible, for they have all disappeared into the dwelling-houses ; but the men who have knotted up their hair are seen shrouded in white linen or muslin cloths, lying on the terraces or under the verandas, or even before the doors amongst the goats ; with the repulsion that all Indians feel for roofs and ceilings, these men prefer to sleep in the mild, warm night filled with the scent of flowers, where all seems veiled in a bluish dust.

X

Sunday, 31st December

When the sound of the morning prayer rising from the sanctuary ceases to be heard, and as the harshly croaking crows disperse in the gray dawn, it is time to start, so I take my seat in the carriage which is to conduct me to the " port " of Trivandrum. Once again at the exquisite hour of sunrise I shall pass through the groves of coco-palms in which the town is hidden, but it will be for the last time.

The stormy wind that has raged during the night has deposited blood-red dust upon the walls of mud and on the thatched roofs, giving more than ever the impression of houses illuminated by the glow of a red fire, but above them the palms that have been bathed in the freshness of the night have an almost supernatural green, tinged with glints of emerald. Here and there bunches of flowers hang down in a falling shower from the summits of the trees till they reach to the ground.

Pickets of the Maharajah's soldiers, looking magnificent in their turbans and accoutrements, pass and repass on their way to relieve outlying posts. Throngs of people are calmly proceeding to mass, for it is Sunday, and I see little girls veiled in muslins holding prayer books in their hands ; nearly all these are Christians of old race, whose ancestors worshipped Christ several centuries before our own. We hear the tolling of the bells of the strange Syrian or Catholic chapels that are built close to the temples of Brahma, and are sheltered by the same verdant palms. The enchanting scene gives an impression of peaceful calm, in which order and tolerance reign supreme.

At length the wharf is reached. It will readily be understood that the port of Trivandrum is not situated on the ocean, but on the lagoon, for the coast of this country is inaccessible.

My boat, which belongs to the prince, lies motionless amidst a hundred others ; it is a sort of long galley for fourteen rowers, having a cabin on the poop in which it is possible to lie down and sleep. These fourteen rowers ply paddles with bamboo handles, and form a wonderful automatic machine of bronze humanity, instinct with force and vitality.

The lagoon, which at first was deep and narrow and shut in by a thick hedge of palms, gradually widens and becomes sunlit. Our rowers work themselves up to a pitch of excitement with songs and cries, cleaving the foul and sluggish waters rapidly, and so begins the peaceful journey which will last three days.

On both shores palms mingled with many-stemmed

banyan trees form an endless hedge, whilst garlands
of unknown flowers hang from the branches, and
great spotted and twisted water-lilies spring from
amongst the rushes.

Barques which are going to Trivandrum pass us
continually, for the lagoon is the chief high-road of
the peaceful country. Huge boats, like gondolas,
that pursue their slow and noiseless course, impelled
by statuesque boatmen furnished with long poles,
these have houses on their poops, filled with Indian
men and women whose black eyes stare with wonder
at our fast boat, manned by fourteen rowers.

Sometimes a marvellous bird, brighter and more
gorgeous than our kingfishers, skims quickly along
the surface of the water, with a cry of joy ; and there
are beds of flowering lilies, and masses of lotus
sheeted with rosy blooms.

The interminable lagoon that serves as a highway
changes its appearance hourly. Sometimes it is
narrow and shady, sometimes overhung like a church
nave by coco-nut palms, whose ribs resemble arches ;
at other times it enlarges and expands and seems to
extend to infinite distances ; then it narrows and the
space between the serried banks of palms is dotted
with countless green islands.

The sun rises, and in spite of the shade and the
moving water I feel myself gradually overcome by
the stifling heat. Our speed is undiminished as the
chief excites the men from time to time by an imperious clack of the tongue, causing their muscles
to stiffen as if they had been struck with a lash, and
to which they reply with falsetto cries like those of
monkeys. Trailing grasses, branches of lilies, and
floating reeds swim quickly past our swiftly flying
boat.

It is ten o'clock, and we are no longer sheltered by
the palms, but journey under the blue sky along a
narrow passage bordered by shrubs bearing white
flowers. The two symmetrical rows of bronzed flesh
continue the mechanical movements—which have

already lasted for six hours—merely a few drops of perspiration trickle down bodies which shine with the polished reflection of metal in the terrible rays of the sun. A wild luxuriance of flowers hangs from the shrubs standing by the shore, the white colour of which stands out harshly against the deep blue sky ; these trees fruit and flower at the same time, scattering plentiful and useless fruits on the water like a hail of golden apples. My boatmen still continue to row, but they now sing in a dreamy manner like that of men wearied with healthy fatigue, whilst their shining teeth are uncovered by a vacant smile.

We pass an inhabited region where there are villages, pagodas, and old churches in the Hindoo style that even the Syrian churches have adopted.

Our waterway suddenly narrows and is hedged in by banks of fern ; then we plunge into dim gloom, filled with the scent of earthy freshness ; we are traversing the long tunnel that the Maharajah has constructed so that boats may reach the more distant lagoons, those of the north, which we shall reach this evening, and travel on to-morrow.

The noise of our paddles reverberates through the tunnel, and as we pass other boats that loom out of the shade like black shadows, our oarsmen utter cries, which are long repeated by melancholy echoes.

Now that midday has come, we change our gang of men. Once through the tunnel we find ourselves again in an open space dotted with palm-covered islands ; a village hidden by trees stands close by the shore, and fourteen fresh rowers await us there. Relays of men are stationed thus at points awaiting orders for the Maharajah's boats.

The fresh men take their places with much noise and excitement, call out like merry children, vie with each other in rowing and laughing, and their white teeth sparkle as they sing. Some are Christians, and wear a scapular across their naked chests ; others have the seal of Siva painted on their foreheads, and the three horizontal lines of Siva traced in gray dust on their arms and chests.

Palms everywhere, a splendid monotony of palms, so many that one is wearied and almost afraid of them. When one thinks that more than two hundred miles of the country round us is given up to their dominion, a feeling of distress is experienced akin to the sentiment that the ancients used to name " the horror of forests."

Palms everywhere, never-ending palms. There are those which rear their plumed heads high into the air, supported by long frail stems ; others again which, like young trees, spring from the surface in the damp warm earth; but all have the same intense green and the same glossy freshness. They shine in the sunlight as if they had been varnished, whilst below them the lagoons look like mirrors of polished tin.

My boatmen display a terrible energy, though the sun beats directly on them with such force that white men could not survive it. They row for hours, the muscles of their arms slackening and tightening under their networks of swollen veins, singing the while at the top of their voices. Sometimes a sudden frenzy seems to seize them, their song becomes panting and broken, and they strike the water so furiously that the foam commences to fly and their oars break. The paintings in honour of Siva disappear, washed away by the sweat which runs down their bodies.

Towards evening the lagoon narrows again, and is inclosed by steep shores covered by ferns and trailing plants. Around us there are hundreds of boats lying at rest, and above our heads rises a bridge of sculptured stone. It is the town of Quilon, one of the large towns of Travancore, and, like that city, is embowered in gardens ; for a while the palms are replaced by trees more nearly resembling our own, and I can even discern lawns and rose bushes.

A large stairway descends to the water, and I can

see the white colonnaded house which has been uninhabited, I am told, for a long while ; the Dewan has given orders that my evening meal should be prepared there. It is nightfall as we reach the shore, and Indian serving-men, in costumes white as the house itself, hasten to the steps to bid me welcome, and to offer me a bouquet of roses on a silver salver. We are to stop here an hour or two whilst my boat-men rest.

After supper I wander round the lonely garden and give myself up to meditation. I dream that I am in an old French garden, fallen somewhat into neglect, but where Bengal roses still cluster round the paths. The sky still retains a note of sombre red where the sun has set—the same dull glow that is seen on our warmest summer days.

Through the stillness of the calm night, sweet and ever-haunting impressions of my childhood days come back to me ; as usual I give myself up to the sad play of my imagination, a melancholy sport that I never weary of indulging in. It was in an abandoned garden surrounded by woods that I received my first impressions of nature, and I dreamt my first dreams of the warm countries on some burning August or September evening when just such a glow lit up our flat horizon.

The same scent of jasmine filled the air in those summer days of old, and the dark wings of bats and owls flitted noiselessly across the copper-coloured sky.

The bats that fly round this house are much larger, but their silent and capricious flight resembles that of our own ; they, however, belong to the larger species called vampire or roussette, and their huge wings scare away my dreams. Then, suddenly from under the great trees which encircle the garden with their shadows, issues a sound of horns and sacred bag-pipes ; it is the hour of Brahma, and I can hear the murmurs of human voices chanting the evening prayer in the recesses of the temple.

Suddenly silence reigns once more, but this time it is pervaded by a nameless melancholy that was not there before. The thought crosses my mind that it is the 31st of December, 1899, and in a few hours the century, which was that of my youth, will pass away for ever. The stars above my head pursuing their almost endless course fill my thoughts with the fearful notion of eternity, and of our poor moth-like existence; and the death of the present century and the birth of the succeeding one, which will be my last, seem to be insignificant nothings when one thinks of the endless terrifying flight of ages. Agonizing thoughts of death and of our short existence are old and familiar, but to be surrounded by these woods and temples, and to think that I am in the heart of Brahmin India, gives me a strange and delightful thrill; this old garden, with its roses and jasmines, seems to conjure up vague and unspeakable impressions in which sentiments of exile mingle with a feeling in other countries, but as the years go by it becomes dimmed, like everything else; this evening it is soon blunted by bodily fatigue, for in the warm languorous night sleep quickly overtakes me.

The stars shine brightly as we resume our journey at nine o'clock; our men are now rested, and will row us for two miles to the village where a fresh relief awaits us.

The slow boats that we had already passed on our way begin to drop behind us once more; their black outlines are enlarged and doubled by the reflections of the water that gives them the appearance of spectral gondolas.

The many-creeked lagoon, which has now widened out like the sea, soon becomes lit up by fires; they are the lanterns of the fishermen and great torches which they use to attract fish, burning bundles of reed, which they swing continually in order to keep them alight. All these flames are reflected by the surface of the shining water, on which the night wind

has traced a few delicate ripples. Though the monotonous rhythm of the paddles begins to make me
drowsy, the sentiment of the intense life which
animates these swamps is ever present. It is truly a
primitive life, however, that hardly differs from that
of our first lake-inhabiting ancestors.

XI

After a warm night, during which the balanced
swing of our oars has never ceased, the first dawn
of the new century rises fresh and rosy upon a world
ever hunting and watching for its fishy prey in the
clear morning light. The immense lagoon, surrounded
by thick clusters of overhanging palms, is thronged
with innumerable fishing-boats, which often brush
past us and cause us to slacken; sometimes these
boats are stationary, at others they wander along
stealthily, making as little noise as possible; men
stand in superb postures on the floating planks, holding nets, lines, and lances in their hands, watching
all that moves in the water. Birds, pelicans, and
herons of all kinds stand on the muddy shore and
dart their inquisitive eyes in all directions, so that
besides hooks, nets, and barbed forks, there are
always hundreds of beaks on the watch. These voracious multitudes are attracted and maintained by
the shoals of cold-blooded and silent little beings of
which the lagoon is the inexhaustible reservoir;
and the commencement of the new century will do
nothing to change a mode of life which must have
existed since the beginning of time.

As the banks draw closer we can perceive under
the great palms tiny human habitations belonging
to people whose very existence is dependent on that
of the trees, they are barriers made from palm fibres
extending from one tree to another, thatches made
from palm, mats, nets, and cords made from palm.

These precious trees not only give them shelter,
fruit, and oil, but also supply nearly every necessity

of those that live under them, and indeed this part of India could exist without the rice-fields which wave here and there in the wind-like expanses of bluish silk.

The lagoons gradually expand, and a slight but favourable wind rises, so my boatmen hoist a mat some three or four metres high upon a mast. What with sails and paddles, our speed grows faster across this peaceful little ocean whose shores are forests, that have a bluish look in the distance. Helped by the wind which fills the mast, the men slacken their energies and commence to hum a different song, a sleepy melody which issues through their closed teeth, and seems like a never-ending peal of bells heard from a great distance.

It is almost midnight in France, the hour at which the twentieth century begins, and the New Year's Festival should be at its height in our land of icy gloom.

The wind commences to fall, and at midday there is a dead calm, and the heat is like that of a stove. We make for the palm-covered shore in order to land the morning relay of men, who withdraw with profound salutes. Our new gang of men set out at a furious speed ; they are of a lighter bronze and wear necklets and earrings, and sacred emblems are traced in gray dust on their breasts. Now the air bears on us with an unaccustomed weight, and seems as if charged with warm vapour. The sky, the dull surface of the lagoon, and the surrounding objects look faded and tarnished in the excessive light, whilst their outlines seem mingled and confused in a glow of dazzling pallor. In marked contrast with this dimness are the drops of water which ripple by our boat and trickle from the paddles and seem to shine from the foreheads and chests of our rowers.

Towards three o'clock we cross the boundary which separates Travancore from the little kingdom of Cochin ; but the surface of the water and the palm forests that have followed us since our departure remain unchanged.

Towards the close of the day, however, towns appear on both banks which lie about the same distance from one another as those of a great river.

The town on the right bank, the one close to us, is Ernaculum, the capital where the Rajah resides ; by the water's edge there are four Syrian churches which look like pagodas, a great Brahmin temple, barracks and schools, red-coloured buildings standing on reddish soil, but neither a boat nor a human being by the landing-place. The dwellings of the haughty Brahmins are concealed under the bluish shade of the encroaching palms, or are hidden amidst trailing plants and ferns, and lie **far** removed from these sad, pretentious buildings.

Signs of life are, however, visible farther along the left bank. First we pass Matancheri, an Indian trading town, with its thousands of little houses nestling under the trees. The town is situated on a bay communicating with the ocean, and countless boats are riding at anchor ; sailing-boats with strange masts belonging to the olden times, which have never ceased to plough the Arabian Sea on their way to trade with Muscat, some even taking grains and spice to Bussorah and the head of the Persian Gulf. A good deal farther on we come to the old Cochin of the Dutch and Portuguese, now fallen into the hands of other masters ; here and there is a port where modern vessels vomit forth their clouds of dense black smoke.

In the middle of the lagoon, and far removed from the three dissimilar towns, there is a wooded island, a sort of park filled with old trees, to which my boat directs its course (half concealed by verdure). I can see white stairways and a white landing-place, and farther back an old white palace. It appears that I am to be quartered here by order of the Rajah of this country, whose guest I am. Neglect and decay are apparent everywhere, and the house, standing amidst lawns and huge trees, reminds me of the enchanted home of the Sleeping Beauty, and the gathering twilight renders my arrival at the lonely isle more melancholy still.

As at Quilon, white-robed serving-men throng the steps and offer me roses, and on my way I pass through an exquisite old garden, with straight walks overhung with roses and jasmine, fashioned in the olden style.

There is nothing but the house on the island, and I am alone in the house. During the times when the territory of Cochin belonged to the Low Countries, this mansion was the residence of the Dutch Governor. It is as massive as a fortress, and the galleries and verandas form a charming series of festooned arches, such as are seen in an old mosque. Within, the colonial luxury of former days, immense whitewashed rooms carpeted by old mats of a fineness that is unknown now; precious old wood carvings; furniture made in India after European models of quaint shape and antiquated style; on the walls coloured prints representing silk, which has faded to a delicious tint.

A messenger has been dispatched to warn me that I shall not see the Rajah who offers me hospitality, as he is at present in mourning. A little prince of the blood, who was quite young, almost a baby, has just closed his black eyes for ever, and the funeral rites absorb the attention of everybody of the palace.

I would have much preferred to stop at Matancheri, in some humble " Travellers' Rest," where I would have been free to mingle with the evening life of the people, than to reside in this official solitude. Both here and at Travancore I am in India, at the same time shut out from it.

The well-mannered and silent serving-men, whose movements have something stealthy about them, light the lamps hanging from the fretted arches; and when I have finished my prisoner's repast, which is served at a table decorated somewhat strangely with flowers and leaves, I wander into the garden to see the first sunset of the century. A dull glow still pervades the eastern horizon on which the trees trace black hieroglyphics; daylight lingers for a few moments, and owls and huge bats with noiseless wings circle madly through the still warm air. Then all at once the stars commence to shine, and night falls quite suddenly.

XII

In the morning, directly the red sun has appeared, my boat is in readiness at the foot of the great stairway to take me across the lagoon towards Matancheri, where I am to visit the Jews' quarters.

After the destruction of the second temple of Jerusalem, which occurred in the year 3828 of Creation, 3168 of Tribulation, and 8 of the Christian era, about 10,000 Jews and Jewesses came to Malabar and settled at Cranganore, which at that time was called Mahodraptna. They were received with tolerance, and from then till now this little colony, which is as much shut off from the nearest Indians as it is from the rest of the world, has kept its ancient traditions intact just like some historic curiosity in a museum.

Matancheri, which must be crossed from one end to the other in order to reach the town of the " white Jews " (as they are called here), is a sort of purely native market, where all the faces have a bronze tinge, and where the open wooden shops clustering at the foot of slender-stalked palms look low and insignificant.

I had already proceeded more than half a mile, and my eyes had grown quite accustomed to the native aspect of the place, when the road suddenly turned, and I was surprised to see a sinister-looking old street that had the appearance of being strangely out of place; high stone houses closely packed together, sullen-looking façades with narrow windows like those of colder countries. The faces of Jews were visible everywhere—at the windows, doors, and in the street—and their appearance was as surprising as the

6

sudden change in the character of the dwellings. The decaying sadness and walled-in isolation of this town seemed to assort ill with its setting of sky and palms; after taking this sudden turning one is no longer in India, and the mind becomes bewildered, and we no longer know where we are; perhaps in the corner of a Leyden or Amsterdam ghetto that has been transported to a land whose tropical sun has baked and cleft its walls. Doubtless this quarter was built by the Dutch in imitation of those of the Mother Country about the time of the early colonizations, when the art of adapting buildings to the climate was not understood; and after their departure these Jews of Cranganore must have taken possession of the abandoned dwellings. Jews, nothing but Jews, a pallid Jewry, whose blood has been impoverished by the stifling houses and the Indian climate contrary to all recognized theory; two thousand years of residence in Malabar have not in any way modified Jewish faces. They are the same people, dressed in the same long robes, that one meets at Jerusalem or at Tiberius; young women with delicate features, old wretches with hooked noses, sly-looking children with pink and white complexions, who wear curl-papers over each ear just as their brothers do in Canaan.

These folk come to their doorsteps to see the passing stranger, for smiling welcome, and I should doubtless be courteously received at any house that I might visit.

To-day there are, at the most, but a few hundreds of these exiles who, as tradition tells, once numbered ten thousand; a sojourn which has lasted nearly two thousand years, and the depressing climate, have weakened even their enduring race; it appears that they live by usury and other underhand commerce, and even when they are rich pretend not to be. The interiors of the houses of two or three of the chief inhabitants, where I rested awhile, presented the same aspect of ruin, decay and filth, together with semi-darkness and the smell of a wild beasts' den; I saw old furniture in the European style, which must have dated from the time of the Dutch, perishing from rottenness ; mosaic images and Hebrew inscriptions ranged round the walls.

The synagogue is at the end of the street, and has a melancholy-looking little belfry, quite warped by time and split with heat. After having passed the first door, we find ourselves in a courtyard whose walls are as high as those of a prison. The sanctuary occupies the centre, and though it is but eight o'clock, the whitewashed temple gleams in the morning sun. There is perhaps no other synagogue in the world where an ancient style of decoration of such an unknown manner is preserved. The crude colours, which time has faded a little, have a singular charm, and there are green doors painted with strange flowers, porcelain pavements of a marvellous blue, milky white walls, glowings of red and gold round the tabernacle, and the surprising radiance of many columns and gratings of turned copper which have been polished like mirrors by the continual rubbing of human hands. Many multi-coloured crystal lustres of ancient make, that must have come from Europe at the time of the early colonization, hang from the ceiling.

Some sallow-faced, long-nosed men dressed in long robes, who were mumbling prayers, rise, book in hand, to welcome me, and a tottering old rabbi, who seems a hundred years old at least, advances to meet me. The magnificence of the carefully turned copper columns is first pointed out to me, and I am asked to note the extraordinary polish. Then my attention is directed to the really priceless pavement of blue porcelain, so rare that one scarcely dares to walk upon it ; it was made in China six hundred years ago, and brought here by sea at great expense.

Finally the tabernacle, which was covered by a long silk cover worked in gold thread, is unbared ; it contains tiaras set with gems of a design primitive as the crown of Solomon, which on certain occasions serve to deck the head of the ancient rabbi; there are also holy books and rolls of parchment, wrapped in cases of black silk embroidered with silver, whose age can no longer be ascertained.

At last the relic of relics is disclosed: the bronzed tablet, that priceless record on which were written some three centuries after the arrival of the Jews in India, in the year 4139 of Creation, 3479 of Tribulation, 319 of this Christian era, the rights and privileges granted to them by the king who then reigned in Malabar.

The characters graven on these venerable tables read somewhat after this fashion: " By the help of God who made the world and set up kings, we, Ravi Vurma, Emperor of Malabar, in the 36th year of our glorious reign here in the fort of Maderecatla Cranganore, grant these rights to the worthy Joseph Rabban. 1st. That he may make proselytes among the five castes. 2nd. That he may enjoy all honours; that he may ride elephants and horses with all due pomp; that his titles may be proclaimed by heralds; that he may use lights in the daytime and that he may make use of all manner of musical instruments; that he is allowed to carry a large parasol, and to walk on white carpet which may be spread out before him; finally that he may cause marches to be sounded on his armour as he advances under a canopy of state. We grant these rights to Joseph Rabban, and to 72 Jewish landowners, together with the government of his own people, who are beholden to obey him, and to him and his heirs so long as the sun may shine on the world.

" This charter is given in the presence of the King of Travancore, Trecenore, Calli Quilon, Krengoot, Tamorin, Tamorin Paliathachen, and Calistria.

" Written by the Secretary, Kalambi Kelapour. As Parumpadpa, the Rajah of Cochin, is my heir, his name is not included among these.

" Signed Cherumprumal Ravi Vurma,
" Emperor of Malabar."

Above the synagogue, close by the side of the cracked belfry, there is a lofty room to which I am taken : here everything is in a state of unconceivable decay and dilapidation ; there are shapeless beams and ruinous walls, and the flooring is full of holes, and bats slumber near the black ceiling. Through narrow windows, pierced like loopholes through the thick walls, the little Dutch town, now passed into Israelitish hands, is seen standing sad, gray, and worn at the feet of the huge palms, whose great heads fill the background, and which merge at once into the forest, whose changeless green extends as far as the eye can reach. On the other side we overlook the thatched roof of a very ancient Brahmin temple, whose low copper cupola seems to crush it against the surface of the burning soil.

This lofty room, this ruin full of shade and spiders' webs, is the school of the little " white Jews." About twenty of them are assembled here, taking advantage of the early morning freshness in order to study Leviticus ; a rabbi, who resembles the prophet Elias, traces passages of Hebrew on a blackboard—for these children of exile still speak the ancestral language now fallen into neglect amongst their Eastern kin.

After the quarter of the " white Jews " comes that of the " black Jews," who are the rivals and enemies of the first. I had been warned that I should give much offence if I did not go to see them and their synagogue after having visited the others. Some were even stationed at the entrance of their street, waiting to see if I would come, whilst above me I could perceive rows of pale, emaciated " white Jews' " faces behind the half-raised curtains, or looking curiously to see which direction I might take.

Let me go to see the poor " black Jews," who pretend that they arrived from India several centuries before the " white Jews," notwithstanding that the white ones proclaim disdainfully that they are only ancient pariahs who have been converted by their teachings.

They are more tanned than their neighbours, but not black, far from it, though they appear to be half-bred between Israelites and Indians. They hasten to bid me welcome. Their synagogue much resembles its rival, but is less rich, and has neither the beautiful copper columns nor the marvellous Chinese porcelain pavement. Just now they are celebrating a service for the children, who are assembled there with their noses buried in their books, and who rock themselves like bears in the orthodox manner of the Mosaic rite. The rabbi made bitter plaints about the pride of their rivals of the neighbouring street, who would never contract marriage nor even hold intercourse with his parishioners. To crown their misery, he told me that the Grand Rabbi of Jerusalem, to whom a collective plaint for intervention had been addressed, had contented himself by replying with this rather offensive generality : " It is only sparrows of the same colour that nest together."

The granite-walled temple with the copper cupola and the roof of thatch that we first saw from the summit is one of the most primitive and sullen-looking buildings of this coast ; it is needless to say that it is as impenetrable as the temples of other places. In an empty and dismal courtyard, whose high granite walls collect the stifling rays of the sun, there are some strange objects of iron and bronze, many-branched candelabra, I am told, whose surfaces have been corroded by the storms of centuries.

Close to, and communicating with the temple by galleries, is an ancient palace of the Rajahs of Cochin, abandoned some time since for the new residence of Ernaculum that lies upon the opposite shore. It looks like a heavy, square, old fortress, though it is impossible to determine the precise age of a building in this country where chronology is interwoven with fables and symbols ; but it gives the impression of extreme antiquity, and the moment we enter we have the impression of an unknown something that must date from a ruder age.

The few little windows, all of which have stone seats carved underneath them, serve to show the thickness of the walls.   All the staircases, even those leading to the rooms of state, are steep, dark, and stifling, hardly wide enough for a single person, and have a look of childish savagery.   The rooms, too, are long, low, and dark, and have an oppressive and prison-like air.

The ceilings are carved into complicated panels, roses, and pendentives out of precious woods that still retain their deep colours, with here and there a few traces of painting.   The walls, on the contrary, have been left flat, and are absolutely smooth from one end to the other ; at the first glance I thought that they were covered by a stuff of many-coloured design, but the semi-darkness deceived me, for they are painted.   The whole palace is decorated with frescoes ; some are slightly damaged by time, but others are in as perfect a state of preservation as some of the paintings on the Egyptian tombs.   Oh ! what astonishing frescoes, frescoes of a special type, in which art displays a prodigal and exuberant luxury : masses of nude forms, in which anatomical details are closely reproduced, though the Indian type of beauty is somewhat exaggerated and the wrists too fine and the breasts too prominent.

Confused swarms of interlacing arms, intermingled thighs, arched backs, and swelling chests.   The ankles and the wrists are braceleted, the foreheads are crowned, and necklets adorn the throats.   Animals also figure in this debauch of copper-coloured flesh.

There is not a trace of furniture ; all is empty. Nothing but complicated ceilings, which seem to crush everything with their weight, and these frescoes resembling tapestries, that cover the walls of all these galleries and prolong the nightmare of animal and human flesh into the remotest and darkest chambers.

The centre room, larger and higher than the rest, is the one in which the rajahs were crowned ; there the frescoes represent a group of cloud-encircled goddesses who are in travail in the midst of a huge crowd of nude spectators.

The sleeping-chamber of the rajahs is the only room that is furnished now, and there a boat-shaped bed, made of panels of precious woods, still offers the repose of its brocaded mattress.

The bed is suspended from the ceiling by red silken cords, for serving-men were accustomed to rock the sovereign to sleep after his meals. Around the royal couch the wall frescoes are of the most sensuous kind, and display an unbridled lasciviousness, and goddesses, men, animals, monkeys, bears, and gazelles roll their frenzied eyes in paroxysms of desire.

There is one other much dilapidated room in which a great bronze lamp burns smokily both night and day; here I am not allowed to enter, as somewhere in the dim background there is a communication with the temples.

It will soon be the midday hour, when every one must seek the shelter of a roof, and as my shady island is too far distant, I will go to Cochin and seek some " Traveller's Rest."

In a little hired carriage drawn by two fleet runners I pass once more through the Indian streets of Matancheri, which were so lately thronged with all the types and costumes of Malabar; now, however, everything seems overcome by midday slumber.

I soon reach Cochin, which is built upon a sand-bank stretching between the sea and the lagoon; an old colonial town that has undergone few changes, and in which Dutch influence is still visible.

The little house which gives me shelter overlooks the shore and the boundless ocean.

The great blue sea of Arabia stretches before me, and its sands glitter with a rose and white splendour under the vertical rays of the sun; crows and fish-ing-eagles fly around, uttering joyful cries, whilst a calm swell throws its breakers on the shore with peaceful monotony. Farther out, where the sea is of a blue and polished tinge, the fins and backs of sharks that are watching for their prey are visible from time to time. But amidst all this dazzling magnificence the horizon is no longer to be seen.

Behind the hut which shelters me, and which is open on every side, the wood of coco-nut palms commences at once, and I can see the green light that filters through them ; from my windows long branches and long feathered tufts of palm droop towards the ground, lit up with a green and luminous transparence that is exaggerated by the dull green background. Now a young Indian climbs noiselessly up a trunk, smooth as a column, ascending by aid of his toes with the ease and rapidity of a monkey in order to obtain the juice that comes from the veins of the leaves, and which is used as a drink ; and this climbing man, who seems half animal in this silent and swift ascent, is the last impression that permeated through my half-closed eyes.

How I love to feel the deep and shining sea so near to me, and to hear its mighty throbbing ! It is the highway that leads freely to all lands, the highway where one can breathe and see far around, and it is the road that I have always known. Truly life is more gladsome in its vicinity, and I find my old self again now that I am near it once more. For an instant I can imagine that I am no longer in this shady, confined, and incomprehensible Indian land.

XIII

After my siesta it is time to return to my isle of the enchanted palace.

The sun is setting as I take my final departure in the boat with fourteen rowers which is to take me to Trichur, the most northerly town in the kingdom of Cochin, a journey that will occupy the entire night. As usual our start is magnificent. The rowers, who are quite rested, seem to snatch shovels full of water at each stroke of the paddles, and a sail has been hoisted to help us. Once more we take the easy road of the lagoon, and the palm-covered banks fly quickly past us.

The evening sun, fast sinking behind the rampart of eternal verdure, droops and dies as ever in flames of rosy gold. A cloudless sky of strangely lovely tint is spread above our tranquil world; once more we are in the midst of fisheries, boats, and spread-out nets, surrounded by the lake-like life we saw last evening—that life of olden days which still lingers upon these Indian lagoons, curtained in on all sides by forests of palms, whose mystery and depth seem increased by the growing twilight.

My boatmen hum once more through their closed mouths the song of yesterday. It appears that this refrain is suited to the hours of ease when, thanks to a favouring wind, they can paddle more heedlessly. Fishermen on the other boats chant the same melody, which does not seem to issue from human throats, but rather resembles a distant peal of church bells floating across the limpid waters from all directions.

This " Land of Charity " is peopled by thousands of beings who, beneath their shady palms, dream with a confiding simplicity of resurrection; Christians, Brahmins, or Israelites all clinging to their old and venerable faiths which, however they may differ amongst each other, seem to contain a shadow of the same truths. I dream, too, of the childish hope that possessed me, that I might have been able to seize a few shreds of the intangible truth, that truth which is so sullenly guarded in the heart of this Brahmin faith. But no; here, as everywhere else, I am the eternal stranger, the perpetual wanderer, who only knows how to appreciate the charm of strange surroundings. My dream is over too, for I am leaving, nursed by songs, in a handsome boat; but even as it is I am amused, and perhaps this is the path which destiny has traced out for me, and with which I must be content.

The curtains of forest which are drawn all round

the horizon have an ever-deepening tone of blue, a blue that merges into black where the sun has sunk. Occasionally their monotonous line is broken by some gigantic tree that rears its black shadow against the sky. The planet Venus is the first of the stars to glimmer through the fading tones of rosy gold, then the moon appears by her side, but it is a moon such as one rarely sees, and only in the limpid air of hot countries. The crescent is faintly outlined by a thin, luminous edge, yet the whole surface can be distinguished with a wonderful clearness ; one feels that it is lit up from behind and that it is no simple disc, but a ball suspended in transparent emptiness, and in spite of all the principles we have acquired, this somewhat shocks our primordial notions of equilibrium and weight. Darkness has at last over-taken us, and the boatmen have lit their fires in order to attract the fish. The songs have died away, and all seems to sleep, all but the sinewy limbs of my fourteen rowers, who hurry me towards the north during the whole night.

XIV

Wednesday, 3rd January

There is a sudden conflagration as the sun rises from behind the thicket of palms. My boat had touched ground several times during the night, and now rests finally in the mud at the foot of a hill of red earth. We have reached the port of Trichur, where the lagoons end, and the waters are crowded by hundreds of other slumbering, gondola-prowed boats.

Trichur, a very ancient and conservative Brahmin town, stands half a mile farther on amongst the trees, but hardly any one is stirring there when I arrive in my ox-cart. The palms which shelter the thatched wooden houses are shaken by a cold wind, which raises clouds of fiery-coloured dust that looks

almost like powdered blood. With its little shops
peopled by grain sellers and copper workers, and its
lanes of hairy banyans, this town resembles all those
other towns of Malabar which, hidden amidst the
woods, continue their ancient modes of existence far
from the coast and all modern things ; but its temple
is particularly large and terrible, and it bears the
name of Tivu Sivaya peria vur, which means Saint-
Siva-great-town.

I alight in front of this temple, which is a fortress
as well, and which sustained the siege of Tippoo, the
formidable Sultan of Mysore, and climb up slopes on
which herds of indolent sheep and zebus are still
sleeping. On seeing my approach some Brahmins,
who had stationed themselves in a doorway to meditate and to watch the sun rise, hasten anxiously to
meet me. Did the stranger think ? . . . But I tell
them that I know, and that I had merely come to
admire the sculptured towers from a respectful distance. On hearing this the Brahmins, with many
smiling salutes, retire to the sanctuary without
troubling further about me. The heavy walls are
whitewashed, but the four doors, crowned with
monstrous sculptured towers that face the four winds
of heaven, have still retained the warm and dark
colour of Indian granite. These four red towers date
from the earliest ages, and are decked with ornaments,
colonnades, and barbaric figures.

Were it not for the wintry gusts of wind which
sweep by everything, and which twist the hanging
branches of the banyan trees, raising huge clouds of
reddish-coloured dust, there would be nothing stirring in the town of Siva. By the roadsides there are
peaceful nooks under trees where the people may
pray ; in such spots we should have placed crucifixes
in the olden days ; here these shady crossways are
decked with granite altars, symbolic stones, and
statues.

There are but few passers-by ; some dreamy-eyed
men going to the temple, beautiful and proud in

their nudity, with their black masses of hair hanging to their loins, and their foreheads painted with the seals of Vishnu or of Siva ; nearly all wear the sacred cord across their breasts, which is the outward symbol of high caste. There are some women going to draw water whose figures are bent under the flashing copper urns which they carry on their shoulders; draperies with many-coloured borders cover them, without in any way hiding their outlines. One of their swelling breasts is hidden by muslin, but the other, the right one, is always left uncovered ; their young bosoms are more developed than those of European races, and seem almost out of proportion with their delicate waists ; yet the outlines are matchless, and have served as models for those stone and bronze torsos that Hindoo sculptors have given to their goddesses from the remotest ages, torsos in which the feminine charms seem purposely heightened.

As I pass these women on the road, their glance meets mine almost stealthily ; it is very tender, but indifferent and far-away—an unintentional caress of the flaming black eyes—then suddenly their eyelids droop.

For the passing stranger they are like a thousand other things in this country, like the great temple itself—unfathomable.

I remain the guest of the Rajah of Cochin till I reach the frontier, and have only to allow myself to be conducted ; all has thoughtfully been provided for my morning journey to Trichur : the guide, the repast, and even the teams of oxen which will take me to Shoranur after a journey of three hours through villages, jungles, and woods.

Alas ! at Shoranur I shall have left the charming India that tourists never visit, and I shall find the ubiquitous railways, and from there I shall take the express train to Madras.

IN THE LAND OF THE GREAT PALMS

CHAPTER IV

IN THE LAND OF THE GREAT PALMS

I

THE WONDERFUL ROCK OF TANJORE

ABOVE the immense plains of this country of Tanjore and above the bushy kingdom of palms, which stretches out like the sea, a huge detached rock rears its head ; [1] standing sentinel, as it has done since the beginning of time, over a region from which it has seen the forests spring and the towns and temples grow. It is a geological oddity, a whim of some primaeval cataclysm, and looks like a helmet, or the prow of some Titan's ship, half-submerged in an ocean of greenery. It is two hundred metres high, and springs without warning from the neighbouring plain ; and its sides are so smooth, that even in this country, where vegetation conquers everything, no single plant has been able to find a foothold.

The early Indians, the great mystics of the olden days, naturally chose this as a place of worship, and for centuries have carefully hollowed out the rock so as to form galleries, stairways, and gloomy temples. Cupolas covered with beaten gold shine from the summit, and every night a sacred fire burns on the very top of the rock, and this fire, which has been kindled for centuries, can be seen shining like a lighthouse from the remotest parts of Tanjore.

As the sun rises on the native village built at the foot of the rock, there is a greater stir than usual, for

[1] The Rock of Trichinopoly.

a solemn Brahmin festival in honour of Vishnu takes place to-morrow, and since yesterday the natives have been occupied in weaving innumerable garlands of yellow flowers. The women and young girls, who are grouped round the fountain filling their copper urns, have already donned their festival attire, their finest bracelets, nose-, and ear-rings. The zebus attached to the carts have had their horns painted and gilt, and are decked with necklets, bells, and tassels of glass. Garland sellers almost block our passage with their displays of floral wreaths ; Indian pinks, Bengal roses, and marigolds, threaded like pearls, are made into many-rowed boa-like necklets, from which hang flowers and ornaments of gold thread. To-morrow all the folk who go to their devotions, and all the gods stationed in the temples, will wear on their flesh, stone, or metal chests such ornaments of rose or yellow flowers. The housewives, who were stirring directly the dawn appeared, hasten to trace geometrical figures on the carefully swept soil in front of their dwellings with the white powder that issues from the little box which they hold in their hands, and with which they weave fantastic designs like intermingling ribbons. One hardly dares to walk along the streets : these networks of white lines, with yellow carnations placed at the points of intersection, are so beautiful. The wind commences to rise, carrying with it clouds of the blood-coloured dust which gives a reddish tone to everything in Southern India, and within an hour all the tracery that has caused so much labour will be effaced.

The houses of the town are painted the colour of red brick, and have the fork of Vishnu inscribed above the door ; all are very low and have thick walls, buttresses, and porches that remind me of the Egypt of Pharaoh's days. There are as many dwellings for the gods as there are for men, and nearly as many temples as there are houses ; and on all the temples and amongst tne reddish monsters crowning the

breastwork of the walls, families of crows are perched
who look at the passing crowds and watch for the
spoils and all the scraps of filth that can serve as
prey for them. A horrible idol can be seen in each
of the little sanctuaries, whose doors are never closed;
it is nearly always the elephant-headed Ganesa,
decked with necklets of fresh yellow flowers which fall
over his many arms and conceal his hanging trunk.

There are temples upon temples, holy bathing-
places for the ablutions of the Brahmins, palaces,
and bazaars.

There are mosques too, for the faith of Islam—
that has triumphed in the north-west and centre
of India—has filtered to some extent into this region
of the great palms. How different from the Brahmin
temples are these simple and geometrical arabesque-
covered mosques that rise from between their slim
minarets, and keep themselves white as those of
Hedjaz in spite of the red dust which gives its tone to
everything in this country.

A swarming as of an ant-heap, and the constant
set of people in one direction suffices to guide me,
even on the evening before the festival, towards the
rock temple that dominates the town. It is made
of three or four monstrous blocks that are without
a crack and almost without a wrinkle; these stones
have merely been thrown one on the other, and the
sides, rounded like the flanks of animals and polished
by running rain-water, hang over in a fearful manner.
A veritable crowd of cawing crows whirls incessantly
round the summit. A monumental stairway plunges
into the dim recesses of the rock, between high
granite columns of laboured design, and past thousands of steeples and idols which have been rendered
almost shapeless by age. Some young elephants,
that are sacred and descended from sacred parents,
are standing by, nearly blocking up the entry; they
are covered with little bells threaded in the same
way as the garlands, and, as I pass, these elephants
caress me with their trunks in babyish glee.

I commence to ascend the stairs, which almost suddenly plunge into darkness ; now religious music, whose volume is increased by the sonority of the grotto, fills the air, seeming to issue from the bowels of the earth.

I need not say that the rock is filled with a number of superposed temples, galleries, passages, and stairways ; some penetrating into mysterious darkness are interdicted to all but the priests. There are statues in every angle and corner ; some are colossal, whilst others are as tiny as gnomes, but all have crumbled with age and have only stumps instead of arms, and their faces are no longer recognizable. As I am not one of the faithful, I must keep to the great central gallery that is open to everybody, and which ascends between splendid columns hewn out of solid blocks. These columns are covered by figures and designs, but the bases, as far up as the height of a man, have lost all shape under the constant polishing which has continued for countless centuries by the nude figures who have pressed against them in these narrow passages. Formerly the walls, and even the pavements and steps, were covered with signs and inscriptions, but age and the rubbing of countless hands and naked feet have rendered them indistinguishable.

First we enter some low and stifling rooms, from which a sound of chanting issues out of the gloom, then higher up we come to a temple, as large as a cathedral, whose ponderous roof is upheld by a forest of columns. The profane are allowed to enter on condition that they do not advance too far ; so it is impossible to see where the temple finishes, and there are passages and sculptured grottos which disappear into the blackness of the rock. In a corner, near a hole through which light comes, some Brahmin children are engaged in the study of the holy books under the tutelage of an old man who is entirely covered with white hair. From the roof prodigious properties belonging to the Brahmin procession are suspended—men, cars, horses, and elephants, all larger than their natural size, strange forms, carefully made from cardboard and painted, or tinselled paper stretched over a thin framework of bamboo.

Tribes of little birds, swallows or sparrows, in that anxiety of reproduction which characterizes the life of this land, have found time between two religious processions to fill these fantastic carcasses with their nests ; so the confused forms of the suspended monsters are gay with the fluttering of wings and musical with the chirping of the young birds whose song falls like light hail on the ground below.

We have to mount higher yet. These polished walls, which are often of a single block, and the semi-darkness remind one of a catacomb ; but a flood of sunlight suddenly pierces through a hole cut in the rock, and we see the pagodas and palm trees stretched far beneath us. There are also some stones which have been brought here as large as those of the early stone age ; these have been thrown, pell-mell and unjointed, one on top of the other, but their huge weight keeps them in position, and time can never shift them from their place.

At every step we encounter Brahmins of superb form and appearance whose chests are daubed with ashes in honour of Siva, the god of death. They hurriedly ascend and descend, busied with the arrangements for to-morrow's festival, disappearing into the passages that are forbidden to me, and bringing out copper vases filled with water or bearing garlands to the gods I may not see.

There is yet another temple. I may not enter it, but only look in from the threshold. It is built over the one I have just left, but is much larger and more magnificent, and much lighter too, for there are many square openings in the roof through which the blue sky can be seen, through which the sunlight falls on the aedicules sheathed in their many-coloured and gilt ornaments.

Above this last sanctuary are the terraces from

which the plains of Tanjore may be seen extending as far as the eye can see, dotted with thousands of other temples that emerge from the green palms.

At last we reach the stone which forms the summit, a single block which the original volcanic disturbance has placed here somewhat unsteadily. This is the stone which looks like the prow of a ship or the crest of a helmet when it is seen from below. The sun is shining on its smooth sides as we ascend by one hundred and forty faintly traced steps, so narrow, worn, and sloping, that we cannot escape a feeling of giddiness.

It is on these final terraces, adorned with golden cupolas, that the sacred fire is nightly lit. Here also, in a dark and heavy kiosk, surrounded by iron bars like a wild beasts' den, the supreme idol is found; their god, the horrible black Ganesa, is the wild beast, and until one approaches quite close to the bars, his crouching form cannot be discerned. His elephant's ears and trunk fall over the protruding belly, and the stone body is half-clothed in gray, dirty, torn rags. Here the captive god, whose expression is fierce and cunning, reigns alone and supreme in the airy temple built above all the rest of temples, from which an uninterrupted stream of music and prayer has poured forth for the last two thousand years.

We stand far above the region of human habitation, and almost above the zone which the birds inhabit. Below us we see the whirling flights of crows and the eagles whose wings are stretched out motionlessly in the air. The country that we overlook is one where religion holds its extremest sway; temples are scattered everywhere, almost as abundantly as trees, and the red harvest of sacred pyramids emerges on all sides above the verdure. So plentifully do the sacred towers rise above the palms that from the height at which we are situated they resemble mole-hills in a field of grass. Those twenty-four monstrous towers down there, grouped like the tents of an encampment, belong to the temple of Chri Ragam, the largest of the sanctuaries of Vishnu—where I am going to-morrow to see the passing of a solemn procession.

The town is situated at the base of the overhanging rock, and the complicated network of streets, the profusion of many-coloured temples, and the mosques, that are so white as to look bluish, are marked out as on a highly coloured map ; the holy ponds, which seem to swarm with black flies, shine like mirrors in the sun ; these are no flies, however, but Brahmins at their morning ablutions.

As at Malabar, the great coco-palms nearly cover the whole of the country, but in the midst of this forest of waving plumes, which extends on all sides of the horizon, there are some occasional gaps ; large yellow patches where the grass has been burnt up by the increasing dryness, which has caused a famine in the north-west provinces, and which is already causing anxiety to the people of Tanjore.

All the sounds of the animated and seething life below mingle as they rise up to us ; the noise of the joyful town, the rumbling of zebu carts, the tom-toms and bagpipes of the streets, the croakings of the eternal crows, the screams of eagles, the psalms from the many temples beneath our feet, and the brayings of the sacred horns that never cease to echo round the sides of the rock on which we stand.

II

AT CHRI RAGAM

The little " Travellers' Rest " at which I find shelter is about two miles from the wonderful rock and two leagues from the great temple of Chri Ragam, and is situated in a sunny cleaving where the feathery palms have been replaced by some mimosas, whose foliage is so poor and scanty that they do not give any shade. The dying trees and the burnt-up vegetation that surround us seem to stretch a warning finger over this

southern land of India, where everything is eternally
damp and green, telling of the fearful drought from
which the whole district of Radjiput is dying.

To reach Chri Ragam from my lodging, I have first
to pass through the town at the foot of the overhanging rock, then to make a journey of an hour or
two in a carriage under a vault of trees and palms of
every age and every shape. On our way we pass
endless temples of varied forms and age, and there are
many stones and sculptured granite monuments over
which the faithful have thrown flowers and garlands—
such strange garlands—in readiness for to-morrow's
festival. Over all the entrances and on every door
the terrible seal of Vishnu, that three-pronged fork
which is inscribed on the foreheads of the men, has
been freshly re-painted in red and white colours.
There are even specially sacred groves of palms which
bear the ensign of the god ; the trunks, smooth as a
column, have been entirely covered with red and
white, so that it is hard to say where the temples end
or the woods commence. The breath of adoration
wafts over the whole of this consecrated place.

When at length we reach the sanctuary itself, an
immense sanctuary which stands in seven inclosures,
the first of which, containing twenty-one pyramids
sixty feet high, is two leagues in circumference, a
feeling of bewilderment, caused by the huge size and
the profuse display of barbaric splendour, comes over
us. The inconceivable plenitude of detail is as startling as the size of the building itself. All that I had
ever read, all that I thought I knew, and all that I
had ever seen at gorgeous performances of fairy
spectacles is astonishingly surpassed here. We are
also forced to recognize that our cathedrals, with their
saints and angels, only compare with these huge red
masses of solid rock on which a thousand divinities
gesticulate with their twenty arms and twenty faces,
as do our modest flowers with those that blossom
here.

We enter an enormous inclosure that is older than

the sanctuary, but whose age is unknown, the work of a generation who had dreamt of a tower as large as that of Babel, but who never lived to finish their work. Access is gained by a doorway which is more than forty feet high, made of simple blocks ten to twelve metres long; at the crown of the archway there are indications of an unfinished pyramid, which would doubtless have struck terror into the minds of those who saw it, but probably its achievement was impossible. The whole structure has acquired a tone of reddish copper, and the sacred parrots, perched in groups on the projecting sculptures, look like patches of brilliant verdigris.

On the other side of the doorway there are magnificent avenues leading to the temples. These avenues extend through the various inclosures and are bordered by religious buildings, ponds, bazaars, gods seated in niches, and many stone kiosks supported on slim columns of antiquated design—everywhere the same four-sided Indian columns with their capitals formed by a group of hanging monsters. The door of each fresh inclosure is surmounted and overwhelmed by an indescribable pyramid, sixty feet high, made up of fifteen stories of colossal gods ranked one above the other. All the statues of the airy kingdom look upwards with thousands of eyes and gesticulate with thousands of arms; there are some who have twenty arms projecting in a fan-like manner from each of their sides, others with twenty faces which look in every direction, their heads adorned with tiaras, and they brandish lotus flowers, deaths' heads, and emblems of all sorts. Numbers of mythical animals force their way through the crowded ranks of the gods: peacocks with extravagant tails, or five-headed serpents. The stone has been carved and chiselled with so much boldness that each subject and each accessory seems to be independent of the rest and looks as if it might detach itself and spring to the ground. The pyramid on which these dense crowds are graven grows narrower as it rises, terminating at length in a series of lance-like points. The almost unfading colours in which these men, beasts, robes, and adornments were painted still retain their brilliancy ; the predominant tone is blood-red, and seen from a distance each pyramid is red, but this tone alters as we get nearer. and patches of green, white, and gold become visible.

The last inclosure is reserved for Brahmins of pure race attached to the service of the gods, who live here with their families.   At last we arrive at the temple proper, and see the sullen and defiant ramparts of its old crested walls rising before us, whilst the customary red pyramid of sculptured gods lowers over the dark and gloomy entrance.   On each side of this last door are terraces on which elephants are chained.   These beasts, which at present are engaged in swallowing some young trees that the faithful have brought, are very old and sacred.   Scattered near, and contrasting strongly with the splendour of the mighty pyramids of crowded figures, are objects that are almost barbaric, straw huts, simple little carts of ancient make, rude and primitive tools.   Everything that clusters at the foot of the old rampart is ruined, worn, and imbued with traces of an uncivilized age that has long since disappeared.

The sun is setting, and it is almost too late to enter the temple, for twilight has already descended amongst the naves and arches of vaulted stones.   If I enter, it is but to inquire about to-morrow's procession of the priests, who flit by like shadows lost in the wilderness of colonnades.   The information I obtain is vague and contradictory ; it may be to-night . . . perhaps later . . . it would depend on the weather and on the moon. . . . I can see clearly that the priests are not anxious that I should be present.

However, in an echoing gallery, whose walls are decorated from one end to the other by two rows of fantastic tigers and horses reared on their hind legs, and of more than natural size, I meet a sweet-faced old priest who informs me it will most certainly be at daybreak, and says that to be more sure I had better spend the night in the temple itself.

I return to my carriage and make for the modest lodging to which hunger calls me. After that I shall return at once and sleep in the temple.

A beautiful silvery moon is shining as I leave my " Travellers' Rest " once more. So white is the moonlight that I should have thought that the walls and the bare ground were covered with snow. The moon's pale rays filter through the thin branches and delicate leaves of the mimosas just as they do through the branches of our trees when winter has stripped off their leaves ; and the tiny flowers, like balls of down, resemble snowflakes and hoar frost. Can this be some northern territory that has wandered into the land of heat ? Everything ceases to astonish in this wondrous land where fantastic and ever-changing images provide a constant feast of unexpected spectacle.

The wintry illusion fast melts away, and as soon as we leave the parched clearing, the well-defined shadows of the palms, banyan trees, and trailing creepers become apparent again. The illuminated fête which is being held in the town is just now at its height ; all the open temples, even the smallest ones, scarcely larger than a cupboard, are adorned with lighted lamps and yellow garlands. As we hasten towards Chri Ragam our carriage passes rapidly through many scenes which fade into one confused recollection. It happens that this is also the month of Ramadan, so the Mohammedans are keeping their festival too. The great mosque, before which surges a crowd of turbans of all colours, is covered by lines of fire, and in order to make their spectacle yet more fairy-like, the white walls, columns, arabesques, and illuminations have been draped with a veil of red muslin which hides the sharp outlines with a rosy glow, and casts a haze of distance and uncertainty over the building ; the minarets and the dome, however, are not sheathed in coloured draperies, and shoot up boldly towards the starry sky, where their snowy crescent-crowned forms glimmer in the moonlight.

III

PREPARATIONS FOR THE PROCESSION

The night has fallen as I get back to Chri Ragam, and the walls of the temple of Vishnu are plunged in gloom. I am standing in the sacred precincts where Brahmins alone may dwell, in the large avenue encircling the sanctuary. The car of the god is stationed here, waiting for the moonlight; it is covered by a sort of dais or fantastic pavilion which sparkles with red, green, and yellow gold, and its roof is much ornamented with miniature towers like those of the temple; the car itself, which forms the base of all this, is a huge and terrible mass of sculptured beams, old as the Brahmin faith, of such dimensions that it seems impossible that it could ever be put in motion. The gilt superstructure, resembling an extravagant and shining pavilion, has only been placed there to-day, and is a thing of no weight, made from silk, tinsel, and paper stretched over a bamboo framework, which, however, gives the impression of heightened effect and magnificence. The moon illumines white groups of men surrounding the car, Indians looking like phantoms in the white muslins with which their heads and chests are swathed. But it seems that the moonlight does not suffice, for torches are brought in order that the wheels, which allow the car to move like a monstrous tortoise, may be attached; these car wheels are solid discs some three feet high made from two layers of timber placed side by side and fastened together with iron bolts. The ropes to which three or four hundred frenzied men will harness themselves to-morrow, ropes, thick as a Brahmin's leg, that serve to draw the huge machine, are already being laid out on the ground.

At present the great stone temple is empty and

shrouded in the gloom of night, and my footsteps echo through the silence in an almost terrifying manner. A few Brahmins, who have come from the country for the festival, have sought shelter here, and wrapped in their muslins lie stretched out on the stones like dead men. The few dim lamps hung at long distances apart and the occasional moonbeams make this forest of columns, and its people of idols, seem more boundless than ever.

The avenue along which the car will travel to-morrow at daybreak follows the four sides of the sullen-crested rampart of the sanctuary, sweeping in a bold, straight line between the fortress wall and the old houses of the Brahmins, with their complicated columns, verandas, and terraces guarded by granite monsters ; it is very gay, for scarcely any one will sleep to-night, and many white groups, whose outlines are sharply defined in the ghostly moonlight, are to be seen wandering along it.

Women and young girls of high caste commence to leave their houses and gather at the thresholds of the doors, where they begin to decorate the venerable earth that the car of Vishnu will plough into deep ruts when the morning comes. The night is beautifully clear, and everything is plain as in the daylight. These women and young girls are so laden with collars of jasmine, and so many garlands of threaded flowers hang on their bosoms, that as they move it is like a swinging of censers.

There is one young and slender girl, wrapped in black and silver muslin, so beautiful that I stop almost involuntarily before her. Each time that she stoops to the ground, and each time that she raises herself up, the click of the precious rings that surround her ankles and arms is heard. The design that she traces on the ground, and which she seems to invent as she goes on, is of a charming oddity. The guide who accompanies me this evening is a Vellana of noble race, and he, at my suggestion, ventures to ask her if she would lend me the white powder for a while so that I may assist in decorating the soil in front of her dwelling. She smiles, and after some hesitation hands the little box to him, so that he may give it to me, for she is too disdainful even to touch my hand. The white ghosts wandering along the avenue surround me, puzzled to know what I am going to do, anxious to know what design will spring up under my hands.

As I trace the monogram of Vishnu very clearly on the dull, red soil, a murmur of surprise and sympathy rises from the bystanders. The little Indian beauty even consents to take the sand-box from my hands and to consult with me as to her plans ; there will be a border of rose ornaments and stars, and hibiscus flowers are to be placed in the centre of each panel.

I feel, however, that I have trespassed far enough, if not too far, and in order that she may not think me an intruder, and that I may receive a gentle smile of farewell, feel that the precise moment has come for me to withdraw.

Some mysterious rite that I may not see is about to be consummated. It is almost midnight. All the white groups have assembled round the gilded car of the god with the shining canopy. To give more pomp and solemnity to the occasion, the great sacred elephants, one of which is a hundred years old, have been tethered close to the car, and, clothed in their gold-fringed robes of state, shuffle about in the moonlight like flabby monsters. Huge parasols terminating in copper balls have been opened, and now a procession of young Brahmins advances carrying torches, whose triple flames are supported on three branches after the manner of the fork of Vishnu.

This is the hour for the accomplishment of the mysterious rite. From a hidden recess at the back of the temple the most sacred symbol, the true and only image of Vishnu, " the one who may not be looked upon," the god of pure gold reclining on a five-headed serpent, will be taken and carried on to the platform which stands in an old kiosk built specially for the purpose. Priests with lighted lamps will watch at his feet, and then to-morrow morning they have only to pass the god into the car through a window and to seat him under the dais-shaped tower that guards him from all prying eyes. Each time that the Vishnu of Chri Ragam passes along the avenue on his way to the kiosk, he is, it is needless to say, swathed in many draperies; and even then the removal always takes place at night, so that no uninitiated eye may catch a glimpse of his form. It happens this year that the festival takes place during the period of the full moon, and I, the only profane stranger here, am warned that I ought to retire, for it is really very light. So I retire from the avenue. I take up my quarters in the distant temple with the Brahmins already reposing there, and wait for the coming dawn. The gloomy place is filled with an immense and peaceful calm, and a feeling almost akin to freshness hovers in the air. As I fall asleep I hear murmured prayers, whose faint whispers echo amongst the vaulted arches; sometimes also the muffled tread of naked feet wandering cautiously over the pavement.

IV

THE PROCESSION PASSES

Croak! Croak! A crow awakens me with the hoarse cry with which it salutes the dawning day, and gives the signal to its fellows sleeping by thousands in the vicinity. The resonance of this forest of stone prolongs and magnifies the sounds of the mournful concert sung amongst these vaulted arches, for the crows are in some manner sacred and nest in the temple itself. Undying echoes repeat "Croak, croak" from all sides; echoes hovering amidst far-distant granite passages, fading amongst lofty naves or reverberating through underground passages, what mazes can be felt rather than seen. The entire

temple vibrates with the answering cries of this
serenade offered every morning to the many gods
who live among these sacred shades.

It is necessary to have the eyes of a bird to perceive that day must soon dawn, and it is darker than
it was last night. The lamps have gone out and the
moon no longer shines. A dampness as of a tomb
is spread over the stones, filling one with a sense of
chilliness. Nothing is visible, only here and there
the faint glimmer of light which filters through a
vent or enters by a hole in the roof. Now another
sound is added to the cries of the birds, a noise of
wings and a rustling of feathers; the black swarm
is about to fly.

Ah! at last the light comes. In this land it
always comes quickly, just as it goes. . . . So quickly,
that the effect is theatrical; prodigious perspectives
of columns stand out suddenly in diaphanous pallor,
a pallor so faint as to make them resemble reflections
from more distant objects, illusionary and impalpable
images of pillars seen through a veil of grayish gauze.
Vast points of view are suddenly revealed, crossways
of naves whose ends cannot be discerned. Now, behind me, appears the avenue where I met the priest
last evening, the avenue of the prancing monsters,
whose outlines I can already see. The human shapes
which were extended on the ground, swathed in their
muslins, rise and stretch their arms, and straightening
their backs take their departure, wan and transparent figures, the sound of whose footsteps seems
strange in this scene of colourless enchantment.

Near to the flagstone on which I slept last night,
a granite staircase leads to the terraces of the
temple; gropingly I find my way to it by keeping
my hands close to the cold walls.

I ascend, and on reaching the top find myself alone.

The terraces which surmount the flat and massive
vaulted arches extend like a desert; a desert of huge
paved stones, that lies round me on all sides; a
desert which appears to merge into the far-distant

clouds. Here, too, I am possessed with a sense of illusion, but the lighting of the scene is quite different ; it is clearer, though the day has not yet come, and yet, just as in the temple, all the objects that I begin to discern seem unreal. These clouds extending round the terrace are formed of vapour that has condensed on the earth during the night ; a vapour so thick that it resembles a bluish-coloured wadding that might be touched if one were near enough ; the whole plain is filled with its fleecy masses, and only a few tufts of the black feathers and black fans that spring from the heads of the tallest palms emerge from it. A greenish light of a deliciously trans-parent shade of beryl gradually covers the eastern horizon, looking like a transparent patch of oil which expands in a wide circle over the veil that night has cast over the sky. A large red globe still lingers in the western sky. Is it some worn-out planet ? or a dead world ? or but the slowly-sinking moon ? By this time all the crows that inhabit the temple are awake, and I can hear the concert of their voices beneath me, and the answering cries that descend from all points of the air, now black with whirling flights of wings.

It takes me ten minutes to walk through the wilderness of stones, across naves, galleries, stair-ways, and passages, to get back to the avenue running round the building where I was last night, and along which the procession will shortly pass.

The golden god must be in his place—his journey from the temple to the kiosk, and from the kiosk to the car duly accomplished—for when I reach the spot no one is near.

The sacred elephants, divested of their finery, are reposing in stalls, which are on a granite balcony extending from either side of the door. The terrible seal of Vishnu painted on their huge foreheads, the same mark that the men have on their own, but ten times greater. Their intelligent eyes are fixed on the car lying near them, which they are so soon to follow.

8

It is almost day, and the sun must soon rise. The four monstrous wheels are fitted to the car, and the cables lie extended on the ground. Now the high priests descend from the kiosk, where they had passed the night in prayer; they are preceded by the procession of youths who carry triple-flamed torches, which they extinguish on coming into the brightness of the growing day. The venerable old men appear separately at the top of the black staircase, at first distantly and surrounded by the smoke of the pine torches, but as they gradually descend the steps their wondrous mystic faces, surrounded with white hair, become defined in the fresh morning light, and I see that their foreheads are shaved up to the crown of their heads, in order that the forked seal of their god may be painted in larger characters. They are almost nude—in their forgetfulness of earthly things; a loin cloth surrounds their body, and they wear a little linen cord indicating their rank, which nestles amidst the fleece of white hair growing on their chests.

Now men are removing the foot-bridge, draped with strange old silks, that led from the car to the window of the kiosk, and which served for the transport of the golden Vishnu. An orchestra of dark-faced musicians plays something deafening, something melancholy and barbarous enough to make one shudder; some beat the tom-toms, while others blow with all their force into gigantic horns that are turned towards the invisible god.

The decoration of the car is at last completed. Four wooden horses, to give the resemblance of a quadriga, have been yoked in front of it; horses with outstretched wings and feet that rear themselves into the air with a look of fury. Around the throne of the god, now concealed by impenetrable curtains of red silk, a kind of suspended garden has been made with branches of natural flowers, whose yellow carnations and marigolds are mingled with golden thread. Naked youths, at first concealed amongst the draperies and the canopies of silk and flowers, are seen stationed at various heights on the rolling structure; these are the guards of honour of the god, and their horns now answer the melancholy howlings that issue from the orchestra stationed on the ground.

The sacred elephants advance towards the car and kneel down of their own will so that the embroidered robes and head ornaments of gold and pearl may be put on them; then they proceed to place themselves behind the priests in the still stationary procession. Meanwhile the younger men fall into rank towards the front of the car, by the side of the four monstrous cables that lie stretched out on the ground.

The wall of the temple which forms one of the sides of the avenue remains dark, deserted, and mournful, but, on the other side, a watching crowd gathers before the houses of the Brahmins, and all the windows, the verandas with their heavy columns, and the pavements, ornamented with monsters, are thronged with children and old men. There are crowds of women everywhere in their gold-embroidered muslins, necklets of flowers, and sparkling jewels; some carry offerings to the priests, whilst others hasten with little sand-boxes in their hands to repair the ravages that have been made in their work, and to place a few fresh, yellow flowers here and there.

The mists that night had thrown over the plain have vanished and melted away, in a single instant, like unsubstantial dreams.

Day dawn in tropical countries is not favourable to any attempts at human pageantry. The spectacle that seemed enchanted but a short while ago when I was on the terraces and whilst the last torches were flaming in the hesitating dawn, now seems unable to bear the pure clearness of the morning sky. Yet I can tell nothing of the sky save that it is infinitely limpid and adorably green, of a pale, resplendent green that cannot be named. But by the

side of it everything looks miserable and faded. The
temple wall displays its decay and its mouldering
red patches. Too much is visible ; the aid of night
or the dazzling brightness of the sun is wanted. The
ornamentation of the car is coarse and childish, and
the robes of the elephants worn-out and ragged. The
clear bronze colour that spreads over the faces and
bosoms of the young women resists a little longer,
it is true, but there are draperies and muslins which
almost look like filthy rags. In this deceptive
moment the decrepitude and decadence of Brahmin
India seem assured, its rites and festivals appear to
have fallen into decay just as its superhuman monuments and its superb race of men. People of a
bygone age, and creeds of a past time whose cycle is
accomplished and now fall into decay.

However, nothing indicates the oppression of the
foreigner ; not a single modern detail intrudes on
this ancient spectacle, and I am the only alien present at the festival.

At last the sun comes, the great magician whose
appearance will transfigure everything. This sudden
bursting forth has something tragic in it, which har-
monizes with the temple and with the god whose
festival is celebrated to-day. A cloud, close to the
horizon, the only visible one, still conceals the sun
from those who are on the level ground, a dark
copper-coloured sky, three pointed flames, resembling
the fork of Vishnu painted on the foreheads of the
men. The great towers, however, can see the sun,
and the crests of the red granite walls, and the
pyramids of gods towering into the air begin to
glisten as if surrounded by a halo of glory.

The sacred parrots, who have thousands of nests in
this forest of sculpture, commence to stir and utter
shrill cries ; their green colour, the green of a Chinese
water-colour, looking still more unreal amidst the red
entanglement of faces, arms, and legs that grimace
and gesticulate on every part of the tall pyramid.

The gildings on the summit of the car commence to

shine now, and the great hour is at hand. The horns give the signal, and hundreds of arms, with tensely knotted muscles, fix themselves on the cables. All the young men, even the most noble Brahmins, join in united effort, partly from pleasure and partly from a sense of duty. Now they make ready. With a grace that is almost feminine, and which contrasts strongly with their proud masculine eyes and thin broad shoulders, they unknot their heavy coils of hair ; then raising their arms, which many bracelets encircle, retie them into a tighter knot.

The second signal, a fury of tom-toms, and a more imperious blast of the horn, is answered by an outcry of human tongues, whilst the cables stretch under the effort of straining muscles. However, the enormous machine does not move, for it has become embedded in the ground since last year's procession.

At the instigation of their leader a better organized attempt is made, and this one will no doubt be successful. More men come to help, and old men, whose chests seem covered with snow, mingle their white fleeces with the black ones. A great cry goes up from the crowd, and muscles and backs are strained more furiously than ever. Still it does not move, and the cables fall, like huge dead serpents, from their disheartened hands on to the ground.

But they know well enough that the car will move. Since the memory of man the car of the god has never refused to budge under the efforts of forefathers, whose arms have fallen back to dust so long ago that their souls must either have been reincarnated or freed from fallacious personality and merged into the one universal soul.

The car will move, as the old priests who stand there unconcernedly with dreamy eyes and souls already half loosened from their emaciated bodies know well enough. Even the elephants know it too, for they stand there quite peacefully, though the thoughts which fill their large brains are quite unfathomable to us. The oldest especially must know it well, the one who has seen three or four generations of arms attached to these ropes, and has been familiar with this scene for the last hundred years.

" Run ! fetch the levers and the tackle, we must have them." Whole trunks of trees are brought on the shoulders of the porters, the levelled end is placed under the wheel which will not move, whilst ten men sit astride on the end that projects into the air and spring up and down, whilst others pull ahead at the ropes and pullies.

The huge structure trembles. There is a great cry of joy, and the car starts off.

The wheels of Vishnu's car commence to revolve, tearing up the earth with four deep furrows. The car moves, accompanied by the groans of straining axles, a creaking of bending wood, and the din of human voices and sacred trumpets. There is an immense overflow of childish joy ; white teeth glimmer in mouths which are opened widely with shouts of triumph, and the air is filled with waving arms.

The car has moved some thirty paces from its original place, but it now stops and becomes embedded again. The elephants who had commenced to walk in procession behind stop also, jostling against one another softly but heavily. So everything must be recommenced.

However, this seems to be the natural order of things, and they prepare to start anew. Whilst the levers and other tackle are being brought, women rush between the serried ranks of priests and almost under the feet of the gentle elephants, so that they may kiss the freshly made furrows in the soil, the ruts dug by the weight of the golden god. The sun's rays have sunk from the summit of the temple on the crowds assembled below and now clothe them with magnificence. Metal rings shine on all the naked arms, and diamonds and rubies threaded on pins sparkle in the noses of the women. Through the transparence of painted or gold-laced muslin, the bosoms of young girls are seen stainless as the breasts of the Bride of Siva, the goddess with the eyes of fishes.

The huge machine proceeds jerkily along; sometimes it makes terrible bounds, then come the never-ending stoppages; thus the procession lasts for two or three hours, in a veritable revelry of strength and movement. The tracks left by the procession of the gods make the ground look as if it had been worked by an army of savage ploughs, the same ground that was so smooth this morning and so garlanded with white ribbons and dotted flowers.

As the procession makes a long halt at one of the corners of the temple, where it is necessary to lever the car round the bend of the avenue, I mount again, with my guide and a Brahmin, to the terraces that extend over the labyrinth of naves—the dim passages and the halls with their myriad columns—in order that I may find a little air and quiet. The terraces are as deserted as they were this morning, but the sunlight shows me that they are decayed and ruined, and that their grayish-red walls are riven by cracks, which look like impresses that centuries have left. The hour is still early enough, and the sun sufficiently low for me to sit or even to lie down in the long shadows cast by the monstrous towers.

The terrace extends before me like a solitary and dismal steppe; close by its edge there are some tiny old gods with bats' wings who bend over to look down below; there is nothing else, only this flat plain with its towers of stony-faced gods rising at regular intervals; but the sanctuary is so vast that some of these towers are quite distant.

Here and there deep ruts like trenches are seen; these are the mouths, the openings of the open-air promenades that have been contrived amongst the gloomy halls below; the one in the centre is planted with banyan trees, whose green heads appear above the terrace, and this is the one that surrounds the holy of holies, the secret and dreadful place of gloom where the unapproachable idols repose.

Perhaps the little divinities who look over the crest of the wall are interested in the procession which I can no longer see nor hear from where I am ; all the turmoil below is hidden from me, so also is the neighbouring town with its houses and its streets, and my strange desert seems to border directly on the forest of palms whose bluish outlines are visible against the horizon.

Crows and vultures wheel around in a dazzling sky, traversed from time to time by flights of green parrots. Lizards crawl about, and the hopping squirrels which haunt the monuments and trees of India play and chase one another amongst the holy stones. I fall into a contemplative silence, and there is nothing to make me uneasy but the pyramids of gods that rise into the air above my head ; the attitude of the graven figures is calm and impassive, but the images seem too grotesque, and the towers are too lofty for my European notions.

An hour has flown whilst I have been resting in the shade of this airy wilderness. My guide and the Brahmin are asleep too, lying comfortably at full length on the warm stones.

Can it be that some hallucination has seized me, or is it giddiness ? One of the towers down there seems to totter, and now it actually moves. For an instant I am stupefied, then I look again and understand ; ah ! it is the mock tower of the car, it is the procession trailing along by the side of the temple wall farthest from me. From where I am the taut ropes, the excited crowd, the elephants, and the procession are all hidden as in a ditch, and I can only see the counterfeit structure covering the throne upon which the invisible god is seated. Neither the music nor the cries of the people are audible. This is the last impression the car of Vishnu leaves on me, that of a tower moving by itself along the edge of the terraces, silently and solitarily, in the wilderness of stone.

V

AMONG THE BRAHMINS AT MADURA

At Madura, the town which was once the capital of a splendour-loving king, there is a temple dedicated to Siva, and to Parvati his wife, the goddess with the eyes of a fish [1]—a temple that is larger than the Louvre and much more elaborately sculptured, and which contains perhaps as many marvels.

Thanks to the influence of the gracious Maharajah of Travancore, I shall be able to enter this sanctuary, descend to its underground caverns, and see the treasures and head-dresses of the goddess. Though the town retains all its Indian features, strangers, who come here in large numbers, are well received, and the temples are not so sullenly guarded as in some of the neighbouring states.

At Travancore letters of introduction have also been given me to families of various castes living at Madura. I first visit the Brahmins, who in India represent all that is most distinguished and select.

This massive and clumsy house, which contains a ground floor and a single story, is typical of all dwellings of the aristocracy of this town. There is also a veranda with columns, whose capitals are carved into the likeness of monsters' heads, and a little stone staircase leading to the chamber of honour, situated on the first floor and overlooking the street with its three tiny festooned windows. The head of the family, a white-haired old man, receives me there; he is surrounded by four young men, who, it seems, are his sons. Their long eyes are underlined by strokes of black paint; as to clothes, they merely wear a scrap of cloth round their waists, but this does not prevent them from having an air of distinction, nobility, and grace. The room, whitewashed and beautifully clean, has a certain air of elegance, and is perfumed by the scent of some unfamiliar incense

[1] In Indian *Minakchi*.

that has been burnt there.   The chairs are of carved ebony.   On the walls, in gilt frames, there are some old water-colours representing the seven incarnations of Vishnu.   On the floor a beautiful Indian carpet and some mattresses covered with a flowered material. The Brahmins are a little surprised at my visit, for strangers do not generally call ; nevertheless, they seem anxious to be courteous and hospitable, and invite me to inspect their house.   First there is a melancholy courtyard surrounded by walls, on which sheep and goats are lying under the shade of a stunted banyan tree.   Then we visit the roofs, whose terraces are the homes of pigeons and the resting-places of countless crows.   From here we overlook the palace of the ancient kings of Madura, an enormous and costly monument of the seventeenth century, built in the Hindoo-Arabian style ; the town, with its temples and its huge red pyramids of gods towering from all sides into a sky black with birds, lies farther off and stretches out till it joins the distant forest of palms.   Finally, I am taken to the library, which is crammed with books of philosophy and religion ; all these volumes indicate a highly-advanced and special culture which contrasts strongly with the simple garb of my hosts.

Before going I return to the reception-room and rest there a few moments, whilst one of the young men takes a long gilt mandoline and plays softly on its muted strings.   Of course I have not seen the women, that would not have been proper, but before I take leave the two youngest children of the house are brought to me, two little girls of three to four years who advance towards me without any traces of fear.   Their costume consists of little heart-shaped plaques of gold, which are suspended from a little chain that is attached round their waists, and some heavily chiselled rings that adorn their wrists and ankles.

They are two little marvels of beauty, two charming bodies of bronze, and with eyes of night in whose depths a smile seems to lurk under their long painted lashes.

VI

BALAMONI, THE GOOD BAYADÈRE

A bayadère, celebrated as much for her charity as for her grace, lives at Madura. In accordance with the usual custom she was at first the favourite of a Nabob, who at his death left her covered with as many precious stones as an idol. Rich and free now, she spends her fortune in works of art and deeds of charity, and in the theatre which she has had specially built, revives with her own charming art classic Indian tragedies that are thousands of years older than our own.

I wander under the splendour of the full moon on my way to the theatre of Balamoni, the good bayadère, and as I pass through the palm woods the long black feathers hanging down in all directions from their slender stems sway and brush softly against each other in the gentle breeze.

Balamoni is on the stage when I reach my seat; she is at the back in a garden of painted flowers, in the golden tower of a fairy palace where she is held captive, and she sings from her windows, accompanying herself on a precious mandoline.

She is a young princess betrothed to the son of a king of one of the neighbouring countries, and her affianced is coming to seek her shortly. At the very first notes one feels the charm of the music and of her voice. Her costume is copied from an antique bas-relief and her outline is charming. At each gesture of the singer the diamonds and rubies with which she is covered glitter.

The rest of the scenery is of an artlessness that is doubtless unintentional, but even whilst making me smile, it gives the impression of an exotic and distant land. The hall is very large and can hold over a thousand persons, though it is simply like one of those light structures of wood, matting, and bamboo that people erect by the side of the temples at the time of the great religious festivals. It has no decoration of any sort, but on each side of the stage there are boxes for the princesses of the ancient reigning family ; the princesses, however, are not coming this evening, for it is not their day. The whole of the pit and other seats are filled by naked-breasted spectators, for the temperature is that of a hot-house filled with scented flowers.

Balamoni sings in a tongue that has long since vanished—in the Sanskrit, which is the mother of our Indo-European languages, and the entire piece will be played in this language just as it was written formerly in the first dawn of time ; but all the listeners excepting myself are sufficiently educated to understand it. The story runs something in this wise. The young princess, whose part the bayadère acts to-night, is loved by seven young princes at the same time, and all these princes are brothers. In order that they may not cause any suffering to each other, they have sworn amongst themselves that none of them should ever wed her, not even the one who was chosen to be her husband by his father the king, the one who was coming to seek her in the palace in which she was kept. In the beginning they are all happy, contenting themselves with her friendship and her smiles. But one day, whilst hunting in a wood, evil spirits, who had assumed the form of white-haired fakirs, came to tempt each one separately and to set them against each other by false statements. Then hatred and unhappiness entered into the palace with a thousand plans of violence and crime. However, the good spirits intervened in their turn, before any wrong had been committed, and after a fearful struggle regained possession of the princes' souls. Once more the princes found calm and peace with their adopted sister, and enjoyed perfect happiness in the fulfilment of their duty. During one of the *entr'actes*, I went to the box of Balamoni, who had been told of my intended visit, in order to thank her for being so beautiful, and for having played the young girl's part with gestures so pure and simple. I found her in a plain little room carpeted with matting, in which the diamonds and ornaments that were strewn about seemed as much out of place as the fantastic presents that some genii might have left in the hut of a shepherdess.

As I reached the door waiting-men, in accordance with the usual custom, place a thick collar of natural flowers, interwoven with gold thread, round my neck, and the hostess offered me her hand with an easy and assured grace. Her proposal, she informed me, was to revive the whole of the ancient Sanskrit plays, and she professed herself much flattered when I mentioned that I would speak of her to my friends in France.

I met the bayadère again next morning in a place that had no romance attached to it; it was at the station of the Madras Railway, for, alas! the railway runs through Madura. She was accompanied by two servants and was going by train to visit her property in the country, just as any modest and prudent house-wife might have done. Truly, in the midst of the rather shabbily attired Indian crowd she seemed to have the air of a peri who had wandered from her way. From afar she could be seen shining like a star, for there were diamonds in her ears, diamonds on her neck and bosom, and her beautiful bare arms were covered with diamonds from the wrists to the shoulders. Others of a wondrous limpidity were attached to the septum of her little quivering nose, drooped over her mouth. Between her yellow waist-band and the short corset of lilac-coloured silk, a portion of her body, smooth as a fair column of metal, and part of the beautiful breasts, whose outlines were modestly concealed by folds of muslin, were exposed to view. (In evening dress our women expose the upper part of the bosom, and I cannot see that it is more improper to show the lower part, it lends itself less to artificial imposition, that is all.)

The bayadère comported herself with so much re-serve and dignity, indeed, that I saluted her, just as I would have done any lady of position. She answered my greeting in the Indian manner, touching her forehead with two ruby-covered hands ; then, accompanied by her maids, took her seat in the carriage " For ladies only."

I follow the good Balamoni with my eyes as I leave the horrible neighbourhood of the station and make my way to the temple of the goddess. During the course of the day some of her kindly deeds were related to me. This one amongst others : last month some European ladies who were collecting money for a Hindoo orphanage came to her, upon which Balamoni, with her beautiful smile, handed them a note for a thousand rupees (about eighty pounds). She is charitable to all, and the poor know the road to her house well enough.

VII

THE TEMPLE

In the temples of India twilight always comes on long before its usual time, under the shadow of low roofs, that are heavy and oppressive as those of sepulchres. The evening sun is still shining in the west, but the little lamps placed at the approach of the temple of Madura, and along the granite-covered avenue that forms a sort of prefatory vestibule where garland sellers are stationed, are already lighted. Any one coming from outside, as I do, sees everything mingled in universal gloom ; men, idols, monsters, human faces and great stone faces, rigid gestures of statues who have too many arms, and the real motions of men who have but two. The sacred cattle, after wandering through the streets all day, have come here too, to nibble flowers and reeds before retiring to sleep in the temple.

After the avenue, there is a door like a tunnel that pierces through a huge pyramid of gods that towers into the sky. Then we reach the temple itself, a silent and echoing city, whose vaulted streets cross one another in all directions, and whose countless people are the stone images graven here. Each column and each monstrous pillar is made of a single block, placed upright by means unknown to us— perhaps by the united strength of millions of sinews— and afterwards deeply sculptured, carved with images of all sorts of gods and monsters. The ceilings are entirely flat, and at the first glance it is difficult to see how they are supported ; then we notice that they are composed of single blocks of stone eight to ten metres long, resting on their two extremities, and that an infinite number of these blocks have been placed side by side, just as ordinary planks are placed with us. The whole structure is built somewhat in the manner of those almost everlasting edifices of Thebes or Memphis over which time has no control. Just as at Chri Ragam, there are serried ranks of prancing horses, that beat the air with their fore feet, and rows of gods that die away into the dimmest distance in lines of fading perspective. The antiquity of the columns is only to be divined from the worn surfaces near their base, or from the blackish polish that covers everything within reach of bodies or hands ; a polish that only the constant and daily contact of animals and men can give. Magnificence and filth, a combination of Titanic luxury and barbaric negligence. Garlands, reeds, and leafy branches of banyan, that have been suspended from one column to the other to celebrate some festival, now lie on the ground in putrefying masses ; properties belonging to the processions, fantastic animals, white elephants of natural size made from paper or paste-board, lie crumbling and rotting in the corners. Sacred cattle and real elephants wander freely through the naves and drop their dung on the greasy and slippery pavements that their feet have polished. Great vampire bats swarm amongst the lofty vaults, but their black wings sweep so noiselessly among the roofs that no sound is heard.

From an inner court that is open to the sky, I catch a glimpse of the fading evening light. It is unoccupied, but some peacocks are perched with outspread tails on the granite monsters. Above the surrounding walls those red and green towers, those surprising pyramids of gods, are visible at varied distances ; half-way up amidst the divinities, swallows and parrots flutter round their nests ; but nearer the bristling points of the summit, still shimmering in the sun, crows and eagles are wheeling madly through the air.

Outside this courtyard, and in a more concealed part of the sanctuary, I chance upon the priest to whom I was specially recommended, the one who can show me the adornments of the goddess.

It seems that I cannot see them to-morrow, for to-morrow is a day of high religious festival. Just as the Vishnu of Chri Ragam makes the yearly round of his temple in a car, so the Siva and Parvati of Madura make an annual excursion by boat in a great lake that has been hollowed out for them ; and this happens to be the evening before the day appointed for the sacred promenade.

But, on the day after to-morrow, so soon as it is light in the temple, the doors of the secret vaults shall be thrown open, and the treasures displayed before me.

VIII

THE BOAT OF SIVA

Need I mention that the boat is a huge and extravagant thing, though it is but temporary, and a new one is built each year ? Upon a hull suited to a three-decked ship, a sort of fairy palace is made from bamboo framework covered with silk or gilt paper ; then there are towers like those of the temples, paper horses and elephants, and the whole surface is covered by waving streamers. All the same our European eyes are fascinated by the extreme strangeness, ar the archaic and Eastern imagery with which it is decorated.

It is two o'clock in the afternoon, and a burning sun pours its fires upon the lake and its deserted banks. The boat is waiting there, moored to a granite stairway, new and resplendent in the midst of the old and unchanging scene. Though this is the hour fixed for the embarkment of Siva, no one comes and nothing even stirs.

The lake on which the boat rests has been dug out by human hands, and is a square some six to eight hundred metres across; granite staircases line its four sides and allow the faithful to descend to its holy waters; in the middle of the lake is a square island that has towers at each of its corners; whilst in the middle of the island an entirely white pagoda stands in a garden of banyan trees. The banks present large open spaces where crowds may congregate, but now these shores are overwhelmed by light and heat; in the vicinity there are curtains of verdure, banyans, palm trees, and some temples; but they are quite distant from the temple of the goddess, and almost in the country.

I hear the sound of approaching tom-toms; the procession is coming. Soon it issues from a shady avenue and advances into the sunlight, into the small burning desert where the lake and the strange ship slumber.

Cardboard giants, some ten or fifteen feet high, that roll and totter on the shoulders of their bearers, come first, followed by artificial elephants carried on men's backs; then six real elephants clothed in long red robes entirely covered with spangles, and a score of huge red parasols of the ancient Asiatic form that was fashionable in the processions of Babylon or Nineveh. Next come the tom-toms and the screeching bagpipes; and lastly the great gilt palanquins of Siva and the gods of his race.

No crowd follows; the procession is quite unaccompanied, and it does not seem to have aroused any

9

interest on its way through Madura.   Slowly it makes
the round of the lake, under the ever-burning rays of
the sun, and at last stops before the boat ; but no
curious eye has even come to look.

They next go through the ceremony of embarkation,
which takes place in the following order : the two sons
of Siva, Siva himself, and lastly Parvati his wife.
Some ancient boatmen, who doubtless have been
attached to this service for many years, advance from
the lake, the water dripping from their hairy bodies
as they approach the palanquins.   How different this
is from the placing of Vishnu in his car, that ceremony
so mysteriously accomplished at Chri Ragam during
the night when the god was hidden by so many veils.
I remain quite close, and no one troubles about me or
even requests me to retire.   The curtains of the
palanquins are wide open, and perhaps on this
occasion I may see the idols that have been worshipped
and dreaded for so many centuries.

Oh ! how can I express the surprise and the feeling
of horror that they gave me as they passed close by,
supported on magnificent cushions, carried on the
wrinkled arms of old and naked servitors.   Evil-
looking little dolls that seemed flexible and boneless,
and whose necks had sunk between their shoulders
under the weight of their jewelled tiaras.   Little
rose-coloured faces of the size of an orange (why rose
when the Indian race is bronze-coloured ?), thin lips
and closed eyes that had no lashes, they might well
be styled human embryos, still-born abortions that
retained a fierce expression even in their eternal sleep.
Yet in spite of their sullen look they have an air of
repletion, an almost drunken weariness in the midst
of the profusion of necklaces, diamonds, rubies, and
wreaths of fine pearls with which their miserable
bodies are loaded.   Great golden ears loaded with
precious rings are hung on each side of their heads,
and false hands of gold, that are much too large, with
long nails, are attached to their hands, whilst large
golden feet dangle from their legs.

A tiny hand, which looks like that of a foetus or of a monkey, has escaped from its huge golden gauntlet and lies there a crumpled mass of the same rosy colour as the idol's face.

The orchestra of tom-toms and bagpipes plays with frenzied fury as the hairy boatmen carry off these ancient still-born children, wrapped in glittering brocades and jewels that gleam in the dazzling sunlight. Now they seat them on thrones that are placed at the bottom of the boat, where they remain invisible enshrouded by thick curtains.

It is all over now. The procession, the elephants, and the parasols vanish, and once more the banks of the lake are deserted. The fantastic boat waits for the evening, then, when the moonlight shines, its wanderings will begin.

Night has come once more, and this old Hindoostan finds peace ; its glaring lights and mad excesses of brilliancy and colour are now swathed in shade. Now, too, the moonbeams penetrate the pall of bluish darkness that has settled on the earth and irradiate everything with their soft and silvery light. Crowds of the faithful hasten to kindle rows of wicks dipped in oil that have been placed along the three tiers of descending steps which extend around the lake ; and soon the immense extent of the square pond is outlined by a triple line of fire. The pagoda on the island in the centre is illuminated also, delineated in lines of palms, though it still remains white in the gleaming moonlight.

The crowd has been assembling since sunset. All the leafy avenues of tangled banyan trees, which lead here from the country and the town, pour forth their floods of humanity on to the shores of the sacred lake. Thousands and thousands of heads are now gathered by the banks, like pebbles on a shore, to pay honour to Siva ; dark and delicate Indian heads that are smaller than those of Europeans, and which seem to find room for feelings of the most ardent mysticism and the most glowing sensuality. (These two things are often associated, though, alas! the recognition of the fact may well fill us with dismay.)

Each one who comes to the lake of Siva carries a long reed, still decked with leaves, across his shoulders, so that the multitude almost looks like a field of grain. The elephants of the great temple, that have been brought back at nightfall, now look like rocks or islands scattered in the midst of this moving plain of vegetation, from which the dark outlines of Hindoo heads sometimes protrude.

Near the fantastic boat, that floating palace with its gilt towers on which Bengal fires constantly burn, an agitated crowd is seen. To the sound of music the towing ropes are brought forward and laid along the ground, then, with shouts of joy, hundreds of the faithful seize them with convulsive grasp. Those who cannot take place by the tightly-stretched rope plunge into the lake bespattering everything; with water up to their waists they push the boat from behind or draw it by its side, or at least walk in its wake.

The noise increases, and the tom-toms and the bag-pipes play furiously; the boat has started and now moves smoothly past the granite edges of the lake. The god and the goddess have begun their oft-repeated journey under a moon that seems to shine with more than usual splendour. The gentle elephants covered with tinkling bells follow along the banks with hesitating steps, fearful lest they tread upon some child or injure the crowds so closely thronged about them.

IX

THE TREASURES OF THE GODDESS WITH THE FISH'S EYES

I went to the temple this morning, immediately the sun rose, in order to see the treasures of the goddess. The inclosure contains two sanctuaries. The larger is dedicated to Siva, under the name of Sundareshvar (the blessed one). The other on the right, opposite the Patramaral (the pond of the golden lily), is dedicated to his wife Parvati, who is also named Minakchi (the goddess with the fish's eyes).

An animated throng already surrounds the labyrinth of stone, and all the niches between the dreadful statues and the granite stalls are occupied by flower sellers, who weave garlands of marigolds, Bengal roses, and gold thread. A continuous stream of half-clothed men passes by, their hair still dripping with water from the morning ablution, and their eyes yet lost in the land of prayer and dreams. The sacred elephants and cattle that dwell in the dusky naves, the birds of the sky that nest in the towers or amongst the red pyramids, all tremble with joy and life in the fresh morning air, and their cries, bellowings, and songs are heard in all directions.

I find the priests awaiting at the appointed place to conduct me to the hidden recesses.

A heavy copper door that leads to the secret part of the temple is thrown open, then after traversing a nave bordered with black gods that loom out of a cavern-like darkness, I find myself in the midst of a pure light by the pond that is named "the pond of the golden lily." It is a deep square of water open to the sky, and its sides are surrounded by granite steps which lead down to the water. Exquisite colonnades, supporting a roof that is sculptured and painted in a grave, formal manner, run round the four sides and form a cloister in which Brahmins can walk and meditate. One side of the jealously guarded inclosure is still bathed in a half light that is fresh and blue, whilst the other is illuminated in tones of rose-red by the morning sun. Above the cloisters that surround the lake with an unbroken line, the towers of the temples, those same prodigious red pyramids of gods that tower over everything and that are seen from all sides, shine in the bright firmament at various heights and unequal distances, each surrounded by its wheeling flight of birds. A sparkling golden cupola is also seen towering into the sky. It is the cupola of the holy of holies, that place of mystery to which no human influence can ever give me access. Oh ! what a strange lake this is, motionless as if enchanted. The columns standing round it are reflected, lengthened, doubled, and reversed in water that is untarnished by a single ripple, in water that seems dead, in a prison of magnificent severity. A nameless peace hovers over this " pond of the golden lily," this mirror of the sun, the clouds, and the stars, that lies hidden in the heart of the immense temples.

I have given up trying to recollect by what ways the priests are leading me amidst the labyrinth of arches. The more we advance, the more monstrous and oppressive our surroundings become. Everything is built of stones, whose mass grows more enormous at every step. Twenty-armed gods, with their huge and varied attitudes, swarm amid the gloom, and I pass by endless rows of them standing in tortured postures. I walk in a dreamland that is peopled by giants and shapes of terror. It is dark around me, and our footsteps wake echoes that seem to issue from a tomb.

The sculptures become more prodigious and every-thing grows more magnificent, but at the same time all is more filthy and more barbarously uncared-for. To the height of a man the walls and ledges are polished and black with filth and wet. We are in a gallery consecrated to the elephant-headed god Ganesa, whose monstrous form is illuminated from below by several smoky flames that burn close by his trunk and feet. Here, in a loathsome corner that is quite dark, a herd of living creatures, whose breathing is plainly audible, stand amidst monsters whose con-torted attitudes are graven out of stone. An idle family of zebu cows, who continue to sleep as though the sun had not risen yet. We slip in the dung with which the stones are covered, but no one dares to throw it out, for all that comes from the cattle is as sacred as the cattle themselves. Above our heads huge bats flutter their widely extended wings in terror and bewilderment.

Once, as we were passing by a high and gloomy nave at the bottom of which I could dimly see some colossal divinities lit up by several lamps, my guides seemed to hasten their footsteps and to be filled with uneasiness. One of the Brahmins who was guiding me turned round and whispered that we had passed the holy of holies, but that he had only told me after we had passed for fear that I might have seen too much. The priests at length halted in a vast and superb spot, a sort of square lying in a forest of massive columns, a place into which several cathedrals seemed to open, for naves led off in every direction, and lost themselves in gloom. We are surrounded on all sides by gigantic gods, hewn from a single block of stone, who brandish lances, swords, and skulls, but their figures are black, shining, and greasy, for they have drunk of the sweat of the countless hands that have lingered on them. There are many altars gleaming with objects of copper and silver ; many pyramids of bronze that time has almost worn out, but which once held torches and played some mysterious part in the worship of the goddess. In the middle there is a swarming crowd of the nude, long-haired beggars who haunt the vicinity of every temple ; the guardians drive and shove them away with many cries, for they throng importunately round a sort of barrier that has been made by attaching two cords from one pillar to another.

A portion of the strained cord is lowered so that I may pass, then raised once more so as to inclose the priests and myself within its circle. In front of me there is a table of great extent covered with a black carpet on which are heaped the treasures of the goddess.

A chair is placed for me near the piles of gold and precious stones, and a garland of marigolds is hung round my neck. Now the priests hand me the ancient jewels they have left their hiding-place for one little

hour ; they beg me to handle them, and find amuse-
ment in throwing them, one after the other, on to my
knees.   There are dozens of golden tiaras, ornamented
with stones of many colours, ropes of pearls, and rubies
that resemble boa-constrictors.

Bracelets a thousand years old ; ancient neck-pieces
so heavy that they can hardly be lifted with one hand.
Great urns like those the women carry on their
shoulders when they go to draw water from the well,
but these are hammered and chased out of fine gold,
There is a chest ornament, a plate of wondrous blue,
made from uncut sapphires large as nuts.

The sound of far-off music reaches me from the back
of the temple as these strange riches are poured into
my hands ; the growling of tom-toms and the deafening plaint of sacred shells and bagpipes.   From time
to time there are sounds of strife behind me, the cries
of the guardians chasing away the horde of famished
beggars, whose thronging threatens the frail barrier
of rope.   Now they show me stirrups of heavy gold
inlaid with diamonds, doubtless used by the goddess
when she rides abroad.   There are the false ears in
gold, with pendants of fine pearls, that they hang on
each side of her rose-coloured doll-like face when the
procession day arrives.   Here, too, the false hands and
feet of gold which they fasten to the ends of her half-
formed extremities each time that she forsakes the
temple's shade to make her solemn wandering.

I believed that all was over when once the treasures, with which the table was so extravagantly
laden, were exhausted.   But it was not so ;   the
priests led me through dark galleries, filled with
dreadful shapes, to a court in which sounds were
heard like those of clear and lively trumpet notes.
There, clothed in red robes, the six sacred elephants
were standing in the sunlight waving their large
transparent ears.   On my appearance they at once
knelt down, though the fan-like motion of the ears
was uninterrupted.   Then when I had bestowed on
each the silver offering that their small, shrewd eyes

sought for, they rose up and departed with the
ambling gait of contented bears. They went haphazard or where they listed, for they have full liberty
to wander through all these passages and naves.

The halls through which I am now conducted are
built and roofed with enormous blocks, and have the
look of cyclopean caverns. Attendants, who accompany us, climb up the walls to draw back the mat
blinds that cover air-holes of irregular shape, but it
is in vain. It is really so dark that we must have
lamps. Naked children run to fetch lamps and
torches of an antique form that burn smokily at the
extremities of long bronze stalks, or on the ends of
supports bent into the form of a horn.

A door covered with iron is thrown open, and our
young torch-bearers enter first.

We are in one of the fantastic stables of the goddess. A silver cow and some golden horses of natural
size are ranged there, bathed in a perpetual night
and a constant damp heat.

Now the children approach the rudely sculptured
figures, and the shining gems with which the harness
is studded are seen to glitter in the torches' flame.
Above our heads, somewhere in the awe-inspiring
granite roof, we hear the shrill cries and the constant
fluttering of featherless wings made by the crowd of
vampires that fly above us in maddened wheelings.

There is a second door cased with iron; another
stable for animals of silver and of gold.

A third and last door. Here live a silver lion, a
huge golden peacock, with fully expanded tail, whose
eyes are made of uncut emeralds, and a golden cow
with the face of a woman of supernatural size, who
wears jewels in her ears and jewels in the division of
her nose in the manner of the Indian women. Golden
sedan chairs for the use of the goddess are stabled
in the corners; state palanquins, wholly made of
gold, wrought with precious carvings and inlaid with
flowers of diamonds and rubies.

The naked children cast the light of their curved

handled torches on these fabulous treasures, but as the torches give more smoke than light I can only see a detail here and there, or the glint of a precious stone, and the rest of the cavern is plunged in a sepulchral and oppressive gloom. The walls are covered with spiders' webs and little stalactites, and in places saltpetre and slime ooze out of them. The startled vampires wheel noiselessly round us, and as they flit by we feel as if a tattered dark material had swept past us, and hear a shrill cry like that of a rat caught in a trap.

X

TOWARDS PONDICHERRY

Leaving the country of Madura in a northerly direction, and ascending towards Pondicherry, we gradually forsake the damp region of the great palms. Their shady clumps are farther apart and give place to fields of grain, plantations, and rice patches. The air gradually becomes less oppressive, but the country is not so well watered and the whole land seems changed.

An air of pastoral tranquillity reigns, though the inhabitants are more sparsely scattered than those of Europe. Troops of goats, and herds of small humped cattle graze on the fast ripening grass that still remains, watched over by naked shepherds, and by shepherdesses wrapped in scarlet cloth.

Each village of mud and thatched house has its Brahmin temple, whose pyramid of gods and whose monsters that lean over the walls crumble away to reddish dust in the burning rays of the terrible sun. At long intervals there are masses of enormous trees, under whose shade gods seated on thrones are ever to be found, guarded by stone horses or cows that have kept watch there for many centuries.

The red dust ; the red dust that hourly assumes a greater mastery. Dryness also becomes more marked, and we hasten through regions which are suffering from a drought that is probably exceptional, and where the sky has a fixed blue limpidity that looks eternal.

On all sides husbandmen are labouring at the work of irrigation, which they carry out by means of the ingenious methods of olden times. Men may be seen standing knee-deep in all the streams that surround the rice-fields, each couple holding an extended sheep-skin by the cords which are attached to it; they swing it with an automatic movement that is guided by the refrain they sing, and in turn fill it and empty its contents into a gutter situated at a higher level, from which the water runs among the furrows of rice that still looks fresh and green.

The wells, which are always placed under the trees, are worked in a different manner, and to the accompaniment of a different melody. A bucket is fastened to the end of a very long pole, which is balanced on the top of an upright mast; two men walk erect on this pole, supporting themselves with the graceful agility of gymnasts by clinging to the branches of the neighbouring trees; they take three steps in one direction, and the pole dips towards the well and the bucket fills; three steps in the reverse direction, and the pole rises and the bucket swings in the air; and so they go on, from morning to night, never ceasing to sing.

As we proceed the dryness threatens to become disastrous, and we soon pass the first dead trees. These are burnt up as if by fire, and their leaves are curled up and coated by the red dust which attacks the monuments of the south, but which here casts its blood-coloured stain over the plants themselves. Face to face with this thirsty land and rainless heaven how impotent our little human efforts seem, little buckets of water hauled up one after the other from the bottom of wells whose springs are gradually drying up. Now we begin to understand the reality and to feel the approach of the frightful famine which before our arrival in India only seemed to us like a pre-historic plague that was quite inexcusable in these days of civilization, when steamboats and railways were at hand to bring food to those who were dying of hunger.

XI

AT PONDICHERRY

The woods of coco-nuts and the great palms re-appear as we approach Pondicherry, our tiny and decaying colony. The region around has so far been spared by the drought, and looks like an oasis which the streams and the rain have not ceased to water, and which in some way recalls the beautiful verdure of the south.

Pondicherry! amongst the names of all the ancient colonies which exercised so great a fascination over my childish mind, those of Pondicherry and Goree were the ones that most readily called up the dreams of strange and foreign lands that ever haunted me. Towards my tenth year, an aged grand-aunt spoke to me one evening of a friend who had lived at Pondicherry, and read me a passage from one of her letters, which even then was half a century old, and in which she spoke of palm trees and pagodas.

Oh! what feelings of melancholy come over me as I reach the charming and far-distant town, where amidst the mouldering walls an entire chapter of ancient French history slumbers.

There are little streets almost like those that are hidden in our own peaceful provinces, little straight streets bordered by old and low whitewashed houses standing amid the red earth; garden walls, over which tropical flowers and bindweeds fall; barred windows behind which pale-faced Creoles or lovely Eurasians, whose eyes gleam with Indian mystery, may be seen. " Rue Royale," " Rue Dupleix "—one can read these names cut in the stone in the ancient

letters of the eighteenth century, just as I remember
to have seen them at the street corners of my native
town on some of the older houses. "Rue Saint
Louis" and "Quay de la Ville Blanche," the word
"quay" spelt with a "y."

In the centre of Pondicherry there is a large, overgrown, and deserted square, ornamented in the middle
by an elaborate fountain whose age does not, I
think, exceed one hundred years, though the glare
of the all-devouring sun has made it look much
older. Somehow this open space conveys an impression of infinite sadness, though I am quite in-
capable of saying why.

From the very first, I, who feel myself so much of
a stranger in the rest of India, am possessed by a
feeling of charm—that olden charm of one's native
land which nothing can replace, and that our newer
colonies of the extreme East do not yet possess, in
that they have had no past.

It is but a tiny little town that exists on its traditions, that lives but because it has lived, systematic-
ally isolated from the rest of India by our hostile
neighbours, and having neither port nor anchorage
on the Gulf of Bengal where our boats can shelter.
Electricity and smoking funnels are wanted also, and
here are no hurrying throngs as at Madras or Calcutta, and neither strangers nor tourists ; for as
Pondicherry is not on the direct route, who would
be likely to come to see it ?

Facing the sea there is a garden where a band
plays at sundown, and is the evening resort of a
number of pale-faced children ; some of them born
in France, others in the land of exile. There,
amongst beautiful tropical trees, a quantity of columns
have been erected around the statue of Dupleix—
columns so tall and fine that they resemble ships'
masts. These precious monoliths, these reeds of
granite, sculptured in Indian style, bear witness to
our bygone greatness, for the Maharajah of the
country gave them to this same Dupleix in olden

times so that he might embellish the palace of France with them. But, alas! the palace was never built.

An angry sea, on which no sails are visible, and whose appearance is as hostile and prison-like as that of Travancore, breaks into foaming billows along the shore. An iron pier juts out into the water, permitting communication with the packets that anchor opposite the shore, but which remain for as short a time as possible. Several large boats are lying wrecked along the sands, of themselves proving the insecurity of the coasts, so massive and solid are they, so well fitted for the struggle.

" Pondicherry, the town of palaces," as it is called in India. There are, in fact, several beautiful old dwellings with Greek colonnades near the Government House Buildings, in the midst of gardens which slumber behind lowered mat-blinds, that may well justify this appellation.

In addition to the officers and functionaries of the colony, some Creole families, who came during the heroic epoch, and who, after four or five generations, have become quite acclimatized, are to be found here. I saw ancient dames whose manners were gentle and old-fashioned ; charming old salons, pervaded by a tinge of melancholy, furnished with sofas and chairs of the eighteenth century, and Louis XVI and Empire clocks, all of which must have made the hazardous journey by the Cape of Good Hope, in the days when the passage by Egypt had not been foreseen. How many hours of languid existence, how many minutes of wearied exile, have not these clocks of olden days numbered ? It is foolish, I know, but the clocks of olden days that I see in the colonies always arrest my thoughts.

The native town that clusters by the " white city " is large, animated, and quite Hindoo, with its bazaars, palm trees, and pagodas. But the Indians are French Indians, and hold fast to France, or at least, are pleased to say so.

I cannot say how touched I was at the reception

accorded me by a certain purely native club that was established by Indian initiative to promote the reading of our books and reviews.

In order to extend further the knowledge of our language a school has been added. Oh! what adorable little scholars were presented to me. Children of about eight years of age, with refined bronze faces and such courteous and well-schooled manners. Some are clothed like little rajahs in robes of gold-embroidered velvet, but they can work out problems on the blackboard and do exercises that would perplex the majority of our school children.

XII

THE DANCE OF THE BAYADÈRE

The young painted face, with eyes of excessive length, draws near. The young face with the impress of gloom and sensuality advances and draws back, very quickly and very lightly. The two pupils that roll, black as an onyx on a groundwork of white enamel, are fixed on mine unwaveringly, in these alternative advances of sensual appeal, and retreats into the shade, that are ever succeeded by a new and provocative advance. The young, bronze-coloured face is wreathed in precious stones, and a band of gold and diamonds surrounds the forehead and descends over the temples, concealing the hair, and in the ears and nose many diamonds sparkle.

It is night, and everything is lit up, but in all this crowd I can only see the woman with the helmeted head whose shining point seems to exercise a fascination over me. There are many spectators gathered around watching her also, scarcely leaving room for her evolutions, only a sort of passage by which she can reach me and then draw back; but they have ceased to exist for me, and I only see the woman and her sparkling head-dress and the play of her black eyes and eyebrows. She has a body lithe as a serpent,

yet firm and plump ; enchanting arms that seem instinct with assurances of embrace, and which twist and
writhe like snakes loaded and encircled up to the
shoulders by diamonds and rubies. But, no! the
attraction lies in those eyes whose expression is ever
changing, sometimes mocking, sometimes tender, and
which look into mine in a way that makes me tremble.
The jewels of her head-dress and the gems in her ears
and nose shine so brilliantly, and the golden band
forms such a brightly defined framing, that the face
underneath, with its soft features and its dull and
dusky skin, seems to have a nameless and far-off
indefiniteness, even when it is quite close to me. The
bayadère goes and comes ; she seems to dance for me
alone. Her dance is noiseless, and only the tinkling
of the precious bracelets on her ankles is heard, for a
carpet receives the cadenced impress of the little
naked feet, whose expanded and mobile toes are
burdened with rings.

All this takes place in an atmosphere so saturated
with essences and the perfume of flowers as to be
almost unbreatheable. I am at a fête given by the
Indians who live here, the French Indians, and I am
in the house of the most wealthy of them. On my
arrival the host placed a many-rowed collar of jasmines of intoxicating odour round my neck, and
sprinkled me also with rose-water from a long-necked
silver flagon. The heat is suffocating. The guests
are mostly seated—a row of dusky heads whose turbans are embroidered with gold thread. Above these
heads great fans of painted palm are waved by naked
and erect attendants—their nudity looking the more
strange amongst this gaily decked crowd, where even
the men wear diamonds in their ears and at their
waists.

The bayadère has been told that the fête was in my
honour, so that it is to me that this comédienne,
accomplished both by nature and inheritance, ad-
dresses herself.

She has come from afar for this evening, from one

of the temples of the south, where she is in the service of Siva ; her reputation is great, and her performances are costly.

She sways backwards and forwards, waving meanwhile her beautiful nude arms, twisting her fingers into strange shapes, and her toes, which have been trained since her infancy to that purpose, into still stranger contortions, the great toe being always separated and maintained erect in the air.

Between the gauze of gold that enwraps her loins and the corset in which her bust is held a close prisoner one sees as usual a little of her pale bronze body, a little of her vigorous and sinewy flesh; and the play of the lower part of her breasts and of her waist is exposed to our gaze.

Her dance consists of a series of expressive poses, a kind of acted monologue, with those oft-repeated advances and retreats, approaching towards me through the lane of human faces, coming quite close with her eyes riveted on mine ; then, with a sudden flight, disappearing into the gloom that envelops the lower end of the hall.

She depicts a scene of seduction and reproach. Behind, at the back, musicians intone the melody of this scene to an accompaniment of tambourines and flutes. She, too, sings as she acts, but only to herself, and in a little voice that is not intended to be heard. This, however, serves to aid her memory, and to allow her to enter more fully into the varied dramatic phases of her part.

Now she approaches from the end of the hall that is shrouded in shadow, a creature glittering in gold and jewels ; she darts towards me with an indignant air of accusation, and menaces me with expressive gestures that call heaven to witness the magnitude of the crime I have committed.

Then suddenly the bayadère bursts into a fit of mocking laughter ; she overwhelms me with bantering disdain and with extended finger, points me out to the jeering crowd. Her irony is, of course, factitious,

10

just as were the superb imprecations with which she but lately encompassed me. But it is a marvellous imitation all the same. Her titter and somewhat sad laughter can be heard to resound in her heaving chest, and she laughs with her mouth, her eyes, and her eyebrows, with her bosom, and with her heaving and panting breasts. As she withdraws, shaken with laughter, the effect is irresistible, and one must laugh with her.

She withdraws backwards, as quickly as her little feet will take her, turning away her head in scorn, so that she may no longer see me. But now she returns with slow and solemn step ; these sarcasms were but spite ; her love is too strong, she returns conquered by the sovereign passion, stretching her hands out to me, imploring pardon, and offering her all in a final appeal. And as she again withdraws, with her head thrown back and her half-opened lips that disclose the pearly teeth glimmering beneath the diamonds in her nose, she wishes me to follow her, even seems to command it, she calls me with her arms, her breasts, and her languorous eyes ; she calls me with all her being, as with a loadstone, and for a very little I should follow her almost involuntarily, for I am at last spellbound by her fascinations. Her promises of love are false, and like her laughter but part of the comedy. One knows it, and indeed it is no worse for that ; perhaps even the knowledge of its unreality only adds a new and malignant charm.

Whilst she acts, a sort of magnetic or invisible bond unites her to those two men who sing in the orchestra, and who, like her, go and come along the human passage ; sometimes advancing, then taking three or four steps backward. They follow her when she comes near me, but are the first to draw back when it is time for her to retire ; they never allow her to escape from out of their sight, and their burning gaze is fixed on her, whilst with widely opened mouths they ever sing in the high falsetto voice of a muezzin. With heads bent forward they, who are tall, look down on her who is short, and they have the air of being the masters by whom she is inspired and possessed. They seem to guide her with their voices, and to fan her with the flame of their breath like some delicate and glittering butterfly that they have tamed to their will, and there is an unknown something in this that seems perverse and uncanny.

In the less brightly lit place where the orchestra is seated there are two or three other gaily-adorned bayadères who had already danced. One had struck me as being especially strange, a sort of beautiful, poisonous flower; tall and thin, with features that seemed too delicate and eyes that were too long already, without their unnatural lengthening of paint; blue-black hair, stretched in tight bands across the cheeks; drapery that was wholly black, a black girdle and a black veil with the slightest silver edging. Her ornaments consisted of nothing but rubies, rubies that covered hands and arms, and in her nose a bunch of rubies that fell over her mouth, so that the ghoulish lips looked as if a spot of blood had yet remained on them.

But I forgot them all so soon as I saw that one, that queen, that star, make her sudden appearance between the musicians who stood aside to let her pass, that creature all decked in gold who had been kept for the last.

Her dance was long, very long, almost wearisome, yet I dreaded the moment when it would end and I should see her no more.

Once more she repeated her reproaches and that irresistible laugh; once more I felt the mockery of her sparkling eyes and again the evermore despairing calls of love.

At last she ceases and all is over, and I wake up and see the people gathered around, and find myself surrounded once more by the realities of the entertainment organized in my honour.

Before retiring—and it is time—I go to compliment the bayadère. I find her wiping her face with a delicate handkerchief; she has been very hot, and the perspiration rolls down her forehead on to her smooth and dusky bust. In a manner that is now correct, cold, and indifferent, the tired and unconcerned comédienne receives my compliments with little bows of mock modesty, little bows made in the Indian style, hiding her face each time with hands on every finger of which she wears diamonds.

What thoughts can there be in the soul of a bayadère of the old race and the pure blood ? the daughter and granddaughter of bayadères, one who has been trained through descent, that has lasted for hundreds and thousands of years, to be a creature of naught but phantasy and pleasure.

XIII

WRITTEN ON LEAVING PONDICHERRY

I am leaving Pondicherry to-morrow for the States of Rajputana, where the famine rages, going by way of Nizam. I have hardly spent ten days in our old colony, and am astonished to find that I cannot leave without regret, though I have hitherto borne my Indian partings with the lightest heart. I might even say that this land of Pondicherry has resumed a sway over me. I might say that I have found my old recollections once more. At the moment of my departure I feel the same feeling stirring within me that I experienced in the bygone days of my youth when the time came for me to quit that other decayed old town, Saint Louis of Senegal, where I had spent a whole year.

I had lodged at the hotel, just as any ordinary traveller might do, for there are two hotels at Pondicherry that exist modestly without any visitors. I had chosen the one by the side of the sea, a house of somewhat stately aspect that dated from the foundation of the town, and whose dilapidations were concealed under a coating of whitewash. In view of the air of abandonment and neglect that prevailed, I entered with some trepidation, and who would have thought that I should become attached to the chance lodging ?

The great and almost bare whitewashed room which I occupied showed plainly the havoc wrought by time, and recalled in a strange and familiar manner that other room which I lived in long ago on the coast of Africa. Green-shuttered windows overlooked the vast plain of the Indian Ocean, whose breezes brought a delicious freshness even during the hottest hours of the day. As in the Creole salons, there were ancient chairs of carved wood, and on a Louis XVI console a clock of the same period, whose persistent ticking told of life and of a soul that was old and worn. All was dried up, worm-eaten and fragile, and I did not dare to sit down too quickly nor to jump into bed hastily. But there was always the same fair weather, blue sky, pure air, and delicious and home-like peace.

Leaning from the windows I could see, besides the shore and the sea, the terraces of some old houses that stood close by. These also called back recollections of Africa, for the roofs were Moorish in style, and the burning sun had riven them with many cracks. From morning till night I am cradled by the sleepy song of a troop of naked Indians who work dreamily in the neighbouring courtyard, and who are occupied in filling mat sacks with grain and spices for the ships.

My room was never closed, neither during the day nor the night, and the beasts of the air made their home with me ; sparrows walked on the mats that covered the floor without ever heeding my presence, and little squirrels, after an inquiring gaze, came in too and ran over the furniture ; and one morning I saw two crows perched on the corner of my mosquito net.

Oh ! how sad and still were these midday hours, when the tropical sun poured down on the silent little streets lying round the house, streets with the strange old-fashioned names. Nothing in my room or my surroundings served to remind me of modern times ; there was nothing on those lonely terraces or on the wide blue plain of the deserted sea by which I could fix the period, though the deliberation of the men occupied in filling their sacks with corn made me think of some colonial scene of olden times. Then forgetting our hurryings, our eagerness, and our rapid steamers, I fancied myself back in the old days when one came here by the Cape of Good Hope on some shapely and wilful sailing-vessel which travelled with a deliberation that made the distance seem ten times as great.

My regrets, as may be imagined, cannot be very deep ; all will be forgotten to-morrow, driven away by the fleeting images of new and fresh scenes. But nothing that I have already seen in this old India, or that I may yet see, will take such a hold on me as this little corner of old France stranded on the shores of the Gulf of Bengal.

IN FAMISHED INDIA

CHAPTER V

IN FAMISHED INDIA

I

TOWARDS HYDERABAD

It is no longer green, there are no more great palms ; the earth is no longer red, and it is quite chilly. . . . These are the surprises that attend my first awakening in Nizam after having journeyed all the night from the regions of Madras and Pondicherry, where yesterday everything was still so green. We have now reached the central plateau of India, and are in the midst of a stony wilderness where all is different—save the croaking of the eternal crows.

Parched lands and grayish plains alternate with millet fields that are vast as little seas. In place of superb coco-nut palms a few sparse aloes and some miserable date trees, almost withered up by the drought, cluster round villages that have also changed their aspect, and that now resemble those of Arabia. Islam has placed its mark on all these things—Islam that seems to love gloomy regions and gleaming deserts.

The costumes have changed too. Men no longer go about with naked chests, but are swathed in white, and they do not wear long hair, but wrap their heads in turbans.

The dryness increases hourly as we penetrate farther among the weary sameness of the plains. Rice patches, whose furrows can still be seen, have been destroyed as if by fire. The millet fields, which hold out longer, are for the most part yellow and hopelessly damaged.

In those which are still alive watchers, perched on platforms made of branches, are to be seen everywhere trying to scare away the rats and birds that would eat everything; poor humanity in the clutches of famine, trying to guard a few ears of corn from the ravages of famished animals.

The night chills have vanished, and the sun pitilessly pours a furnace-like heat on the earth, whilst the sky extends above our heads, limpid and blue as a great sapphire.

The scenery towards the end of the day becomes strange and wonderful. Scattered amidst fields of burnt-up millet and parched jungles there are heaps of monstrous brown stones, great blocks with polished sides and fantastic outlines that have wandered here somehow. They seem to have been purposely piled up into strange and unstable postures; some are upright, and some lean so strangely that these groupings, which are often of great height, have always the most absurdly improbable appearance.

The sun is setting, and Hyderabad is at last visible, very white amidst clouds of white dust, and very Mohammedan with its terraced roofs and slender minarets. The trees, fast dying of drought, are shedding their leaves and give the false impression of the decline of the year. The river that flows in a large bed at the foot of the town is almost dried up, and the water is so low as to be nearly imperceptible. Troups of elephants of the same grayish colour as the mud banks are slowly wandering along, trying to bathe and drink.

The day declines and the Eastern sky is lighted by a burning glow; the whiteness of the town fades slowly into an ashy blue, and huge bats commence to flit silently through the cloudless sky.

II

HYDERABAD AWAITS THE NIZAM

The inhabitants of this country, however, have not felt the tortures of famine that tread at the heels of their neighbours of Rajput, and the glittering splendour of their capital is at its brightest now that they await the return of their king, of the Nizam as he is called here.

" Long Live the Nizam, Our Prince," is seen in great gold letters on all the floating banners and at the top of the many triumphal arches, decked with silk and muslin, that cross the roads and streets.

Hyderabad, the white city that overhangs the almost dried-up river, in whose fresh mud the hordes of elephants are wandering, Hyderabad, beflagged and gay, has been waiting day by day for a week for the king who does not come.

" Welcome to the Nizam, Our Ruler," is the inscription written above the archway thrown over the great stone bridge leading to the town, an archway gaily decked with red crape and covered with gold spangles.

There is a constant stream of passengers dressed in many colours, of horses, waggons, and attendants, passing over the bridge.   I am surprised after journeying through such a succession of sad plains to find hidden amongst these gray and stony steppes a city so teeming with life and colour.

The streets extend before us, white, broad, and straight, thronged by a crowd that glitters with all the colours of a flower-bed.   First of all we are astonished by the luxury and the infinite variety of the turbans.   There are rose, salmon, and cherry-coloured ones, and some with the tints of peach blossom ; here lilac, amaranth, yellow, or golden ones are seen. All are worn large, immoderately large, wrapped round the little pointed caps with their free ends hanging loosely behind on the wearer's robes.

The streets extend white, broad, and straight, crossed here and there by triumphal arches, which are taller than the houses, and from which spring minarets crowned with golden crescents.   In addition to these stone arches several others, made of silk stretched over bamboo frames, have been raised in honour of the prince who does not come.   In the middle of the town there is an archway of enormous proportions, a four-sided arch with four minarets which tower above all the others near, tower, too, above the tapering spires of the mosques and dart into the air, far above the dust of Hyderabad, into the purity of the unchanging sky.

The Arabian ogive, as it is seen here, has been much complicated by festoons and indentations, the Indians having even enriched the fanciful beauty of the original models. On the ground floors of all the houses rows of arches succeed one another in infinite variety, either very pointed or very obtuse, the rose-pattern predominating, although the many-leaved trefoil is often seen. Along the whole length of the street merchants are seated on cushions and carpets, under the shelter of the porches, the arches of which have been elaborated with such studied refinement. The back of their shops is in open-work masonry like the front, and the blue, green, and gold with which it is painted make it resemble the outspread tail of some huge bird of the peacock tribe. Here is the jewellers' quarter, where collars, bracelets, and glass trinkets glitter in every shop, side by side with precious gems, and tinsel glitters next to virgin gold. Here is the quarter of the perfumers, where the essences of all the flowers are stored in ancient Chinese vases, brought here long ago by caravans. There is also the sparkling street where slippers are sold, all gilt and bespangled, with the tips bent backwards like the prow of a gondola. Intermingled everywhere, as if by chance, are the stalls of the flower-sellers, where masses of roses, broken from their stems, are piled up into tiny mountains. There are piles of jasmine flowers, too, that children thread as they would thread beads. We pass by sellers of arms, lances, and the great two-handed swords of olden days, knives for tiger-hunting, these of a special shape and destined to be flung into the tiger's gaping jaws as it leaps upon its victim. Marriage robes for men, gilt all over, are on sale, and marriage turbans glittering with spangles. Here is a quarter where the space between the houses and the middle of the street is occupied by people engaged in printing light muslins, some of which seem transparent as the mist. Little designs in silver and gold are strewn over green, rose, or yellow grounds. The fabric may not be lasting, for the first drop of rain would spoil all, but the colouring is always admirable, and the smallest piece that issues from the hands of these artists of the street looks like the magic veil of some peri. Gold, gold, there must be gold everywhere, or, failing that, tinsel or gilt paper, or anything that will glitter in the gorgeous sunlight and fascinate the eye.

The dust is white, the houses white, and the garments of the people white ; a snowy whiteness is the prevailing note of the streets and their moving multitudes, and it is from the whiteness of the robes that the glowing colours of the muslin turbans stand out in such relief.

" Honour to the Nizam ! " The amount of silks, muslins, and velvets hung out in honour of the long-absent prince is quite incredible. Hyderabad glories in the expectation of its king, and for the last eight days everything has been ready, even the flowers that the sun has now withered. But the Nizam is at Calcutta, driving through the streets with Asiatic pomp, followed by a dozen gilded carriages. He neither returns nor sends any news, but drifts at the mercy of his inclinations. The Indians, who would do exactly the same in his place, are not at all surprised at his proceedings, and merely continue to expect him. Alas! however, there is no danger that the rain will come to spoil the light draperies, to wash away the gildings of the triumphal arches, for there is never a cloud in the sky.

Each day, as the hours advance, there is an increasing bustle, and from an ever-thickening cloud of dust a volume of sound arises, the cries of the streets, the braying of the bands, that swells and swells, until nightfall comes and silence returns.

There is a constant stream of horse-drawn carriages and of carts to which trotting zebus are yoked. These are skiff-shaped coaches of basket-work in which mysterious ladies sit, enveloped in hanging curtains pierced with holes, through which these painted beauties can gaze upon the crowd. There are splendid horsemen, with pointed caps and streaming turbans, riding with couched lances. Long strings of drome- daries belonging to some caravan, elephants of burden returning from their work, all covered with dust or mud, elephants of state marching to the sound of bagpipes in wedding processions, with little towers on their backs in which the bridal pair are concealed behind curtains drawn close.

The monotonous chaunt of the palanquin bearers is heard, as, running with nimble steps, they carry on piles of embroidered cushions some important and be- spectacled old gentleman, or some grave priest lost in prayers. Beggars in rags, covered with shells, drag themselves along, and there are mad folk of disquiet- ing aspect, who are sacred, and whose eyes have the far-off look of those who discern other worlds. Long-haired old dervishes, all bedabbled with ashes, hurry along ringing bells, seeing nothing as they forge ahead, while people respectfully stand aside to let them pass. We meet bands of Yemen Arabs, whose presence the Nizam is pleased to encourage. Now the chief of some far-off province advances, a man of savage and magnificent mien, who dashes along at a breakneck pace, followed by horsemen bearing lances.

The air is filled with the scent of burning perfumes, scented, too, by the red roses which are heaped up be- fore the sellers of wreaths, scented by the white jasmine flowers that overflow their baskets and fall like snow into the dusty street. Who would think that famine is approaching from the west, or that it had already made its voracious presence felt on this side of the frontier ? And with what water and in what sheltered gardens have all these flowers been brought to bloom ?

Towards sundown the characters of the Thousand and One Nights begin to appear, dandies whose eyes are painted with blue and whose beards are tinged vermilion ; they wear robes of brocade, or of velvet trimmed with lavish gold, many necklaces of pearls or of precious stones, and carry tamed birds of prey upon their right hands.

" Welcome to His Highness the Nizam " is seen once more : this time over an archway hung with orange-yellow crape, decked with citron- and sulphur-coloured streamers of the same material, and spangles of gold. This archway is outlined against a large and snowy mosque, adorned with crescents and with points of gold, and as it is the hour of evening prayer the mosque engulfs the white-robed crowd of worshippers, whose heads are wrapped in muslin, and who from afar look like great flowers of many hues that have been scattered over the ground.

However, the news circulates that the Nizam is not yet returning ; certainly that he will not be back till after the moon of Ramadan. At the next moon perhaps he may return . . . or it may be later. Allah alone can say.

III

GOLCONDA

AT the corner of one of the outlying streets of Hyderabad, this inscription can be read upon an old wall— " Road to Golconda." It would have been equally true to have written up " Road to Silence and Ruin."

Passing along the deserted road, from which our horses' feet raise clouds of dust, we first see a number of abandoned little mosques, and many crumbling little minarets of rare elegance and exquisitely beautiful design. Then nothing more. We plunge into the parched and ashy-coloured steppes and see heaps of granitic blocks of such strange shapes that it seems as if they could not belong to our terrestrial sphere.

After driving for an hour we arrive on the banks of a lake, whose waters are so low that its muddy bed is exposed to view. Behind the lake the whole horizon is walled out by a phantom town of the same ashy-gray colour as the surrounding plain. This is Golconda, the city which for three centuries was one of the marvels of India.

It is well known that all cities, palaces, and monuments that man has erected look larger when they are

in ruins ; but really these ruins are too overwhelming.
First there is a crested rampart, at least thirty feet
high, furnished with bastions, parapets, and stone
watch-towers, which appears to extend for miles into
the desert country ; then above this already formidable inclosure there is a cyclopean fortress tower.   It
is made out of a mountain, one of those strange
mountains, one of those agglomerations of granite
blocks that give the country its appearance of fantastic
unreality.   The desire for what is gigantic and superhuman which possessed the kings and peoples of the
olden days must surely have found here everything
to its heart's wish.   Amongst the monstrous blocks
walls have been built, inclosed within each other and
poised one above another, whilst their crested ramparts
intermingle bewilderingly.   Close to the edge of the
boldest rocks bastions have been thrown out that
overhang terrible precipices ; mosques have been
poised at various heights, and there are complicated
arches and prodigious buttresses.   The topmost stone
of all, from superstition or the whim of design, has
been left in its natural state, looking like some great
round-backed beast crouching on the highest summit.

At the gates of the dead city, near piles of cannon
balls of stone or metal, and of implements from many
an ancient siege and battle, there are modern repeating
rifles stacked in sheaves.   The soldiers of the Nizam
and many sentries are on guard, and we have to show
a special permit.   Access to these ruins is not granted
to any comer, for they still constitute an impregnable
fortress, and it is reported that the sovereign conceals
his treasures here.

Terrible gates, those of Golconda, which will only
swing round under the combined efforts of many men.
The double leaves of the doors, now lying back in the
recesses hollowed out in the thickness of the ramparts,
are armed with long and pointed, dart-like, iron spikes,
a formidable armature which serves to ward off the
elephants, who used to delight in destroying the huge
beams with their trunks as they filed past into the city.

As we enter, my little convoy suddenly assumes the appearance of European shabbiness in spite of my two drivers with their gilded turbans and the runners who wave large fly-fans round the horses' flanks.

The first street that we come upon after passing through the thick walls is the only one that is at all inhabited. A few poor wretches live here in ruined palaces, and keep modest booths for the benefit of the soldiers.

The rest of the immense inclosure is occupied only by silence and a feeling of emptiness. Golconda is but an ashy plain, bestrewn with fallen stones and ruins of all sorts, from amongst which the rounded and polished backs of primitive blocks, that look like slumbering beasts, are seen to rise. The entire country is covered with such blocks of stone, which sometimes rise to the height of mountains, which dwarf and outlive the puny constructions of man.

The Indian story about these stones of Nizam is that after God had finished the creation of the world He found Himself in possession of a quantity of superfluous material, which He then rolled up in His fingers and cast haphazard down upon the earth.

The doors of the citadel, fiercely sheeted with iron spikes, like the gates in the city walls, give access to confused masses of granite, from which one ascends to the open air by roadways or by dismal staircases that lead through fortifications and passages cut out of the naked rock. The whole building is of a vastness which fills us with stupefaction, even in this land of India where colossal things are passed unnoticed. The crested walls, intermingling with the rocks, form, even to the very summit, a series of impregnable positions. There are cisterns, consisting of deep caves hollowed out from the bare rock, in which water can be kept during times of siege. There are dark holes leading to subterranean passages, which descend to the very heart of this fortified mountain and through which the open country may be reached in cases of supreme danger or of despairing flight.

Mosques are built at various heights, so that when
11

danger is nigh prayers may be said to the very last.
All has been foreseen and prepared, as if for indefinite
resistance against a race of giants, and it is not possible
to understand how, some three centuries before our
modern guns were invented, the sultans of Golconda
could ever have been driven from such a stronghold.

As we ascend, an ever-widening circle of desolation
—bathed in a glare of sunlight—lies before us.   The
masonry becomes more bold and terrifying, but ever
more ruined ; towers and walls bend and lean, so that
our heads reel ; great masses seem ready to fall, and
we see arches riven by gigantic cracks.   There are
also the remains of monuments which we cannot
comprehend, of which neither the use nor the age is
known ; and in the caverns there are gods who ruled
before Islam, monkey-headed images of Hanouman,
that live among the bats, before whom tiny flames
flicker and smoke, doubtless lighted here from time
to time by some mysterious worshippers.

On the last terrace, at the topmost height of all,
there is a mosque and kiosk from which the sultans in
the olden days used to overlook the land and watch
for armies approaching from the remotest distances.
The view from here, the gardens and the shady nooks,
was celebrated in bygone days, but now life has
departed from these plains.

The climate has changed and rain is wanting, and
it would even seem as if India becomes more parched
as the forces of its people wither and decay.   Beyond
the chaos of the walls and ramparts of the citadel,
which extends far down the silent plain, the outer
crested wall of the city, still kept in repair by the
Nizam, wanders away into the far distance, serving
to mark out the limits of the city which was once
Golconda, Golconda of the wondrous diamonds.   But,
one asks, what good purpose can such a wall serve by
merely inclosing a patch of desolation which has grown
to resemble the immense desolation by which it is
surrounded ?   Here is the same gray plain with the
strange smooth stones that look like heids of monsters

crouching amongst the ashes. Farther off, Hyderabad is just visible as a white streak, and scattered here and there at the edges of the plain those everlasting blocks of stone, which, heaped into rugged mountains and the semblance of fantastic fortresses, give the impression of an infinite and mournful succession of cities that have perished. At a little distance from the walls of the dead city there are some carefully whitened domes which do not appear to be in ruins. They rise out of inclosed gardens whose verdure still looks astonishingly fresh and green amidst the parched surroundings. They are the tombs of the ancient kings of Golconda, that, thanks to the respect of the Indians for their dead, have been spared from destruction. Nay, more, the great mortuary gardens surrounding them have even been replanted during the last few years.

Many sultans and sultanas of the fairy kingdom slumber under the beautiful and stately cupolas. Only one is wanting to this silent company, that last one who, after having built the dwelling-house that was to last him for eternity, was driven from home and sepulture by the conquering Aurangzeb, driven forth to exile and to death.

Their resting-peace is exquisite. Near by stand rows of cypress trees which resemble ours, though the heats of India have caused them to spindle. Nevertheless, such trees are the favourites, chosen of the dead in Eastern cemeteries as they are in our own. The sandy walks, too, with their rows of rose bushes, ruddy with bloom, are as straight as those of our old French gardens. Numbers of women and young girls, whose duty is to tend the artificial luxuriance of this oasis, are occupied from morning to night in pouring the water from the earthen jars which they carry over the flower beds, the precious water that has been drawn by men with much toil from wells that are as vast as huge abysses.

Seen from a distance, the coating of whitewash conveys a false impression of preservation to these domes, but all traces of painting and ornamentation have vanished from the interiors of these vast mausoleums, and the luxury of former days has been swallowed up in grayish mould.

However, there are garlands of flowers on each of the little marble tombs standing under the hollow cupolas—reverential and charming reminders of a dynasty which passed away three hundred years ago.

The strange and homelike charm of these gardens, standing in parched wildernesses which are only kept green by constant waterings, is that tall and delicate cypress trees are found side by side with palms, and that humming birds fly boldly over vases of roses just as our butterflies do at home.

IV

THE DREADFUL CAVES

The grottos are consecrated to all the divinities of the Pourana, but the greatest of them all are sacred to Siva, the god of Death.

Men, possessed by an inspiration which was both terrible and colossal, laboured for centuries in the hollowing out of these granite mountains. Some of the caves are the work of the Buddhists, others of the Brahmins, and there are some dating from the times of the Jaïna kings. Civilizations and religions passed away without ever interrupting that tremendous work of excavation and sculpture.

Towards the thousandth year of our era, according to the account of the Arabian Maçoudi, the earliest author who mentions these grottos, they were then in the fullness of their glory, and countless pilgrims from all parts of India came to them in a never-ending stream.

Now they are forsaken and long periods of drought have laid waste the austere regions which surround them, but their ageless existence is continued indefinitely in the midst of the silence and abandonment of a country whose life is fast ebbing away.

The modern road leads across a ruddy-coloured little desert, out of which strangely regular little hills, that resemble great citadels or donjon towers, emerge at intervals, breaking the monotony of a plain which, but for them, is smooth and flat like the shore of the sea.

It was in an Indian cart that I traversed the waste on which the sun was beating down, following a road that was outlined by dead trees.

Towards evening a phantom town, that resembled the Tower of Babel as it is represented in old pictures, drifted past us. This was the once celebrated town of Dalantabad, where the last of the Sultans of Golconda died in exile three hundred years ago. A city that is a mountain, a fortress, and a temple ; a rock which the men of olden days have trimmed and walled and smoothed from its summit to its base, so that it is more astonishing than the pyramids of Egypt, standing in their deserts of sand. Hundreds of crumbling tombs are scattered around, and the great rock is encompassed by countless crested ramparts, bristling with lances, each inclosed within its fellow. We entered through formidable double doors which, like those of Golconda, still retain their iron sheathings.

Within there is no one ; only silence, ruins, and withered trees whose rootlets hang trailing from their leafless branches like tresses of long hair. We left the fortresses, passing through double doors which were just as fiercely armed and just as useless as the others.

Towards the east a rocky barrier extended across the horizon, and as the road wound up in zigzag fashion, I had to descend and walk behind the slowly trailing cart. It was the hour of the setting sun, the hour when the gorgeous and unchanging glow covers the land that knows no clouds. Dalantabad, that crested mountain of ramparts and temples, seemed to rise with us into the air, outlined against the sky in a halo of glory, whilst ever extended round us the still immensity of red and burning plains from which all traces of life had vanished.

On the summit of the ridge another group of ruins, called Rozas, awaited us ; a Mussulman town crowded with ruined mosques and delicately tapering minarets.

Here many cupolas that have covered graves were clustered near the ramparts, which now loomed through the twilight. Though it was almost dark in the streets, several turbaned men were seated on the stones strewn by the roadside : a few last stubborn inhabitants, old people who would not quit these walls because of the sanctity of the mosques.

Then, during the next hour, nothing but the mono-tony of the rocks, the ever-widening plain, and the deep silence of the night.

Suddenly there is something so surprising and so impossible that a feeling almost like fear steals over us during the moment that it takes us to comprehend. The sea ! the sea ever before us, though we know that we are in Nizam, in the very centre of India.

There is a sudden dip in the ground, and the ever-changing sea lies extended before us. We overlook it from the summit of the immense cliff along which our road runs, and we feel the mighty wind coming from below, a wind chilly as that of the ocean.

But these are only plains which extend before us, plains from whose surface the wind raises the clouds of dust which so resemble the foaming billows.

Now we reach our journey's end, and the grottos, of which there is as yet no sign, lie underneath us, along the mournful shore : they are hollowed out in these enormous cliffs and their dreadful mouths of terror are open on to this waterless ocean.

It is night and the stars are shining as my cart stops before the " Rest Houses," out of which the hosts, two white-haired Indians, hasten to receive me, calling loudly the while to their serving-men, who are idling about the neighbourhood.

No one would consent to conduct me through the grottos of Siva. " It would be better," one said, " to wait for day." At last a shepherd, who was bringing back his goats, was persuaded by offer of money, and we set out, carrying a lantern that could be lighted when we got down to the dismal cavern mouths.

The night is moonless but clear, so when our eyes

become accustomed to the gloom we can distinguish our surroundings.

First we descend by a slope, some five or six hundred metres long, to the plain that looked like the sea. We descend through great silence : above us the twinkling magnificence of the stars, around us strange-shaped rocks and cactus plants. No doubt these plants are withered up like everything else, but they are still erect, and their stiff branches resemble waxen lights held in a candelabrum. The gloom becomes more pronounced as we reach the bottom and walk along the edges of the tideless shore at the foot of the over-shadowing cliffs. The wind which blew so strongly as the night was falling has subsided ; there is not a rustle audible anywhere, and a strange solemnity has come upon the place.

On the face of the cliffs we see the yawning mouths of the caves, more intensely black than all the surrounding darkness, seeming too vast to be the work of man, yet too regular to be natural. But I had expected to find them thus ; I knew that they must be fashioned so.

We pass them by without stopping ; then the shepherd suddenly hesitates, turns round, and retraces his steps. Religious dread, or perhaps even fear alone, prevents him from approaching the place to which he had proposed to take me, doubtless some place of nameless dread. Then with a manner which seems to say " No ! You will have to be satisfied with this one," he plunged forward amidst masses of fallen rock, stones, and cactus plants, into the mouth of the nearest of the gloomy excavations.

Already we are surrounded by a fearful beauty— though I understand that this is nothing to the one that he did not dare to show me.

There are courts open to the sky, great as places of stately festival, hewn out of the solid granite, out of the mountain itself. Their walls rise vertically to an overwhelming height, outlined by three or four tiers of galleries, placed one above the other, and between whose massive pillars rows of gods of superhuman stature are ranged—a dead audience assembled to witness the spectacle of Death. The darkness of night enshrouds everything, but the ceiling of the Titanesque hall is the star-strewn sky, whose vague and diffused light allows us to distinguish the crowd of solemn giants who watch us as we approach.

There are so many of these sculptured caverns that one almost forgets the number, though each one represents the work of an entire generation.

My goatherd, recovering from his first timidity, becomes more and more bold as we proceed on our Dantesque journey. He now lights the lantern that we may enter a cavern which is quite dark, one that must date back to some early and barbarous age, one where we shall no longer be safeguarded by the stars, for the sky will be hidden by the granite masses of the mountain. It is a kind of avenue, high and deep as the nave of a Gothic cathedral, from the smooth walls of which spring jutting arches which resemble ribs. It is as if we were in the inside of some animal, or the carcass of a monstrous whale. So poorly does our little lantern light up the surrounding darkness that it at first seems as if the long hall is quite empty. But now a form becomes visible, and the outline of some one stationed at the back acquires distinctness ; it is the image of a solitary god some twenty or thirty feet high, seated on a throne whose shadow covers the wall behind him and reaches to the roof, where it dances at the pleasure of the little flame we have brought with us. The god is hewn from the same granite, and is of the same colour as the rest of the place, but his giant's face has been painted red and the great eyes are white with black pupils. These eyes are lowered towards us as though in surprise that we should thus disturb him in the midst of his nightly slumber. The stillness of the cavern is so deep that the vibration of our voices continues to be heard long after we have finished speaking, and the horrible stare of the god causes a feeling of embarrassment.

However, the goatherd is no longer afraid now that

he has satisfied himself that all the stony images are as motionless during the night as they are by day. On leaving the grotto he extinguishes the lamp, and from the deliberation with which he retraces his steps, I gather at once that he is going to take me to something which he did not dare to face at first. We walk hurriedly across the sand, which resembles that of the seashore, and following the line of the cliffs pass, without stopping, before the mouths of those caves whose mysteries are now already explored.

The night is far advanced as we reach our destination. The man lights the lantern and then hesitates as if to collect his courage. Evidently the place to which we are going must be very dark.

A touch of unexpected horror is imparted to this cave, the entrance of which is much larger than any of the others, by the fact that the guardians of the threshold, instead of being calm like those we had lately seen, are twisted and contorted in convulsions of suffering, rage, or agony ; but in the dim light it is difficult to distinguish, amidst the black masses that surround us, which are images and which are but the jagged shapes of the mountain itself, for the very rocks and the huge overhanging fragments have writhing attitudes and the convulsive forms of pain. We stand before the dwellings of Siva, the implacable god of Death, he who slays for the very joy of slaying.

Even the silence that guards the threshold has something about it that is peculiar and terrible ; rocks and great human forms, those stark and agonized shapes over whose tortured heads ten centuries have already passed, are enveloped in silence whose sonority is so awe-inspiring that we dread the sound of our own footsteps and listen with anxiety to our very breathing.

But now we are prepared for everything except noise. Hardly, however, had we penetrated into the first vault before a sudden and startling report resounded through the air, just as if we had touched the mechanism of a spring gun, a report that instantly spread through all the temples—a flapping of great black wings, the maddened wheelings of great birds of prey, eagles, owls, and vultures, sleeping in the crannies of the roof. This rushing noise of wings is swollen by the hollow echoes into a mighty symphony of sound which rises and falls, and dies away into the distance ; then it is no more, and silence reigns.

Leaving this vaulted archway, which was but a peristyle, we again perceive the stars above our heads, though they are only visible at intervals and have the far-off look of stars seen from the bottom of some great cleft. The successions of open courtyards which have been made by removing half a mountain, by taking away enough granite to build a town, are peculiar in that their walls, which rise to the height of two hundred feet, with galleries of gods in full array of battle, *are nor perpendicular* but lean over us threateningly. The solidity of the rock, which extends the whole way down in a single solid mass that has neither flaw nor crevice, was relied upon to produce the effect of a chasm that is closing in—a chasm in which we must be instantly engulfed.

And then, those first courtyards were empty, while these are filled with many colossal objects, obelisks, statues, elephants on pedestals, porches, and temples. It is no longer possible to form any idea of the arrangement of the grotto, for midnight is near and our lantern flickers feebly amidst the gloom. We can only discern a profusion of horrible images ; here the face of a dead man figured in the rock ; there the form of a grinning skeleton or ogling monster starting out of the obscurity through which we wend our way, only to fade instantly out of sight amidst the confused shapes of darkness which surround us.

At first we only saw single elephants ; now there are troops of them, standing upright with pendant trunks, the only things that seem calm amidst the rout of phantoms that are tortured and twisted by all the agonies of death. These elephants form the supports of the triple sequence of monolithic temples that occupy the centre of the cave.

We pass between these temples and the leaning walls that surround them so threateningly. On our way we have occasional glimpses of the stars, which, however, have never seemed so far away as they seem now. Around us a confused medley of furious forms, fighting monsters, and of shameful and horrible embraces, disembowelled and headless human beings still locked in each others' arms. Siva, Siva at every turn, Siva decked with a necklace of skulls, Siva, who engenders and who slays, Siva, who has many arms, so that he may slay the more, Siva, whose mouth is twisted with a grin of irony, making hideous love, so that he may slay the children whom he begets, Siva, who dances with mad shouts of triumph on quivering tatters of human flesh, on limbs torn from their sockets, or amongst the entrails which he has snatched from mutilated corpses. Siva, in an ecstasy of joy and pleasure trampling on the bodies of little girls whose skulls have been battered in by his cruel heels. These horrors emerge one by one from the surrounding gloom. Our flickering light plays under them for an instant, then they disappear, and darkness enshrouds them once more. In places the groups are nearly effaced, for the flight of centuries has left its trace, and their faint outlines are hardly visible before they fade into the indistinctness of the deep shades to mingle with rocky shapes that seem vaguely instinct with the horrors that animate the place. I no longer see, I no longer know where they end. I only feel that the whole mountain, even to its very heart, must be crowded with these dim forms of horror, thronged with this luxuriance of immortal agony.

The elephants that support the central temples upon their backs seem out of place here, for their attitudes are calm and tranquil, but on passing round to the other side of the temples we find that the corresponding elephants are animated by the prevailing madness of torture and of strife. Some are embraced by tigers and other wild beasts, fantastic beasts; others are torn by their cruel teeth; here, half-crushed by the temples on their backs, the elephants wage combats to the death. On this side the great encircling wall, that solid mass of granite, leans over more than ever, and the confused luxuriance of figures only commences to be outlined some twenty feet from the ground, while the lower part of the wall—which bellies out like the side of some overhanging ruin that is just about to fall to pieces—is smooth, with here and there a few soft curves. I can fancy myself in the inside of a deep-water shell, or in the hollow of a gigantic wave that has lifted all these edifices on its mighty crest, from which they must instantly fall, burying me in chaos.

We have now completed the circuitous course which leads between the lofty monolithic temples and the graven mountain walls that dominate them on every side. The interior of the temples is now the only thing left to see, but my guide again hesitates and suggests that we should wait till the morrow, till the sun has risen.

The staircases which lead upwards are in disorder; all the steps are broken, and the constant passage of naked feet has given them a dangerous and slippery polish.

We maintain silence as we ascend, involuntarily and almost without knowing why, but the smallest stone that totters, or the tiniest pebble that rolls down makes an alarming noise that is repeated by the echoes. Around us on every side are manifold images of horror. Siva in varied attitudes, Siva tortured by convulsions, slim-waisted Sivas expanding their heaving chests in the drunken delight of passionate love and of slaughter.

Even amidst the darkest gloom I did not regret that I had forgotten to bring either a firearm or a stick, and the possibility of being interfered with either by man or beast never once crossed my mind. But now the terror of the goatherd communicates itself to me, a grisly fear that is nameless and indescribable.

I had expected that horror would run riot in the sanctuary, that I should find forms of unspeakable dread; but no, all is simple and peaceful. It is like the great calm that must inevitably greet one on the other side after the terrors of death have done their work. There is not a single graven image, not even the suggestion of human or animal shapes. There is absolutely nothing : the grave and solemn temples are quite empty. Only if we walk or speak the echoes are louder and more mournful than they were. Otherwise there is nothing to affright us, not even the flapping of a night bird's wings. Even the square columns that have been hewn from the solid rock and which extend from the ceiling to the floor are decorated with a sober and severe pattern of intercrossing lines.

It is evident, however, in spite of the ruin and ravage wrought by time, that the place has always been sacred. We feel this the moment we enter, for we are immediately inspired with a feeling of religious dread. These walls would not be so blackened by the smoke of torches and lanterns, nor would these floors of granite be so smooth and greasy, unless the place were still visited by crowds of worshippers. The god of Death has not deserted the mountain that the people of another age have hollowed out for him, and a soul still dwells in this ancient sanctuary.

There are three chambers, three temples, each situated above the other, all cut out of the same block of stone. The last of the three is the holy of holies, the forbidden place which I have been debarred from visiting in all the other Brahmin temples.

There, at least, I expected to see something of nameless horror, but, again, there is scarcely anything to see. Yet that which is there astonishes and terrifies more by its primitive simplicity and its brutal daring than all the collections of horrors piled up outside. On a crumbling stone altar is a little black pebble that shines like polished marble ; its shape is that of an elongated egg that stands on end, and on the sides of the pedestal on which it is placed are graven those mysterious signs which the followers of Siva never fail to trace with ashes on their foreheads when the morning light appears.

Everything around is blackened with smoke, and the niches that are hollowed out in the walls to receive the lights that the faithful bring are covered by a thick coating of soot, while thousands of wicks, that no one dares to remove, swim in oily filth. All this foulness tells of an old and stubborn creed, an uncivilized and timorous worship.

But this black pebble, the centre, the reason, and the cause of all this tremendous task of sculpture and of excavation, is the most expressive and the most concrete symbol that the Indians of former days could find to typify the god, who ceaselessly engenders that he may ceaselessly destroy: it is the Lingam : it represents the god of procreation who labours but to nourish death.

A faint light is hovering over the expanse which resembles the sea as I quit the travellers' shelter where I had slept on my return from the dreadful caves. The day has hardly dawned, and under the cloud of dust which hangs over it like a mist, the expanse has a tone of blue, that neutral blue of the fog-enshrouded sea, but the sun rises quickly and discovers a reddish plain, parched and waterless, dotted here and there with a few dead trees. I am on my way to the temples of Siva, to see if all those things were real or if they were but phantasms which will not bear the light of day. This time I am alone, for I know the road that leads down among the rocks and the tall cactus plants standing erect like candles of mellow wax.

Though the sun has only just risen, its rays are already powerful enough to make my temples burn, a wicked and destructive sun that spreads death and desolation over the Indian land with daily increasing force.

Three men carrying long sticks, shepherds without flocks, ascend from the plain, saluting me profoundly as they pass. They are terribly emaciated, and fever glows in their great eyes. Doubtless they have come from the land of famine, on the threshold of which I am now standing. Thousands of little plants that formerly carpeted the mountain side are now changed into a sad and lifeless coating of felt, but the beasts that yet remain still carry on their endless struggle for existence, and the ground is strewn with the bodies of little birds on which eagles have lately preyed. Huge and voracious spiders have spread nets everywhere to catch the last butterfly or the last grasshopper. And the glory of the sun, whose fierceness increases every moment, till it becomes like a scorching brazier, is as sinister as the glory of Siva . . . the god who engenders and who slays. How my thoughts are fixed on him this morning as I descend to his horrible sanctuary ! How well, too, I can understand him, as the Brahmins know him, the god who kindles life in man and beast with mad and mocking profusion, but who takes care to invent an enemy especially fitted to destroy each species he has created. How joyously and with what inexhaustible and detailed art has the god made teeth, horns, claws, famine, plagues, and the venom of serpents and of flies. He has sharpened the beaks of the birds which skim over the ponds teeming with fish, and for man, who has acquired the mastery over savage beasts, he has cunningly kept disease, exhaustion, and old age ; and into the heart of all he has thrust the foolish and maddening dart of love. For all he has designed the countless, impalpable swarms of what is infinitesimal, filling even the streams of clear water with myriads of destroyers or with the spawn of cruel worms ready to batten on the vitals of those who come to drink. . . . " Suffering exists to elevate and purify the soul," I grant it, but what about our children, our little ones, who died without ever having understood, choked by a disease which has been specially invented for them ? For that matter, too, I have seen suffering, nay, even anguish and useless supplication in the eyes of the humblest creatures. . . . Poor little birds that linger in the agony which imbecile sportsmen have inflicted on them, is this to elevate their souls ? And the tiny-winged things whose life-blood is drained by fierce spiders ! What boundless cruelty infests the whole seething mass of creation, a loathsome cruelty the reality of which has been acknowledged by the peoples of all ages, but whose pitiless truth has never struck me so forcibly as it does now that I am once more seeking the grottos of Siva. Yet I am one of the happy and fortunate ones whom famine cannot touch and for whom fate seems to have no immediate menace. At the most I have but to fear the burning sun or the bite of some black-ringed cobra that may be lying under the withered grass.

When I reach the bottom and stand on the plain of dust and sand I have only to turn to the right in order to find myself within a few minutes' walk of the huge and yawning entrance. No alarming noise startles me this morning as I enter the dreadful sanctuary. The eagles, vultures, and falcons which sleep in the roof have already started out in search of prey and hunt with ever-ready claws and beak. Everything is silent, but the silence is less terrible than it was on my midnight visit.

Once more I see the monolithic temples supported on the backs of the elephants, and the obelisks that stand in front of them, rising up in the centre of this deep cleft from whose overhanging walls the graven images look down. But by the light of the rising sun all seems less colossal and less superhuman, and not horrible enough to celebrate the god as he deserves. These were the works of a childish race who had not lived long enough to understand the terrible ferocity of life or who did not know how adequately to symbolize it.

There is nothing to recall the impression that was made on me during my midnight visit when I came here in the dark with a feeble lantern that only lighted up the images from underneath. The morning light reveals a state of extreme dilapidation. It is not only that centuries have passed by, reaping their harvests of heads, bodies, columns, and capitals, but that these temples, like all the temples of Siva, were assailed at the time of the Mussulman Conquest by hordes of fanatics intent on worshipping God by some other name.

When I saw these horrors enshrouded in the gloom of night, I did not suspect that they had once been painted, but now that I can plainly see the whole crowded assemblage gesticulating wildly under the shadow of the overhanging rocks, I perceive that they are still tinted with a cadaverous green and that the backs of their niches are yet of the reddish colour of dried blood.

The monolithic temples in the centre were also in those days painted with many colours and tints like the temples of Thebes and Memphis ; whites, yellows, and reds still linger on the more sheltered places. This morning, however, I shall ascend by myself. I wish to be alone. The presence of a sentient being, even so rude and uneducated a one as the goatherd who was with me the night before, would disturb my colloquy with Siva.

Within there is such a silence as I had foreseen, but I had thought that there would have been more light. It is almost dark in spite of the rising sun, under whose fierce rays the great red plain is already glowing. A little of the freshness which night had left still lingers on, as if imprisoned by these granite walls, but within the secret sanctuary, whose walls have been befouled by the smoky torches of bygone ages, an eternal gloom surrounds that black pebble, the Lingam, which represents the god of Life and Death with such irony, yet with such perfect truth.

V

THE SONG OF FAMINE

It is especially the little children, poor little skeletons who look at me with eyes filled with mute wonder at their own sufferings, who sing or wail this song.

They stand at the entrances of the villages, or in the open places by the roadside, clasping tightly with both hands their hollow bellies, which resemble empty leather wine-bottles, so loosely do the folds of their skin hang down.

To hear the full blast of this dread song, one must travel about one hundred leagues from the cave of the

12

destroying god, towards the north-west, towards the land of Rajput, where men die by thousands for want of the little rice which no one sends them.

In this land the forests are dead, the jungle is dead, everything is dead.

The spring rains, that used to come from the Arabian Sea, have failed for many years past, or they have gone elsewhere, expending themselves uselessly on the deserts of Beloochistan. So the torrents have no more water, the rivers are dried up, and the trees can no longer clothe themselves with leaves.

It is by the little frequented route of Rutlam and Indore that I journey towards the land of famine, and I am on one of those railways which now furrow India in every direction. The train is almost empty, and the few passengers are all natives.

For hours an endless succession of forests passes before us, no longer forests of palm trees, but of trees like our own. Indeed, were it not for their extent and for those wild backgrounds, we might fancy ourselves at home. Their delicate branches are of a grayish colour, and the general tint is that of our oak trees in December. Ancient Gaul in late autumn must have looked so; but it is April and we are in India, and this tropical spring heat, this fiery glow which pours down on the wintry landscape, only serves to plunge our thoughts into a bewildering maze. There is nothing, however, which we see during our first day's journey which seems to point to a pressing want, still we seem possessed by a feeling of something abnormal, of a desolation that cannot be alleviated. Indeed, one might almost fancy oneself to be travelling through a planet of which the end were threateningly nigh.

Need I say that India, the mother and the cradle of the European race, is a land full of ruins! The spectres of towns which perished ages and ages ago are to be found almost everywhere, towns whose names are now forgotten, but which were great cities in their day, and which overlooked abysses from their lofty mountain perches. There are ramparts extending for miles, and palaces and temples that are now only the home of monkeys and of snakes. By the side of such ruins, how pitiful our donjon towers, our manor houses, and all the remnants of our feudal age appear!

Ruins and forests of the colour of ochre or burnt sienna follow one another all along the line, plunged, till the evening comes, in a shimmering haze of heat. At last the burning sun sets behind the masses of dead vegetation and the ruins of the legendary cities; but the air is so dust-laden that the glory of the sun is dimmed, and its colour is of that faded rosy hue which we see on a chilly winter's evening.

Next morning we wake and find ourselves on the boundless jungle. At the first village at which we stop a sound is heard directly the wheels have ceased their noisy clanking—a peculiar sound that seems to strike a chill into us even before we have understood its nature. It is the beginning of that horrible song which we shall hear so often now that we have entered the land of famine. Nearly all the voices are those of children, and the sound has some resemblance to the uproar that is heard in the playground of a school, but there is an undefined note of something harsh and weak and shrill which fills us with a sense of pain.

Oh! look at the poor little things jostling there against the barrier, stretching out their withered hands towards us from the end of the bones which represent their arms. Every part of their meagre skeleton shows with shocking plainness through the brown skin that hangs in folds about them; their stomachs are so sunken that one might think that their bowels had been altogether removed. Flies swarm on their lips and eyes, drinking what moisture may still exude. They are almost breathless and nearly lifeless, yet they still stand upright and still can cry. They are hungry, so very hungry, and it seems to them that the strangers who pass by in their fine carriages must be rich, and that they will pity them and throw them something.

"Maharajah! Maharajah!" all the little voices

cry at once in a kind of quivering song. There are some who are barely five years old, and these, too, cry " Maharajah ! Maharajah ! " as they stretch their terribly wasted hands through the barrier.

The Indians who are travelling in the train are only humble occupants of the third and fourth classes, but they throw what they have, scraps of cake and copper coins, for which the famished children rush like wild beasts, trampling each other under foot. What use can they make of the money ? It seems that there is yet food in the village shops for those who have money to buy it with. Even now there are four wagons of rice coupled to the train behind, and loads pass daily, but no one will give them any, not even a handful, not even the few grains on which they could live for a little while. These wagons are going to the inhabitants of those towns where people still have money and can pay.

What is it that is stopping us ? Why are we forced to stay so long at this dismal place, where the crowd of the starving swells in size, as every minute passes, the song of their distress becoming fiercer and fiercer ?

The land around the station is so dry and dusty that the fields which used to be cultivated with rice and other crops merely resemble a desert of ashes. Now the women approach, or rather the skeletons of women, with hanging breasts which look like leather bags. They seem almost exhausted by their efforts, for they, too, have hastened here in the hope of selling the heavy and stinking bundles which they carry on their heads, skins stripped from their cattle which have perished of hunger. But the price of a cow which still shows signs of life has fallen to a quarter of a rupee (about fivepence), for it is impossible to provide food for cattle, and nothing in the world would induce the people of this Brahmin country to eat the flesh. So who wants to buy a stinking hide that swarms with flies ?

I have already thrown out all the small coins which I have by me, but, my God ! why do not they start ?

Oh ! the despair of a tiny mite of three or four, from whom a somewhat bigger child has snatched the coin that it held clenched so tightly in its little hand.

At last the train moves and the outcry dies away. Once more we plunge into the silent jungle, but the jungle is dead, that jungle which ought to swarm with life now that the spring has come. The thickets and the grasses will never be green again, and April has no power to awaken their languishing sap. So, like the forest, the jungle keeps its wintry appearance in spite of the fierce and scorching sun. Here and there we see thin and scared gazelles wandering about, poor beasts that cannot find food, and that do not know where to search for water. Sometimes we see a young branch projecting from the trunk of an old and withered tree, a tiny twig that seems to have collected all the flowing sap, so that it may put forth a few tender leaves, or even a great red flower, which blossoms sadly in the midst of all this desolation.

At each village where we stop a famished horde watches across the barrier. The song that we so dread to hear, that heart-rending and high-pitched reiteration of the same notes, greets us directly we approach, then it swells, and at last breaks into a despairing wail as we disappear into the parched and desolate wastes.

VI

THE BRAHMINS OF THE TEMPLES OF ODEYPOURE

About one hundred and fifty miles beyond the dreadful grottos—in the north-west direction of ever-increasing drought—the white city of Odeypoure, in the land of Meswar, still forms a delicious halting-place on the famine track, whose traces I have now commenced to follow.

As we approach, the white masses of the palaces and temples are visible from a great distance, sur-rounded and inclosed on every side by a background of peaked and lofty mountains, the sides of which are clothed with forests.

Notwithstanding that the want of rain has changed the green of the leaves to tones of withered brown, and in spite of the sadness of a land whose trees have become bare and yellow in the springtime, the city, as seen from a distance, still retains a privileged and a smiling aspect, standing as it does at the foot of wooded hills that make for it a sort of nest of peace and mystery.

But as we come nearer the distress is only too painfully apparent. Pitiful beggars wander through the avenues of dead trees leading to the gates. I have never seen such creatures elsewhere, and it scarcely seems possible that they are alive. They are but mummies or dried bags of bones that walk abroad, that still have eyes in the depths of their sockets and voices in the depths of their chests with which to ask for charity. They were once labourers in the fields, and they have dragged themselves towards the town because they heard that food is still to be had there. But ofttimes they fall by the roadside, and here and there we see them lying in the dust, which gives a ghastly tint to their nude forms, and which will soon form the shroud of their death-agony.

Along the avenue we pass an endless succession of sad and silent inclosures belonging to the Maharajah of Odeypoure. Projecting above the walls that surround them are the roofs of mausoleums, the ruins of temples, stone and marble kiosks, buildings with cupolas, which have been used for the cremation of dead princes, and great dying trees denuded of leaves, on whose branches monkeys are seated.

At last we reach the tall and white doors that lead out under the ramparts. These are guarded by Indians armed with naked sabres, and the flood of starving beggary is brought to a standstill as a river by a lock. Here they remain, a dreadful mass of outstretched hands—not, indeed, that they are prevented from passing through, but city gates have ever been the chosen spot, in all the countries of the world, of those who beg.

Odeypoure was only founded some three centuries

ago (after the destruction of Chitor,[1] the ancient capital of Meswar, whose ruins lie some miles farther towards the east), but the town, wrapped in its shroud of whitewash, has already an air of extreme antiquity. It contains a number of Brahmin temples, filled with white columns and white obelisks, the largest and most sacred of which is the temple dedicated to the god Chri-Jannath-Raijie. Very white, too, those great palaces of the Maharajah that stand upon a lofty rock, one side commanding the whole town, the other reflecting its whiteness in a deep, clear lake, which is surrounded by forests and mountains.

Immediately on my arrival I was able to win the friendship of two young Brahmin brothers, both priests of the great temple. It was their custom to pay me a modest daily visit during those silent and scorching hours when I could no longer leave the little hostelry, which was situated in a lonely and dusty plain outside the walls. Both brothers were clothed in white robes and wore small turbans, both had the same exquisitely refined features, and the same mystic expression illuminated the eyes of each.

Their noble lineage dates back, without a break or flaw, for two or three thousand years, and they are the children and the great-great-grandchildren of those dreamers who, since the beginning of time, have set themselves apart from our common humanity, in that they have never given themselves up to intemperance, nor mingled either in commerce or in war. They have never slain even the humblest created thing, nor have they eaten anything that has ever lived. It would seem that they are moulded from a different and a purer clay than ours, one that has almost shaken off the trammels of the flesh, even before death has done its work. Their senses, too, must be more acute than ours, more capable of appreciating the things that lie beyond this transitory life.

Alas! my hopes of attaining a little wisdom from

---

[1] Chitor, built in 728, sacked in 1533 by Bahadur, Shah of Guzerat, and finally destroyed in 1568 by Akbar.

them were futile. From generation to generation their Brahminism has become obscured by the abuse of ritual observances, and they no longer know the hidden meaning of the symbols.

" The King Chri-Jugat-Singhie, son of Chri-Karan-Singhie, great worshipper of the god we serve, began the construction of our temple in 1684, the year of his accession to the throne. This prince built the other temples on the lake, and twenty years were occupied in the construction of these three buildings. Several princes from the neighbouring countries came in great state, with many elephants, to the ceremony of in-auguration, which took place in 1708, when the image of our god was placed in the sanctuary."

This history was told me by one of the brothers in the midday silence and shade of the " Travellers' Rest." Its shutters were closed against the sun, the flies, and the parching wind of famine. They are very well informed about the temples of Odeypoure, and all the deities of the Pouran Pantheon, but when I question them about the nature of their eternal hopes, and as to what they can see of the life beyond, they do not know how to answer me in any way that I can understand. We seem accordingly at once to lose touch of each other ; we no longer feel ourselves to be souls bound by a common tie, and a curtain like that of night falls between us. Doubtless they are seers, as indeed are the majority of priests, but they are also simple-minded men who cannot explain themselves.

The two priests bring me simple presents daily, flowers or modest cakes made in the native fashion. They are gentle and courteous, too, but an abyss seems to separate us, and, mingled with the respect with which they treat me, there is a kind of insur-mountable disdain. For instance, not only would they rather die than partake of the horrible dishes tainted with blood and flesh to which my forefathers have accustomed me, not only would they refuse to take a glass of water from my hands, but even to eat or drink anything in my presence would seem to them a dishonour that nothing could efface.

This morning they pushed my door ajar a little before their usual hour, letting in a ray of blinding light, clouds of dust, and the breath of a furnace. They came to tell me that this was the day on which their god held festival, and that they would not be at liberty to come back, but that I might find them at sunset in the first inclosure of their temple.

They left some garlands of jasmine, such as the people of this part wear about their necks during the festivals, but they were made of true French jasmine, a sort that is unknown in the more central parts of India. This was the first time that I had seen the little white flowers threaded into a childish garland since the early summers of my life, since the time when, seated in the shade of the old walls which surrounded the courtyard of my parents' house, I used to delight myself by weaving necklets like those my Indian friends had brought to me. Suddenly the memory of those far-off summers came back to me, once more I saw the foliage hanging from the wall, and all the plants and flowers of that courtyard, which used to represent the world to my childish eyes. Then for a little while the Brahmin land and the city of Odeypoure, with its deities, its sun, and its famine, were blotted from my mind, and seemed to fade into immeasurable distance.

As the day declined I sought the temple of the god Chri-Jannath-Raijie.

His temple is white as the freshly fallen snow, and one ascends to it by a monumental staircase of thirty or forty steps, guarded by rows of stone elephants.

Here in the North of India the Brahmin pyramids no longer resemble those of the South with their madly mingling crowds of divinities and animals : they are more sober, more mysteriously calm, and from a distance resemble those tall, funereal trees that grow in cemeteries. The temple of Chri-Jannath-Raijie is adorned with several of these pyramids, which are white too, white as the fallen snow.

As I knew that none but Hindoos of noble caste were allowed to pass within the temple, I stayed in the courtyard and sent a message to my friends. Though they appeared at once, a change seemed to have come over them since we last met in the " Travellers' Rest," and the gulf that separated us had widened even broader. They at once excused themselves for not taking my hand as was their wont, for in the exercise of their priestly office they had to handle sacred things.

For the first time I saw them nearly naked, as it is usual for priests to be when serving their god. The little cord of the " true sons of Brahma " was looped round their finely shaped bronzed chests, and their dilated eyes had a far-away look which I had not seen before.

With unvarying courtesy they seated me in a place of honour, at the foot of a copper image of Vishnu, which stood opposite the door of the sanctuary.

The courtyard of the temple was blocked with flower sellers, whose baskets were filled with necklets of white and yellow jasmine, and with strings of Bengal roses, but amidst all these flowers the spectres of famine wandered in ever-increasing numbers, poor skeletons with fevered eyes and of earthly hue.

Processions of Brahmins passed before me, ascending or descending the steps of the temple, passing between the great stone elephants that reared their trunks towards the sky from the topmost flight of steps. All the men were clothed in white and wore sabres at their waists, while from their chests several rows of flowers hung down. There were old men whose snowy beards were brushed back after the fashion of Rajput, which makes them look like old white cats ; and many little children, whose legs were hardly long enough to let them climb the stairs, but whose expression, however, was always grave and concerned, and who wore the tiaras of velvet and gold, with which their heads are adorned, with much solemnity ; the women were marvellous, draped in the antique style in coloured muslins whose designs were worked in gold, or in black muslins adorned with silver stars.

A hollow-sounding music reached us from the depths of the dark and impenetrable temple, and sometimes the noise proceeding from a gigantic tom-tom rumbled amidst the roofs like thunder. Each person, before ascending, stooped down to kiss the lowest step and even those upon the topmost stair turned round to kiss the threshold of the doorway before they left the temple's holy shade. But the spectres of famine were ever at hand, discountenancing the gaily dressed throng with their ghastly nudity. Sometimes they attempted to stop the worshippers with their withered hands, clinging to their muslin veils, seeking to extort charity with gestures that were brusque and sudden, like the hands of snatching apes.

Then the wind rose, as it did each evening at the same hour. It brought, however, no refreshing coolness to the burning city, but merely a haze of dust, in which the sun set yellow and dull as the sun of our northern climes.

In spite of everything the festival continued in the streets till nightfall. People threw whole handfuls of coloured and perfumed powder at each other, till faces and clothes were almost covered, and sometimes there were seen those who emerged from the fray with one side of their faces bedabbled with violet, blue, or red. All the white robes bore the imprint of hands that had been dipped into dyes of brilliant colours—the impress of five fingers stamped in rose, in yellow, or in green.

VII

THE ENCHANTED WOOD OF ODEYPOURE

Three fakirs live in this enchanted wood, their thatched shelter standing close to the roadside at the foot of a hill which mirrors itself in a tranquil lake. Three young men with beautiful regular features, long-haired and nude, powdered from head to foot with dust of a pale gray stone colour.

All day and every day, at no matter what hour one

passes, the three fakirs are there, seated under the humble shelter which is open on all sides.   Their legs are crossed in the posture of Buddha, and they sit motionless on the ground, in front of the waters which reflect the mountains, the dismal forests, and the white palaces of the King of Odeypoure.

Directly we have passed through the great pointed gates that lie behind the city the silent woods commence, woods which climb to the lofty peaks which surround us, so that they may join on to the distant forests and the jungles where the tigers dwell.

The trees are of medium height, and the bushes, with their slender twigs, are like our own, but both trees and bushes are as leafless as trees and bushes are in France at the end of the autumn.   And yet it is springtime here, a tropical spring, and the air is hot and stifling.   Overhead is a cloudless and unchanging sky that stretches over the whole of India just as it overhangs these forests.   The weather is brilliantly fine, and so it has been for three years past, which is the reason why everything is dying.

It is astonishing how lovely and calm this shady place has remained, lying, as it does, outside the city gates.   All the life seems to congregate towards the other side of the town, and scarcely any one passes along the road which leads in front of the three fakirs who sit in meditation by its side.

In the woods there are wild boars, monkeys, and a quantity of birds, flights of turtle-doves, and droves of parrots.   Flocks of superb peacocks strut up and down among the dead trees, under the grayish bushes and upon the ashy-coloured soil.   We see them running along in single file with outstretched tails, the wondrous sheen of which looks like a spurt of green and incandescent metal.   All these animals are free and unrestrained, yet their demeanour is not that of wild animals and birds, for in these lands, where they are never slain by man, the idea of flight does not animate them as it does at home.   As to the tigers that live on the other slope of the mountain, no living man has ever seen them wandering amidst the thickets of this enchanted wood.

The first glance that we get of the three stone-coloured men who are seated so motionless by the roadside skirting the edge of the lake is one that fills us with the vague dread of something supernatural. They differ from statues in that their long hair, moustaches, and eyebrows are black, but their eyes are so strangely fixed that we cannot be certain.

These men are merely fakir novices of about twenty years of age; fastings and penances have not yet altered their gracious forms, and their legs, which after a while will be withered and contracted into one fixed position, are still plump and almost feminine. The designs in red that are inscribed on the dust-covered foreheads in some way resemble those on the bedabbled faces of clowns, but their expression is so grave that we never think of making the comparison.

Behind them, under the shelter of the thatch, we can see the orderly and gleaming rows of copper vessels that serve for their morning ablutions and for their frugal meals. The dead branches stretching above their heads are the chosen resorts of birds. Parrots, turtle-doves, gorgeous peacocks, and the thousand feathered songsters that have been robbed of their living by the long drought, come here to pick up the grains of rice that the three sages have scattered on the ground for them, after their frugal meal.

The wanderer who stops to speak to the three fakirs is sometimes invited by a gesture or by an absent smile to seat himself under the shelter of their roof, but as the ground has been swept so carefully they beg their guests to remove their shoes before drawing closer. Then their eyes plunge into dreamland again and one is free to depart at will, for they speak no more, nor do they ever seem to see.

This lake, lying amidst the woods, belongs to the King of Odeypoure, and the palaces and a few old white temples are the only buildings reflected therein. On the two islands in the centre there are more palaces and walled gardens, but everywhere else the banks are covered by an interlacing thicket of trees and shrubs. On every side the lake is shut in by steep and lofty mountains, whose sides are clothed by dying forests, though we sometimes see the white glitter from a little citadel of olden days, or the reflection from some tiny Brahmin sanctuary perched on a jagged summit, far above the flights of soaring eagles.

Close by the edge of the water, which grows lower every day, the branches are still tinged with green : everywhere else, no matter where we may look, only the tones of rusty autumn or the chill grays of winter are to be seen.

To-day I saw one of the fakirs move for the first time. I had gone to the enchanted wood about sunset—at the hour when a thick cloud of smoke always overhung an abandoned house belonging to the Maharajah that lay on the opposite shore. It was not smoke, however, but a simple whirlwind of dust raised by the trampling hoofs of wild boars, of which hundreds come every evening to scramble for the maize that is thrown from one of the upper windows by order of the King, since the dead jungle can no longer sustain them.

Suddenly one of the fakirs rose up and went to look for the mirror, powder, and carmine that were in the shelter behind him ; then, after having again assumed his former cross-legged posture, he whitened his face and carefully painted the sign of Siva on his forehead. No living thing was near, save the peacocks and the turtle-doves, which had begun to cluster on the trees in anticipation of their evening meal. In whose honour, then, can he have made this evening toilette ?

At last, however, the sound of horses galloping quickly through the trees is heard. It was the King who passed with some thirty of his courtiers on beautiful horses, whose harness flashed with a thousand colours. All the horsemen were clothed in white, and long robes enwrapped their slender forms. Their beards and moustaches were worn brushed upwards towards their foreheads after the fashion of

Odeypoure, a fashion which gives a cat-like expression to the chiselled bronze features that are at the same time both intellectual and manly.

The King galloped at the head of the troop. His beard was worn like the beards of the others, but a matchless beauty and distinction graced his features and his bearing.

As I watched them disappearing through the leafless glades my thoughts were carried back to our own middle ages, and I fancied some prince or duke returning from the chase, followed by his train of knights and barons on the beautiful evening of a century that had long since passed away.

VIII

A VISIT TO A RAJPUT PRINCE

The stylishly appointed landau which by order of the Maharajah of Odeypoure has fetched me from the " Rest House " gallops up sanded slopes bordered by balustrades and clumps of rose bushes. We are near the shore of the lake on that rock from which the palaces rise in a clustering amphitheatre. Here and there marble elephants are seen emerging from the flowers and foliage. As we sweep up the steep and sharply winding slopes, pulled by two powerful and fiery horses, the horizon rapidly enlarges and the panorama of the enchanted wood and the blue lake studded with its island palaces unfolds itself before us, but it seems as if the wall of forests and mountains, which makes such a mysterious background to everything at Odeypoure, were rising with us too. The Maharajah, Prince of Meswar, whose palace I am about to visit, is descended from the ancient and the most powerful of the royal families of Rajput. He is one of the survivors of the " dynasty of the sun." Centuries and centuries before our oldest and most princely European families had emerged from obscurity his ancestors had levied arms to conquer kingdoms or to free queens who had been led into captivity.

Rama, the founder of the " dynasty of the sun," the hero who attained divinity, had, as we are told in the Ramayana, two sons, the elder of whom established Lahore. The descendants of the second extended their sway over the people of Rajput towards the middle of the second century. However, at the epoch of the great incursion of barbarians from the north in the year 524 all the princes of the family were massacred, the queen only excepted, she being at the time on a pilgrimage. Finding herself pregnant, she took refuge in a cave, where she died in giving birth to a son. The child was adopted by some pious Brahmins, in whose care he was only with difficulty retained, for his royal blood impelled him towards the warlike practices of the Bhils who inhabited the neighbouring mountains. These soon after chose him for their chief, and one of their warriors, after cutting his finger, made a bloody mark on the young man's forehead in token of his sovereignty. About 723 the descendants of the cavern-cradled king established themselves here as sovereigns, and since that time their line has never ceased to reign. Even to-day the custom of marking each successive king on the forehead is still observed, and the bloody seal is imprinted by the rough hand of a Bhil, in token of the sovereign's rude origin.

The landau stops in an inner courtyard, planted with palm and cypress trees, and here a white-robed officer of the royal household receives me. As is usual in India, the princely establishment consists of several palaces, but the one into which I am first shown is modern, with European drawing-rooms, looking-glasses, sideboards laden with silver, and billiard-rooms, appointments which we had been far from expecting to see in so indigenous a town.

The Maharajah, however, prefers the ancient dwelling-place of his ancestors, and it is there that audience will be granted to me. I must now prepare for it.

At first we thread our way through a number of little gardens and silent passages, then suddenly, after passing under a tall and pointed archway with doors of wrought copper, we come upon a noisy crowd revelling in deafening music. We find ourselves in an immense courtyard, in a place built for the combats of elephants, a site overlooked on one side by the majestic white façade of the old palace, with its ancient sculptures, its decorations of blue tile, and its golden sun, whilst on the other side, rows of stalls are ranged against the wall, in which chained elephants are placidly chewing their fodder. In the middle three or four hundred men of savage mien—Bhils—who have come from the mountains for the festival of their god, are holding sticks which they strike one against the other in the manœuvres of a war dance which is being played for them on bagpipes, horns, huge tom-toms, and cymbals of bronze. Hundreds of women are leaning over a terrace watching this dance —a wondrous exhibition of beauties with dark eyes and splendid bosoms veiled in muslin.

What a number of passages have still to be traversed before the sovereign is reached! What a number of courtyards, where great scented orange trees are flowering between arcades of white marble! How many ante-chambers, whose recesses are littered with slippers, and where men, armed with long sabres, are seated in every corner! There are passages, too, which barely allow us to squeeze by, and dark little staircases of the olden times, hewn from the solid rock, which are so narrow, steep, and slippery as to be almost alarming. As we thread our way through the gloom we encounter endless successions of guards seated amidst the slippers that trail on the ground in every direction. Often, too, horrible divinities glare at us from their hiding-places as we pass by. At last, after having clambered to a great height through the rocks and rooms that are built upon the rocks, a door is reached before which the officer, who has been guiding me, stops respectfully. Then, after saying in a low voice "His Majesty is here," he retires and leaves me to enter alone.

13

I am in a white gallery with marble arches, which overlooks a huge white terrace. On the ground is a linen cloth of snowy whiteness. There are no attendants present, and in the whole extent of this fresh, airy, and spotless little desert there is no furniture save two gilt chairs that are placed in the centre. In the figure that stands there, alone and upright with outstretched hands, I recognize the horseman whom I saw the other evening, the one for whom the fakirs made their toilette. Now, however, he is clothed in a simple white robe with a necklace of sapphires.

Now that we have seated ourselves with becoming ceremony on the light gilt chairs, an interpreter, who has entered noiselessly, places himself behind me. Each time that he speaks he holds a napkin of white silk before his mouth, so that his breath may not annoy his lord—a useless precaution, however, for his teeth are white and his breath is sweet.

This silent prince, so rarely accessible to strangers, possesses both charm and grace, together with an exquisite courtesy that is tinged with a certain shyness, the kind of timidity that I have sometimes noticed in very great aristocrats. At first he deigns to ask if I have been well treated in his country, and if I like the horses and carriage that he had sent for me—the usual trivialities of a tentative conversation between persons who are separated from each other by difference of race and diversity of opinion. Afterwards, when the conversation turns on European affairs and on the countries which I have just left, and on Persia, whither I am so soon to go, I can perceive how many thoughts, that would be curious alike to both of us, we might interchange did not so many barriers stand in the way.

Now, however, some one comes to remind the prince that this is the hour of his evening ride in the enchanted forest where the fakirs dwell. To-day he proposes to ride round the shores of the lake as far as the house where the wild boars assemble daily. Serving-men with large Oriental parasols were already in attendance, so that he might be sheltered as he passed along the terraces on his way to join the knights and barons who are even now waiting in the saddle. Before dismissing me he is kind enough to give orders that the unfinished palace which he is building shall be shown, and that a boat should be in readiness to take me to the island palaces of the olden times.

It would seem then that even in these days of change there are still Indian princes who plan dwellings such as their forefathers dreamt of in the bygone days of splendour.

The new palace is perched loftily on a flat and circular space that juts out upon the lake. It is composed of a number of white halls and white kiosks, almost covered with festoons, and traceries of stone and marble, so placed as to overlook the varied aspects of the lake. A sumptuous staircase, lined by elephants of stone, leads down to the waters which lie embosomed amidst high and savage mountains and gloomy virgin forests. Within, mosaics of glass and porcelain deck the walls. In one room there are sprays of roses, each flower of which is made from porcelains of twenty different colours ; in another room, aquatic plants, water-lilies, herons, and kingfishers. One room has just been finished. Here rose-coloured lotus flowers wander over the moss-green walls in a simple, antique, and formal design, which reminds us of what we call " the new art." In the middle of this room there is a crystal bedstead, with satin cushions of the same tone of green as the walls and velvet mattresses that match the rosy colour of the lotus flowers. I step into the boat that is waiting for me near an old Brahmin temple that lies amidst the trees, a temple so dilapidated that it seems ready to crumble into the water through which we row towards the isles. The usual evening wind has already risen, the wind that daily strews the land of Rajput with dust and death. On the lake, however, it becomes fresh and pure and but flecks the waters round us with tiny blue waves.

We first touch the smaller of the two islands. The

palace on this island is barely one hundred years old. How secluded and shut in it is ! For my part, I should have thought that it was sufficiently isolated by the deep waters which surround it. There are little gardens surrounded by mosaic-covered walls, now overgrown by rank weeds, thickets of brambles, inextricable tangles of vegetation, and great tufted bunches of mallow flowers. There are labyrinths of low, dark rooms, decorated with mosaics or with fast fading paintings. These rooms are so constructed that freshness and shade might be enjoyed at all times of the day. Here, too, the kings of bygone times could meditate before an everchanging prospect, inclosed and melancholy gardens, wild and distant horizons, the forests where the tigers dwelt, or the fairyland of white palaces that rose on the opposite shore. Oh ! who can say what strange dramas or what lingering agonies these little rooms have seen, these little deserted rooms, now slowly mouldering in the damp emanations of the lake ! Sometimes we see curios that stand in dark and gloomy niches in the walls, trifles that came from Europe, things which must have been valued here a hundred years ago, old-fashioned porcelains, Dresden figurines in the costumes of the time of Louis XVI, artificial flowers in Empire vases. . . . Who were the queens and who were the young princesses who received these fragile presents, who shut them up so carefully, and who have passed away leaving them behind ?

The palaces of the larger island, which we now visit, were built by a glorious potentate who lived about three hundred years ago. They are more extensive and elaborate, but even in a more advanced stage of ruin than those on the other island. The huge landing-place, the white steps of which are partly submerged in the water, is ornamented by great elephants of stone that seem to be stationed there to await the arrival of the boats. The mournful gardens are as much shut in as those of the neighbouring island, but their walls are more elaborately inlaid with mosaics and much more richly sculptured. The great branched palm of the South is found here, but it does not grow naturally, and it can only be seen near the abodes of princes. The air is deliciously scented by groves of orange trees, the flowers of which are strewn like a coating of hoar-frost over the ground and over the dead leaves which lie thick upon it. It is already late as we reach the palace, and the sun has sunk behind the steep and tall mountains that enshroud the lake with a primitive twilight. Now is the hour when the parrots roost, and I notice that they have chosen the branches of these jealously guarded orange trees for their resting-place. We see them arriving in flocks from the enchanted wood in little green clouds, clouds of a green more vivid than that of the fading leaves, for even at the water's edge everything has commenced to turn yellow, and the wintry tints of the surrounding forests will soon be universal. The wind that bears famine and drought on its wings blows ever more strongly, and amidst the ruins of this lonely isle the evening seems instinct with an almost menacing melancholy.

IX

THE BEAUTIFUL ROSE-COLOURED CITY

I have journeyed a hundred leagues farther north, but since leaving Odeypoure desert has followed upon desert, and the whole land seems accursed. The remains of what were once villages, jungles, and cultivated fields have disappeared under a sad and monotonous winding-sheet of white-coloured ash that looks as if it had been strewn there by some immense volcano. At last, after passing through this land of desolation, we came upon a city which seemed full of Oriental glow and charm. The avenues leading to the crenelated walls and arched gateways of the city are thronged by white-robed cavaliers, by women wrapped in long red and yellow veils, by ox carts, and by strings of camels decked in gay accoutrements.

Surely the times of plenty could not show a more dazzling display of life and colour !

But what can be the meaning of those miserable heaps of rags lying at the foot of the ramparts ? There are human shapes hidden under them. What can all these people be doing on the ground ? Are they ill, or are they drunk ? Ah ! these are heaps of bones, or the withered and mummified carcasses of the dead. No, it cannot be that, for there are some who still move, their eyelids tremble and they can see, and there are some who can even stand on the tottering bones that serve as legs.

After we have passed the first gate another is seen, cut through an inner wall which is painted in rose colour up to its jagged crests, a bright rose colour so regularly flecked with white flowers as to resemble a piece of chintz. The tatters of humanity are there also, but the dark forms wallowing in the dust look more frightful close to the charming rose colour of the flower-spangled wall. They look like skeletons with leather overdrawn, and their bones stand out with horrible precision. Elbows and knee-caps make great swellings like the knots upon a stick, and the thighs, which have only one bone, are thinner than the legs, which have two. Some are grouped in families, but others are abandoned and alone ; some lie extended on the ground, almost at the point of death, whilst the rest sit huddled in crouching attitudes of stupid immobility, with grinning teeth and eyes which sparkle with fever. In one corner a fleshless old woman, who appears to be alone in the world, weeps silently upon her rags.

What an enchanting surprise awaits us as we pass through the second gate and behold the interior of the town !

What an astonishing and kingly caprice it must have been that planned a whole rose-coloured city, where all the houses, ramparts, palaces, towers, balconies and temples are of one colour, evenly diapered with similar posies of white flowers. One might almost think that all the walls had been hung with an antique

chintz of floral design, or that the town had been hewn
out of onyx in the style of the old cameos of the
eighteenth century. It is so different from anything
that we have seen elsewhere, and the whole effect is
one of complete and charming improbability.

There are streets laid out in straight lines, some
almost a mile long and twice as broad as our boule-
vards. These are flanked by high palaces, the façades
of which display an endless succession of Oriental
fantasies. I have never seen such extravagant luxury
of superposed colonnades, of festooned arches, towers,
windows, and balconies. All, too, of the same tint, a
rosy tint whose colour is that of a flower or of an old
silk, and even the tiniest moulding or the tiniest
arabesque is outlined by a white thread graven in relief.
It almost looks as if a delicate tracery of white lace had
been nailed over the pieces of sculpture. On the flat
surfaces, however, the decoration which resembles
chintz with old-fashioned posies is again to be seen.

A seething crowd fills the whole length of the streets
with a dazzling and ever-changing play of colour.
Each side of the pavement is encumbered by merchants who have spread out their wares of cloth,
copper, and arms on the ground before them. Wandering amongst the crowd are busy throngs of women,
who are decked in muslins emblazoned with all manner
of fantastic designs, whose naked arms are encircled
with bracelets which go right up to their shoulders.

In the middle of the street there is an unending
procession of armed horsemen bestriding gorgeous
saddles, of heavy carts drawn by zebus with painted
horns, of long strings of camels, and of elephants with
gilded robes whose trunks have been ornamented with
complicated networks of coloured patterns. Drome-
daries, on which two people ride one behind the other,
also pass by with ambling gait and outstretched necks
like those of running ostriches. Nude fakirs, covered
with white powder from head to foot, walk past, and
palanquins and chairs that are borne on men's
shoulders are carried along ; an Oriental fairyland

parading in all its splendour in a setting of rosy magnificence inconceivable in its beauty.

Servants lead tamed cheetahs belonging to the King through the streets. These are led on slips so that they may become accustomed to crowds. They wear little embroidered caps tied under their chins with a bow, and they pace along, putting down each velvet paw with infinite precaution as though stepping over eggs laid on the ground. . . . For greater security they are also held by their ringed tails, and four attendants always walk behind. But there are also many hideous vagrants—graveyard spectres like those lying at the rampart gates. For these have actually dared to enter the rose-coloured city and to drag their skeletons through the streets. There are more of them than I should have thought possible. Nor are those who wander tottering and with haggard eyes through the streets the only ones. There are horrible heaps of rags and bones lying on the pavements hidden amongst the gay booths of the merchants, and people have to step aside so as not to tread upon them. These phantoms are peasants who used to live in the surrounding districts. They have struggled against the droughts which have brought destruction to the land, and their long agony is imprinted on their incredibly emaciated bodies. Now all is over ; their cattle have died because there was no more grass, and their hides have been sold for a mere trifle. The fields which they have sown are only steppes of dusty earth where nothing can grow, and they have even sold their rags and the silver rings that they used to wear on their arms and ankles so that they might buy food. They starved for months, till at last famine definitely appeared, hideous famine which filled the villages with the reek of a charnel-house.

They are hungry and they wish to eat, that is why they have come into the city. They thought that people would take pity on them, and would not let them die, and they had heard that food and grain were stored here, as if to resist a siege ; they had heard, too, that every one in the city had something to eat.

Even now carts and strings of camels are constantly bringing sacks or rice and barley that the King has procured from distant lands, and people are piling them up in the barns, or even on the pavements, in dread of the famine which threatens the beautiful city on every side.

But though there is food it cannot be had without money. It is indeed true that the King gives food to the poor who dwell in his capital, but, as to helping the peasants who die by thousands in the surrounding fields, how can that be done if there is not a sufficiency ? So all heads are turned aside from the poor wretches who wander through the streets, and who haunt the places where people eat, still hoping that a few grains of rice may be thrown to them, till at length the time comes when they must lie down anywhere, even on the stones of the street, to wait for death's deliverance.

At this very moment they are piling hundreds of sacks, which the camels have brought, on to the pavements : room cannot be found in the barns—so three starved and naked children, whose ages range from five to ten years, must be driven from the place where they had sought a rest.

A woman who is standing by tells us that they are three brothers and that their parents, who brought them here, are dead (of hunger, I suppose) : that is why they are here, and they stay because they have nowhere else to go.

The woman appears to see nothing unusual in all this, yet she does not seem heartless or unkind. My God ! what sort of folk are these ? What can be the material from which the souls of these people are fashioned ?—people who would not kill a bird, but who feel no compunction when little children are left to die upon their doorsteps ?

The tiniest of the three children seems to be almost dead, for he is motionless and has no longer strength enough to drive away the flies that cling to his closed eyelids : his belly is so empty that it resembles the carcass of an animal that has been drawn for cooking, and he has dragged himself along the ground so long that at last his hip bones have rubbed through the skin.

But they must move on elsewhere so that there may be room for the sacks of grain that have been brought here.   The tallest of them gets up and takes the little child tenderly to his bosom, and after giving a hand to the other brother, who can still walk, he silently moves away.

The eyes of the little one open for a moment.   Oh ! what a look of unspeakable anguish is written on the face of this innocent martyr ! what an expression of reproach, of astonishment, of surprise that any one could be so unhappy, and be left to linger in such suffering !   But the dying eyes are soon closed ; the flies return to settle there, and the poor little head falls back on the wasted shoulder of the elder brother.

With a wonderful look of resignation and childish dignity the small elder brother totters forward with his charges, but he neither murmurs nor sheds a tear, for is he not now the head of the family ?   Then after having made sure that he is far enough off not to be in the way, he lays his brothers very gently on the ground and stretches himself out by their side.

The wonderful luxury of the city attains its most curious effects in the open space from which the principal streets diverge.   There the pyramids of the Brahmin temples are coloured pink up to their extremities, and, rising through flights of black crows into the dusky sky, give us the impression of rosy yew trees dotted with flowers.   The façade of the king's palace is also rose, overlaid with white flowers : this building even surpasses in height the fronts of our cathedrals, and is composed of an endless repetition of kiosks placed one above the other.   Each kiosk is like the one below it, and each has the same colonnades, the same lattice-work and the same complicated domes, whilst on the topmost pinnacles are royal standards whose coloured bannerets flap in the parching wind.

Rose are the palaces, rose are the houses lining the streets that lead on all sides into the dusty distances.

In the central square the crowds are more animated and more noisy, and many jewels sparkle amidst the dazzling diversities of colour that the revellers wear. The spectres of famine are more numerous, too— especially the shadowy forms of little children who are drawn hither by the smell of the rice-cakes and the sweets of honey and sugar that are being cooked in the middle of the open space. Of course, no one gives them away, but they stay on all the same, their dilated eyes sparkling with a fevered longing, even though they can hardly stand on their trembling legs.

And the invasion of these hunger-smitten ones increases rapidly. It is like a ghastly tide that flows from the country towards the town, and the roads leading across the plains are strewn with the corpses of those who have died before reaching the city gates.

A woman has just stopped to beg at the stall of a bracelet-seller, who is even now eating hot and savoury pancakes. The woman is a mere spectre, who clasps to her bony bosom and withered breasts the skeleton of a child. No, the trader will give her nothing ; he does not even deign to look at her. Then the mother, whose breasts are dried up and whose child must die, flies into fury and the cry of a maddened she-wolf hurls itself forth through her unclenched teeth. She is quite young, and was doubtless beautiful ; youth still glimmers in her ravaged cheeks, indeed she is almost a child and can hardly have seen more than sixteen years. But at last she understands that no one will take pity on her and that she is doomed. Then her despairing wail rises into the yell of a hunted beast that knows that its pursuers are at hand. Meanwhile the huge and pampered elephants walk past with heavy tread, munching the costly forage which has been brought from distant lands.

The outcries of the crows which swarm in thousands on the roofs and in the air can ever be heard rising above the clamouring of the crowd. This eternal and perpetual croaking, that dominates all other Indian sounds, here swells into a mighty crescendo, into a scream of delirious ecstasy, for the times of famine, when the odour of death is rife in the land, are the times of plenty for the crows, the vultures, and the flies.

It is now time to feed the royal crocodiles that live in the shadow of high-walled gardens.

The kingly palace is almost a world in itself, with its endless dependencies, its stables for elephants and for horses. In order to reach the artificial lake where the crocodiles are to be found, we must pass through many doors bristling with iron, and through many courtyards broad as those of the Louvre. All these courtyards are flanked by sullen-looking buildings whose windows are barred with iron. Naturally, their walls are painted in rose colour and scattered over with nosegays of white flowers. To-day these quarters are crowded, and the roll-call is being read out. It is pay-day, and soldiers of barbaric aspect and superb bearing are waiting with standards and lances in their hands. They are paid in heavy coins of the olden time, in round pieces of silver or in squares of bronze.

We pass through a marble hall, with arches and columns sculptured into arabesques. Here a cloth of purple is stretched over a gigantic loom, and dozens of workmen are occupied in covering the surface with raised flowers of gold embroidery. This is only a new trapping for one of the favourite elephants.

The gardens, by dint of laborious watering, have been kept almost green, so that they seem a wondrous oasis in the midst of the parched land. A crested wall, some fifty feet in height, incloses vast and park-like slopes over which a gentle melancholy broods. There are cypresses and palms and little woods of orange trees and many roses that load the air with fragrance. There are marble seats where one may rest in the shade, kiosks of marble, built for the pleasaunces of bayadères, and marble basins where princes may bathe. There are peacocks and monkeys, and occasionally the furtive muzzles of jackals peer out from under the orange trees.

At last we reach the formidable walls which surround the great pond, and at once see that its waters have almost disappeared through the long drought. Enormous old crocodiles, that look like rocks, slumber in the mud. Soon, however, a white-haired old man advances and stations himself on the steps leading down to the water's brink, singing as he walks in the high falsetto voice of a muezzin calling to prayer, and as he sings he waves his arms as if to call the slumbering reptiles. Then the crocodiles awake, and their first slow and indolent movement gives way to a fearful agility and suppleness of motion. They approach quickly, swimming across the pond, accompanied by great greedy tortoises who have also heard the call and wish to be fed too. All now form a circle at the foot of the steps on which the old man stands with his serving-men, who carry baskets of meat. The livid and viscous jaws now distend cavernously in readiness to swallow the goat's flesh, the legs of mutton, and the lungs and entrails which are thrown to them.

Yet outside in the streets no one, with muezzin's call, summons the starving to come and be fed. Those who have just arrived still wander about with outstretched hands, tapping, should any one chance to look their way, upon their hollow bellies. The rest, who have lost all hope, lie down anywhere, even under the feet of the crowd and in the track of the horses.

A French stranger has ordered his carriage to stop at a crossing where two of the avenues of rosy palaces and temples join, a spot much thronged by merchants, horsemen, and women in gay muslins. Here he alights and advances towards one of these dreadful, inert heaps of starving human beings and stoops down to place pieces of money into their lifeless hands.

Immediately it is as though a horde of mummies had suddenly risen from the dead. Heads emerge from the rags that covered the heap, and withered and bony forms rise slowly from the ground. " What !

He is giving money ! we can buy something to eat ! "
The ghastly resurrection suddenly extends to other
heaps lying hidden behind the piles of merchandise,
the crowds and the furnaces of the pastrycooks, for
they seethe and stir and grovel on the ground.   Then
a swarm of phantoms advances with faces of dead men,
with horrible, grinning teeth, with eyes whose lids
have been eaten away by the flies, with breasts that
hang like empty bags on their hollow chests, and with
bones which rattle as they walk.   Instantly the
stranger is encircled by these spectres of the charnel-
house.   They throng round him, they seize on his
clothes, and try to snatch the money from his hands
with finger-nails which look like claws.   And all the
while their poor pleading eyes seem to ask pardon
and forgiveness for their importunity.

Then silently the phantoms melt away.   One of the
spectres who was too weak to stand tottered and fell,
causing the spectre nearest to him to fall also.   This
one in his fall brought others to the ground, but as
each one in tumbling over clung to his neighbour, all
gradually collapsed, fainting and exhausted, into the
dust, from which they had no longer strength to rise,
like a troupe of marionettes or like a set of ninepins
that are bowled over.

Now the sound of approaching music is heard, and
I can see an agitated crowd.   It is a religious procession
that has been sent out to announce that a festival will
be held on the morrow in the Temple of Brahma.
One of the attendants, whose duty it is to keep the
road clear, notices that an old woman has fallen on her
face into the roadway, so he picks her up and throws
her back on to the pavement out of the way, where
she lies bruised and groaning.

The passing procession is one of great beauty.   A
black elephant, ornamented with designs in gold, leads
the way ; behind him musicians walk, playing a solemn
air in the minor mode on their bagpipes and their
copper instruments.

Then four gray elephants advance, bearing on their

backs young men adorned like gods. These graceful youths wear tall tiaras on their heads, and throw perfumed and coloured powders over the people standing beneath them. These powders are so light and subtle that it almost looks as if they were scattering clouds. Gradually, too, the colours of green, violet, yellow, and orange settle on the elephants and tinge them with strange fantastic tones. The joyous youths throw the scented dust by handfuls, and the robes and turbans of the crowd are coloured at their will. Even the little, starving children, who look up from the ground on which they lie, are covered with the sandal-scented powder, and often their eyes are filled, for the motions of their enfeebled hands are too slow to shield them.

Now the day suddenly declines and a universal pallor seems to irradiate from the rose-coloured walls. Overhead the sky is blue, but the air is so charged with dust that the moon looks wan. Flocks of black-winged birds swoop down to roost, and crows and pigeons nestle so closely together on the cornices that the rosy palaces are outlined by strings of sombre hue. Vultures and eagles still swoop in wheeling circles through the air, and the monkeys, who live freely on the house-tops, grow lively as the night comes, and chase each other with nimble feet : strange little shadows running with lifted tails along the edges of the roofs.

Below, the streets grow empty, for there is no night life in Eastern cities.

One of the tame cheetahs, who is on her way back to the palace to sleep, has seated herself on her haunches near the corner of a street. Just now she is on her best behaviour and with her cap all awry wears an expression of well-fed contentment. Her attendants have seated themselves in like fashion around her, though one of them still holds her by the tail. The cheetah's mystic eyes of pale green jade are fixed on some of the starving children who lie panting on the ground, only a few steps away from her.

The merchants hasten to fold up their many-coloured stuffs and to pack their plates, vases, and vessels of copper into baskets. Then they retire to their houses, leaving more heaps of starving wretches, who had been hidden amidst their gay merchandise, exposed to view. Soon these will be the only human beings to be seen, and during the night they will be the masters of the pavement.

Gradually the heaps of death-smitten wretches become more clearly defined, and they are more numerous than I could have fancied. The square becomes deserted, and these rigid forms and hideous heaps of rags will soon be left to the loneliness of the night.

In the deserted country outside the city walls all the trees swarm with life in this twilight hour. Eagles, vultures, and splendid peacocks flock there in troops, each forming a little colony on the slender and leafless branches. Gradually their outcry ceases, and the stillness is only broken by intermittent calls which soon become less frequent. The complaining voices of the peacocks still linger in the evening air; then, as night comes on, the mournful cries of jackals take up the song. It is ten o'clock, a late hour for the city whose life almost ceases with the day. The country around has become exquisitely silent. A mist seems to veil the distance, but it is only the dust rising from the parched sand. The pale moonlight glistens on the white and dusty ground, the dead trees, and thorny cactus plants. Night has brought a sudden chill, and we seem to see the snows of winter. How cold it will be for the poor children who are lying naked and starving on the ground ! The silence of the desert has now penetrated within the walls, and nothing can be heard but the rumbling of muffled music issuing from the depths of the Brahmin temples. A few white-robed men still move up and down the lofty staircases, which are flanked by elephants of stone. No one else can be seen, and the streets are quite deserted—those long, straight streets that seemed broader and larger now that they are no longer thronged with people and equipages. The beauty of the palaces, and their fretted windows, seem even more imposing in the calm moonlight, and the rose-coloured city is still rosy in the whiteness of the moon.

But the black and sinister heaps are still there, those horrible piles of panting rags, those starving herds which have collapsed by the side of the sacks of corn that have been piled hastily on the pavement, and which are now being guarded by men armed with bludgeons.

Now we are able to see many niches of stone that were hidden during the day by the teeming multitudes. Each one shelters a god, maybe the elephant-headed Ganesa, or maybe Siva, the king of Death, but each idol is decked with flowers, and each has his little lamp which will burn till dawn comes.

Soon the heaps of rags become transformed into dark shapeless masses, patches of black which befleck the rosy gray of the enchanted city; but ever and anon a cough or a groan may be heard, and sometimes a leg or an arm protrudes from the ragged heap and stretches itself quiveringly into the air. To those who lie on the ground what matters the joyous day, the calm night, or the radiant dawn ? No one will pity them ; they have lost all hope, and they know that their weary heads must remain where they have fallen, and that they have naught to expect but the last pangs which will end all.

X

THE TERRACE ON WHICH THE COUNCILS WERE HELD BY MOONLIGHT

The pale, full moon that hangs in the twilight sky has not yet commenced to shed its wan light over the masses of ruins that stretch out beneath my feet, and though the sun has sunk behind the mountains more than an hour ago, these ruins are still irradiated by its yellow glow. I am stationed on the lofty terraces of the dwelling of the ancient kings, a sort of formidable and unapproachable eyrie standing in the midst of a great abandoned town. Once it was filled with

14

priceless treasures, but now it is empty, save for the few serving-men who have charge of it.

I am already at a great height, and if I lean over the luxuriantly carved granite slabs that serve as balustrades to these terraces, I overlook abysses, at the bottom of which lie the remains of houses, temples, mosques, and other splendours. I am already at a great height, and yet I am overlooked on all sides, for the rocks on which the palace is built stand encircled by mountains that are still more lofty. Around me are great pointed peaks of reddish stone rising almost vertically into the air, whose topmost summits are crested by ramparts, the jagged edges of which are outlined against the yellow sky. The towering wall is one of those ancient works whose audacity and enormity fill us with perplexity, for it is built of huge blocks poised on almost inaccessible mountain peaks, and it incloses a circle of several miles. It seems, too, to rise so loftily and with such confidence into the air that I can hardly look at it without a feeling of giddiness. Surely the people of olden times could hardly have imagined a more wonderful defence for the now decayed city and the palace where I am standing, for they have transformed the summits of the whole encircling chain of mountains into one huge fortress. And there is but one entrance into the forbidden circle, a sort of natural cleft, through which I can see distant deserts that look as if they had been ravaged by fire.

The sun was declining as I set out for the ancient capital of Amber, whose ruins now lie beneath my feet, a capital replaced nearly two centuries ago by the town of Jeypore, which I have lately quitted. I was accompanied by guides and horses, placed at my disposal by the Maharajah of the beautiful rosy city, the successor of the kings who formerly inhabited this palace of Amber, on whose terraces I now stand. I had hastened to make my escape from the fairy splendours and the Dantesque horrors of Jeypore, and was glad to reach the open plains, where at least all the agonies would be over and the silence of death would reign.

Yet I knew through what regions of terror I should have to pass directly I left the rampart gates : it would be like a battlefield over which a conquering enemy had long since swept. Withered corpses would lie in the parching sun, and these corpses would breathe, and some even would be able to rise and follow me or seize me with their poor bony hands in supreme and despairing appeal.

Yes, indeed, I found all that awaiting me.

Amongst the dreadful heaps of bones and rags were many old women whose descendants had probably perished of hunger : abandoned grandmothers who lay there, calmly waiting for their turn to come. They did not beg, nor even move, though their great eyes expressed an infinitude of despair. Above their heads multitudes of crows, perched on the branches of the dead trees, were keeping anxious watch until the time should come.

But children were even more numerous than on the previous days. Oh ! the little faces that seemed astonished at so much misery and destitution, and that looked at us so appealingly from the ground. We got down and stopped before some of the most emaciated, though we could not stop before them all, for they were legion. Poor, little, weary heads, attached to skeletons that could no longer support them. We lifted them up gently, but they fell back confidingly into our arms, and the eyes closed as if they would sleep under our protection. Sometimes we see that the succour we have brought comes too late, but often the tiny spectres get up and take the piece of money that we have given them to the merchants who sell rice.

My God ! It would cost so little to keep these infants from starvation ! The frugal nourishment of an Indian costs about three half-pence a day.

After issuing from the rosy gates we had to pass through two miles of ruins before the open country was reached. The gardens that adjoined the road were filled with dead trees and with interminable suites

of cupolas and carved stone kiosks, now only inhabited by monkeys, crows, and vultures. The outskirts of all the towns of this country resemble each
other in that they are crowded with burying-places
and with vast relics of former civilizations.

It is needless to say that there are no signs of cultiva-
tion, and that no living person can be seen in the
villages, which swarm with flies.

When at last we reached the foot of the mountains,
it seemed as if the regions of reddish stone in which
we found ourselves were heated by some artificial
means. Even in the shade each gust of dry and dusty
wind seemed like a breath of flame. The only vegetation of this neighbourhood consisted of great plants
of dead cactus. These still remained standing, and all
the surrounding rocks bristled with their thorny spears.
My two guides rode on horseback with bucklers by their
sides, carrying their lances erect, just as the soldiers of
Bahadur or Aktar may have done in the olden times.

The declining rays of the evening sun were flashing
in our eyes as we at last saw the narrow cleft which
gives access to the inclosed valley of Amber. A formidable door barred the only entrance, but, when we
had passed through it, the ancient capital lay before us.

We ascended by paved slopes, on which our horses
could scarcely find foothold, to that kingly palace of
stone and marble, so proudly enthroned on the rocks
that overlook the other ruins.

Close by the entry, near one of the first windings of
the ascending road, we came upon a black and evil-
looking temple, the floor of which was stained with
pools of blood, and which reeked with the stench
of a slaughter-house. In a niche at the back, the fearful
Dourga lives. She is quite little and almost shapeless,
and has the look of a malevolent gnome cowering
under a heap of red rags. At her feet lies a tom-tom,
almost as large as a tower. For centuries past a goat
has been slaughtered here each morning at daybreak
to the sound of the enormous tom-tom. Then the
priests offer the warm blood to the goddess in a cup

of bronze, and place the horned head before her on a plate. How can the goddess have slipped into the Brahmin Pantheon even under the title of Spouse of the God of Death, this Dourga, this fearful Kali, who is so greedy of blood that even human sacrifices were formerly offered to her in the very land where for ages all slaughter has been forbidden?

Where can she have come from with her red cloak, from what dark ages, and from what gloomy night?

At different points on our route, heavily studded bronze gates have been thrown open for us, but at last we had to leave our horses and continue our ascent on foot, through courtyards and gardens and winding staircases. We pass through marble halls, whose thickset pillars are decorated with tiny designs of barbaric taste. The vaulted arches were once clothed with glittering mosaics, and patches of shining looking-glass still shimmer under the damp incrustations that make the walls resemble the sides of a stalactite cave. The doors, too, were of sandal wood inlaid with ivory. As we climb higher we see piscines which still contain a little water, and there are baths hollowed out of the rock in which the ladies of the harem used to bathe. In the central space there is a cloistered, hanging garden, from which the rooms of the queens, princesses, and beauties of former days opened out. As I passed through on my way towards the topmost terraces, the air was scented with the perfume of ancient orange trees, but the old guardian complained bitterly of the monkeys who now seemed to think themselves masters of the place, and were even bold enough to gather the oranges.

Now that I had reached the topmost terraces, I waited for the night to come. The ancient kings had built these places and surrounded them by rich balustrades so that they might give audiences or hold councils there by moonlight, and I had wished to see these terraces at their allotted hour, under the moonlight which will soon pour down upon them.

The eagles, vultures, peacocks, turtle-doves, and

swallows have now retired for the night, and the abandoned palace seems doubly abandoned in the pervading silence. The sun has been hidden from me for a long time by the lofty mountains, but it must have set by now, for on the terrace below me I can see the Mussulman guardians, who ever wait for the holy hour of Moghreb, turn towards Mecca, and say their evening prayers.

Just at this moment a hollow sound reaches me from the blood-stained temple. It is the Brahmin hour of prayer also, and the tom-tom commences to roar, the tom-tom of the witch-like goddess with the scarlet cloak.

These heavy and resounding blows are but the prelude of, and signal for, an orgy of savage sounds. Groaning bagpipes and iron cymbals join in, and a horn howls unceasingly on two ever-repeated notes, which swell and fall and become blurred in their passage through the hollow and empty rooms on which these terraces are built. Suddenly an answering peal of bells floats through the air. It is the little temple of Siva whence this insistent ringing comes, a little chapel perched on the top of the pointed peaks which surround me, a temple leaning against the lofty wall whose crests stand out against the evening sky like the teeth of a black comb.

I had not expected to hear so much clamour amidst these ruins, but in India the destruction of a town and the decay of its sanctuaries do not prevent the performance of the sacred rites, and the gods still continue to receive service in the midst of the most deserted regions.

For the last few moments my eyes have been turned towards the little temple from which the pealing bells resound, and when I next look towards the ground, I am almost shocked to see my shadow suddenly and sharply defined there. Instinctively I turn to see whether some one has not lighted a strangely bright lamp behind me, or whether an electric search-light has not enveloped me in its wan rays. But no, it is the great full moon, the moon of royal audiences that

I had quite forgotten, but which has already commenced its nightly offices, almost without any intervening twilight, so quickly in this country do the days
make haste to die.

Other shadows, the shadows of motionless things,
are now thrown everywhere in alarming contrast with
spectral brightness, but the terrace of the moonlight
audiences is bathed in the full white glory of the moon.

I shall descend when the clanging music has ceased,
for I should hardly care to traverse so many narrow
staircases and passages whilst it lasts, or to walk alone
at this late hour through the palatial halls that must
now be given up to wraiths and monkeys.

But the music lasts a long while, so long that I can
count the kindling stars.

How commanding and yet how hidden the place is,
and what kings of phantasy these sovereigns must
have been who planned these moonlight terraces!

In about half an hour the sounds of the tom-toms
and the howls of the sacred horns become less deafening and less frequent. Their vibrations linger and
grow feeble, and their outbursts of renewed and des-
perate frenzy are of ever-diminishing duration. I feel
that the sounds express a lingering agony, and that
they are dying of exhaustion. At last silence comes
back again, and from the bottom of the valley, where
the ruins of Amber lie, I can hear the melancholy
flute-like voice of wandering jackals.

It is not really dark in the stairways and the low
halls of the palace as I make my way down. Everything seems bathed in moonbeams of bluish whiteness,
and silvery rays enter through festooned windows and
cast the charming outlines of the pointed arches on to
the pavement : the faded mosaics on the walls glow
with new life, so that the halls seem studded with gems
or sparkling drops of water. As I passed through the
gardens, now heavy with the scent of flowers, the
upper branches of the orange trees became all alive
with the agitated and noisy awakening of the monkeys.

My guides await me at the lower doors, where, after

the freshness of the terraces, the air seems hot and stifling. They are already in the saddle, and carry their lances in their hands. We trot tranquilly through the night towards the city of Jeypore, which I am leaving for good to-morrow.

I have decided to avoid Beckanire, a town lying a hundred leagues farther north. I had intended to visit it, but I have heard that the horrors of the famine culminate there, and that the streets are lined with corpses. Alas! No! I have seen enough. So I shall take the road that leads back to less desolate lands, to places where, being near to the sea of Bengal, life can still thrive.

XI

THE TOWN OF FRETTED STONE

My last halting-place in the land of famine was the city of the King of Gwalior, a city which is entirely overhung with lace-like carvings, and is renowned throughout the whole of India for the imaginative luxury of its sculptured stonework. It is almost too pretty, and the complicated perforations look laboured. The houses seem to resemble scene-paintings, punched out of fine cardboard, but they are made of stone, and their delicate traceries are by no means fragile. The thousands of little columns surrounding the festooned doors of the windows, from which stalactites hang down, have capitals of foliage, whilst their bases seem to spring from the heart of a flower. The streets are overhung by a prodigious number of loggias and balconies, rising one above the other, all fashioned from stone from the neighbouring quarries. Should any one desire to make a trellis for their balcony or a screen behind which beautiful ladies may sit unseen, it is only necessary to take a huge slab of stone, sawn to the thinness of a plank, and then to cut out arabesques of exquisite refinement. Once in its place, the slab resembles a fragile piece of wood-carving or even imitates the delicacy of paper. Then it is coated with snowy whitewash, and the surrounding walls are painted with gaudy representations of flowers and processions of gods or of elephants.

The nightmare of famine is almost forgotten directly one enters this fairy city, in spite of the surrounding desolation which draws nearer every day. Here the people are rich enough to buy grain and there is still water enough to keep the gardens green. Baskets of roses are still on sale in the open places, waiting for people to buy them for their scent, or for the adornment of their persons.

We are in a Brahmin town, yet turbans are as plentiful as in the land of Mahomet. It must be admitted that they are of a special shape, being always wound tightly round a rigid framework, but there are endless varieties of form and colour dictated by the position and caste of the wearer. Some resemble a sea-shell, others the hats of the Louis XI period; here are some which remind us of the caps worn by women in former days, and we even see some which have two horns and long turned-up flaps. They are made of silk, and their colours are scarlet, pink, sulphur yellow, and celadon green, and, just as at Hyderabad, their fresh hues are thrown into relief by the whiteness of the crowds and of the streets. The sign of Siva, carefully painted on the foreheads of the men, is here transformed into the shape of a white butterfly with wings extending from either side of a red ball. The fork of Vishnu, however, remains just as it was in the south of Hindustan.

This is a town of horsemen, for they can be seen everywhere galloping on prancing steeds decked with golden harness. Many people ride on elephants, and strings of camels walk past in slow procession. There is no lack of mules, nor of little asses whose gray skins are faintly tinged with pink.

The carriages are very varied in kind, and all are extravagant. There are some tiny ones plying for hire which are made of glittering copper, with tops fashioned like pagodas. These are harnessed close up to the horse's tail, and are constantly shaken by the trotting. Then there are others which roll along with slow and solemn majesty, drawn by a pair of huge and sleepy zebus, yoked so far apart from each other that the whole road is taken up. These are invariably shaped like the arched prow of a ship, but the prow is so narrow that the people in the carriage have to sit cross-legged, one behind the other. The largest carriages shelter mysterious and hidden beauties. These are shaped like a monstrous egg, and their interiors are jealously shielded from view by red curtains. Sometimes one may catch a glimpse of a beautiful, beringed and amber arm reposing amidst the draperies of these slowly moving vehicles, or perhaps even the vision of a naked foot loaded with many rings. Then there are litters of every description. On some, young dandies, whose eyes are extended by paint and whose ears sparkle with diamonds, are being carried, dressed in robes of mauve or orange silk ; in others, nabobs, severely garbed in mantles of purple or violet velvet, are being borne along, their beards spread out in fan-like waves over the velvet folds of their garments, beards which are generally snowy white, but which sometimes have been tinted with bright vermilion dyes.

Many salutes are exchanged in the pretty streets, whose houses look as if they were made of white stone *tulle.* People are very courtly in Gwalior.

It is incontestable that the beauty of the Aryan race reaches its highest development of perfection and refinement amongst the upper classes in this country, where the pale skins are scarcely darker than those of the European races. Oh ! the wonderful eyes and the almost too exquisite and too regular beauty of the women who walk past in groups of dazzling colour, each one draped like a Roman matron in tinted and transparent muslins.

How remote is the India where the great palms grow, and where a bronze-coloured race walks about. with no other adornment than their flowing hair.

The muslins of Rajputan, that enwrap these people from head to foot, are, by intention, archaic in design, and the colours are always thrown on in patches and blurred forms which have no distinct outline. Here a woman has chosen a moss-green fabric strewn with rose-coloured spots for her veil, another who walks by her side is in golden yellow shaded with blues which alternate between tones of lapis lazuli and turquoise, whilst another is in lilac stained with a marbling of bright orange. The lightness of these tissues, the floods of sunbeams, and the transparency of the shadows cause all these colours to flash prismatically. And sometimes in the midst of all these flower and morning hues, another beauty passes, dressed like the queen of the night, bringing the marvellous contrast of black, black veils, zigzagged over with long stripes of silver.

Colours exercise such a fascination over the people of Gwalior that there are whole streets whose inhabitants are solely occupied in dyeing muslins and tinting them with tones in harmonious relief. This charming art is exercised quite openly, and it is usual for the people who pass by to stop and express their opinions on the work in progress. When a piece is finished, it is hung over one of the carved balconies, or given to two little children to carry about in the sunlight till it is dry. The dyer's quarters seem to be in a state of constant festivity with these gay and airy stuffs thrown like veils over the houses, and others that float in the air like waving flags.

Many bridal processions promenade slowly through the city, preceded by tambourines and bagpipes, the husband riding on horseback under the shelter of an enormous parasol that serving-men hold over his head. Funeral processions hurry past us with excessive haste, the corpse tightly swathed in linen and carried joltingly on the shoulders of the bearers; following these, a breathless crowd that howls and bays as dogs do at the moon. At the street corners there are fakirs bedabbled with ashes, who lie in convulsed and epileptic attitudes, and who pray with the expectant fervour of instant death. The great market-place is surrounded by temples and mosques, covered with the most delicate traceries, and the stalls of the merchants who sell silks, carpets, prints, cakes, and grains are besieged by crowds of women in multi-coloured veils.

Those horrors of death and slaughter, those sickening displays of carcasses of animals and of reeking fish, of guts and scraps of quivering flesh, are nowhere to be seen, for the people of Brahma do not eat anything that has ever lived. In the place of such exhibitions we see heaps of roses plucked from their stems, which are used in the making of essence, or simply to be woven into necklaces.

White doorways, over which are trellised balconies, give access to the immense royal quarters. There are snowy palaces surrounded by beds of white roses and by languishing trees, whose foliage is that of late autumn rather than of April. There are lonely parks that grow more parched every day, and even the king cannot prevent this from taking place. There are little lakes, now almost waterless, on whose shores stand marvellously sculptured kiosks, in which the Court was wont to take the air in the rainy seasons, when water abounded and the trees were thick with leaves.

Peacocks and monkeys wander disconsolately through the fading walks where the roses are still kept in flower with infinite care, but even these animals seem anxious about the drought and the encroaching desolation.

The King of Gwalior is at present in the neighbouring mountains, where he seeks relief from the fever that preys upon him. I have his authority to enter his palace, so that all doors fly open before me.

The rooms are furnished in the European style with gildings, brocades, and mirrors, so that we might fancy ourselves in the Palais Bourbon or at the Elysée. But in the midst of this commonplace luxury we can feel that India is hidden behind the silken hangings on the walls ; we can feel the sadness of the parks that are withered in the spring, and the anguish of the suffering country. The young lord who guides me with such distinction through the palace is quite a denizen of fairyland, for he is clothed in white, and a cap of rose silk rests on his head, pearls are in his ears, and he has a necklet formed of two great rows of emeralds. His face recalls the incredibly beautiful features that we see in old Indian or Persian miniatures. The eyes, which are already too long, are lengthened by lines of paint, the nose seems too delicate, and the black moustache is almost too silky. His cheeks are almost too red with the blood under the skin of amber.

The resting-places of the ancient kings of Gwalior occupy an immense and silent quarter on the other side of the city, and the dead monarchs lie in the midst of gardens, and under temples of stone and marble, on which the pyramids have the shapes of huge cypress trees or churchyard yews.

Amongst all the mausoleums that raise their pointed towers towards the sky, the most sumptuous is the one in which the late Maharajah sleeps. The stone and the white marble of this tomb are magnificently worked, and a black marble cow (venerated symbol) reposes in its sacred shades. This royal tomb is barely finished, yet the birds have already taken possession of it. Owls, doves, and parrots nest in flocks on its pyramids, and the steps are strewn with their gray and green feathers. The pyramid is very high, and through the wheeling flights of crows and eagles that encompass its summit we can see the whole city and its sculptured houses and palaces, its dying gardens, and its monuments. The outskirts are, as usual, encumbered with ruins ; ancient cities of Gwalior, ancient palaces and city quarters, abandoned because of their age and decay, or deserted during the stress of war or at the fancy of their rulers. One side of the horizon is bounded by a Titan citadel, such as the noble Hindoos used to build in the heroic ages of

their country in the days before they were tamed by
strangers, and when they led a free and warlike life.
A league of ramparts, donjon towers, and fierce old
palaces crowns yonder precipitous rocks, more than
a hundred yards in height.   The dim background is
filled with tones of ashy gray and tints of withered
leaves, and these dead forests and jungles that are
dead, seen in the extreme and vague background,
throw menace, silent menace, at the city which is yet
so free from care, so blithe—the menace of the approaching famine.

Yesterday evening I took a farewell ride through
the city of fretted stone, mounted on one of the king's
elephants and accompanied by an amiable Court
official.   It was at the cooler hour, when the ladies in
painted muslins, or in muslins worked with silver, take
the air of the balconies, which are like gems.

Every one seemed to know my companion by sight,
and to recognize the liveries of the two attendants who
ran ahead of us, so that we passed along amidst a
shower of salutations.

The elephant on which we were riding was a female
about seventy-five years old, and so tall that we were
on a level with the first floors of the houses.   The
streets were so narrow that we could even touch the
delicate traceries of the sculptured galleries on which
fair ladies were sitting, who saluted us as we passed by.

In one of the squares a space has been partitioned
off by mats high enough to prevent people looking
over them ; but we, from our lofty perch, could see
into the airy inclosure and overlook the marriage
festival which was being held in the street, because
the house of the bridal couple was too small,   We
could see bejewelled young women in gold-spangled
veils seated in a circle listening to singers and
musicians.

Many salutes greeted us from the market-place, and
the petty traders and poor folk bent to the ground
with deep obeisances.   The dashing horsemen merely
bowed their heads, reining in their horses, which

reared and plunged, frightened by our elephant, up-setting baskets of roses. Even little children of five or six, delightful little girls with painted eyes, stopped and saluted us by placing their hands on their fore-heads. Their curtsies seemed to rise up from the very ground beneath us, from under the very feet of the monster which trod so gently lest she might hurt these little ones.

I recollect that we stopped with a sudden jolt at the corner of a street, which was scarcely wide enough to let us pass; then the head of an enormous male elephant with long tusks appeared in front, coming towards us. There was a moment's pause. It almost seemed as if the two colossal beasts were holding a courteous consultation, as indeed may have been the case, for they both came from the royal stables and must have known each other well. At last the new-comer retreated thirty paces till he came to a court-yard, and as we passed by he stroked us gently with his trunk.

XII

THE ROYAL MOUNTAIN

Midday already looms, dazzling and sad, upon the desolate plains of India. My elephant gently ascends the huge slope that leads up the mountain side to the ruin-crowned summit, which seems a burial-garden of the gods, strewn with palaces and temples.

The climbing elephant zigzags across the road so as to mount more easily; the undulations of his gait rock me as with soft cradling, yet each footstep betrays the might of the colossus, for the dust flies up under the weight of his puissant feet. Hardly any sound accompanies the muffled tread, and in the utter silence of my surroundings I can hear little else than the jingling of the two silver bells that hang from the animal's side, bells that chime in sad and melancholy cadence. Sometimes, too, the flapping wings of passing eagles or vultures resound through the stifling and motionless air. The stiff ascent hugs close the flanks of vertical rocks. On the side of the abyss a low and massive wall with parapets juts out over grayish distances, which lie bathed in a glare of sun and dust.

On the mountain side gigantic things tower over us, huge jagged rocks, crowned with castles and turrets, such as the people of our time neither dare to build nor know how to build. Looking up we see a prodigious expanse of palaces of the olden time and of unknown style, palaces with watch-towers and balconies which jut out over the abysses, into which they look unflinchingly. For more than a thousand years dynasties of kings, of whose existence we know nothing, piled stone upon stone on the mountain which was already a fortress by Nature, so as to raise to the clouds this impregnable stronghold. Truly, the fortified châteaux and manors of our country squires seem ridiculous in comparison with the stupendous ruins with which India is filled.

The cumbrous elephant still ascends, the two bells ever repeating their soft and monotonous plaint. The overhead sun outlines the dancing shadow of the animal on the path, and paints in black outlines the image of his waving trunk. The two escorts who precede us climb sleepily, carrying long silver-mounted wands of state in their hands.

At different heights gateways bar the road which we ascend with Oriental slowness. What need is there to say that these are terrible gates with loopholed keeps rising above them, and that they are guarded by native troops, stationed there, perhaps, because the king has taken up his abode amidst the ruins of the glorious past ? Around us a widening circle of dim plains, whose withered trees look ashy in the dust-laden atmosphere. The gray horizon seems to mingle with a gray sky, thick with incandescent haze and flights of birds of prey, weary of wheeling over plains, which reek of drought, exhaustion, and of death.

A fiery glow reverberates from the rocks, and no breath of wind stirs through the air ; even the birds are slumberous and as though overcome by the mid-day glare. Eagles and vultures settle with folded wings to watch us as we pass by. The motion of the elephant gradually benumbs me, like the constant rocking of a gondola ; my dazzled eyes close, and soon I see nothing but the immediate objects that start out from the midst of the surrounding grayness, for water-less years have even enwrapped the red granite of the rocks with a winding-sheet of dust.

First I see the gilt turban, the brown neck, the back draped in white, and the little sharpened dart of the Hindoo driver, who sits, lance in hand, crouched like a Buddha on the animal's neck ; then a little of the scarlet cloth of the elephant's headpiece ; then his two huge pink ears marbled with black, that wave fan-like so as to drive off flies and other winged tormentors.

The docile beast ascends untiringly, pulverizing the path under his heavy feet. By his side and close to the rocks there are great rounded masses of stone that recall his shape, and that have been engraved with his image by the people of a long-forgotten age. Here vague carvings resembling trunks of tusked heads ; there curved backs whose outlines are almost those of the rocks themselves. There are also inscriptions in several dead languages, and many gods stand in niches cut from the solid rock, the work of the Pals or the Jaïnas, who were the first inhabitants of this formidable spot.

Down below in the burning plains the ruins of ancient Gwalior begin to be visible amidst the floating clouds of ashy dust, and I can see also the white out-lines of the new city that the Indians disdainfully call Lachkar (the encampment), and the great stone pyra-mids of the Brahmin temples. It is midday ; ardent flames pour down upon our heads, and the overheated rock glows like a furnace ; eagles, vultures, and crows sleep, overpowered by heat and silence.

Ever ascending, we arrive at the foot of the awe-inspiring palaces that stand on the precipitous edge and seem to raise the mountain's crest higher into the

15

air. These towered façades are of incomparable splendour, for they are built of regular courses of monstrous blocks of equal size, extending along the whole length of the building, their surfaces adorned with bands of green, gold, and blue mosaics, depicting many races of men and animals. Formerly these were the homes of the powerful Kings of Gwalior, who, up to the sixteenth century, lived here lofty and inaccessible.

A huge final gateway, glittering with bright blue mosaics and bristling with the Maharajah's soldiers, at last admits us to the level space which extends for more than a mile along the summit of a plateau which is entirely surrounded with ramparts and said to be the most impregnable stronghold in all the Eastern Indies. From the earliest times this place has never ceased to be a loadstone to the envy of warlike kings, and volumes of history are filled with the accounts of marvellous battles that have been fought here. Now it is but a lofty desert covered with palaces and tombs and with the temples and idols of every age and every civilization. Nowhere in Europe can such a place be found, such a tragic museum of bygone splendours.

The elephant kneels down so that we may alight and enter a mosaic-covered palace that seems less archaic and better preserved than the others.

It is barely five hundred years old, but the colossal foundations date from the time of the Pal kings who reigned at Gwalior from the third to the tenth century of our era. We wander through low, frowning rooms whose ceilings are formed from blocks of granite, and encounter the strange silence by which ruins are ever haunted. A dim twilight and a sense of freshness, grateful after the burning glow of the air outside, prevail. Nothing remains of the magnificence of olden days but the luxury of the carving and the marvellous enamels on the walls, that represent winged beasts, phoenixes and blue- or green-winged peacocks in glowing colours, colours of whose permanence the secret has been lost. The view of the outer world only reached these palaces through sheets of perforated granite embedded in the masonry of the walls. Such were the windows where beautiful captives stood lost in dreamland, and here, too, kings must have come to watch the clouds and the far-off plains with their armies and their battles. The whole of the front which overlooks the abyss, and which is three hundred feet long, with a height of not less than a hundred feet, the whole of these halls and rooms, whose walls are as thick as those of casemates, breathe alone through these fretted slabs, which open neither for flight, nor suicide, nor love, more dreadful far than the iron bars of a prison. Everywhere under the stones there are secret staircases leading to cellars, basements, and dungeons, and no one now knows to what depth the rock is hollowed out into abandoned wells and dark passages.

Other palaces, yet more barbarous, lie by the side of this one. There is one that is built of huge blocks that dates from the Pal kings, another belonging to the Jaïn period, an almost shapeless mass of rock pierced by tiny triangular windows that resemble loopholes.

In another direction the fortified plateau is covered with temples whose diversity relates the whole history of Brahminism, with tanks large enough to satisfy the wants of thousands of men in the event of a siege, and wherever we may look a wilderness of tombs and statues.

I stop before a Jaïn temple whose gods were formerly mutilated by the soldiers of the Great Mogul, and dreamily compare it with the old monuments of the Christian faith. Even our most beautiful churches are built of stones of uneven size embedded in mortar. Here, on the contrary, huge smooth, regular blocks are so adjusted and mortised into each other that they stand upright by themselves, miracles of precision, which forms an almost imperishable whole.

Now I and my Indians have resumed our seats on the back of the slowly swaying elephant, and to the accompaniment of the same tinkling bells we slowly descend the other slope of the mountain into a ravine of red rocks which soon cast shadows over our heads. We pass ascending horsemen whose steeds take fright and rear, and a dromedary which wheels round in terror, letting his burden fall to the ground, for even in this land of elephants it seems that there are few animals which learn to pass them without fear.

The gorge down which we journey is peopled by stone giants, colossal figures of Tirthankars, cut from the naked rock, that have their homes here in niches and caves, where they stand or sit.[1]

Some are twenty feet high, and all are completely nude, and their vastness of detail gives them an obscene appearance. Both sides of the valley are lined with staring figures, and our road runs through the midst of them.

But the iconoclastic army of the Great Mogul passed along this road in the sixteenth century wreaking vengeance on these images, breaking the heads and hands of some and disfiguring others in another way, so that all are mutilated.[2]

Now it seems that fresh figures loom through the dusty haze which veils the country. In other valleys which open out before us amongst other rocks the motionless throng continues in apparently never-ending succession. It is as if the air were ash-laden, yet the glare of the sun is everywhere. The heat and the tranquil tinkling of the bells dispose us to slumber. As we draw near to the plains everything grows more and more indistinct, and sleep almost overcomes us as we pursue our swaying march through ranks of giants whose outlines seem to melt into the vagueness which environs us.

---

[1] The largest of the statues are those of Parvasnath and of Tirthankar Adinath, the founder of the Jaïna faith, and do not date farther back than the fifteenth century.

[2] Mutilations ordered by the Emperor Babar in 1527.

TOWARDS BENARES

CHAPTER VI

TOWARDS BENARES

I

THE THEOSOPHISTS OF MADRAS

" A HEAVEN with no personal god, an immortality without a separate soul, and purification without prayer."

This was the formula, the supreme conclusion, that rang in my ears in the melancholy silence that followed our conversation. A dark sadness filled the lonely house that stood by the riverside amidst strange trees and palms. The severe library in which we sat was still illuminated by the light that fell through the window panes, but the transparent images that represented all the emblems of man's faith gradually faded. Here, as in a mortuary museum, were emblazoned in coloured glass the triangle of Jehovah, the lotus of Cakya-Mouni, the fork of Vishnu, and the symbols of Isis. I was in the house of the Theosophists of Madras, of whom I had heard so many wondrous things. For though I scarcely believed in them, I had come, almost despairingly, to beg for a ray of hope, and this was all that they had to offer, the cold consolation of the doctrines of Buddha, which I already knew, the light of my own reason.

" Prayer," they said, " who is there to hear it ? Each man has to face his own responsibility. Remember the laws of Manou. *Man is born alone, lives alone, dies alone, and justice alone awaits him.* Who is there to hear prayers and to whom would you pray ? *for you yourself are God. You must pray to yourself* by means of your own actions."

A silence fell upon us, one of the saddest that I have ever passed through, and in the midst of this silence it seemed as if my last faint beliefs fell from me one by one with almost imperceptible rustlings, like those of falling leaves, withered by the breath of the cold, calm reasoning of my companions.

Nevertheless, the two men who had listened to me were kind and well-intentioned. The first was a European who, wearied of our anxieties and perplexities, had come here to seek the spiritual detachment which Buddha used to preach, and had become the leader of the Theosophical Society ; the other was a Hindoo, who, though he disdained our Western philosophies, had returned home from Europe vested with our highest academical honours.

" You have told me," I replied, " that our fading individuality persists for a little while after death. Can you at least give me this absolute proof of what you say ? can you show me, can you give me some evidence of its truth ? "

" Yes," he replied, " we can prove it, but only by reasoning. As to giving you visible proofs, tangible proofs, no. To see those who are wrongly called the dead—for there are no dead—special senses, special circumstances, and special temperaments are essential. But you may believe our words. We and many others worthy of credence have seen the departed, and have written down a description of what we have seen. Look, you will find in this bookcase books which relate . . . To-morrow when you have become one of us you shall read them."

And was it for this that I had come to India, to the old cradle of religion, and was this all that was to be found in the temples ? Brahminism tinctured with idolatry, and here, a rearranged Positivism of Cakya-Mouni, and the Spiritualistic books which have been lying about all over the world.

After another silence I asked, like a man who has given in, and knowing that my question merely verged on childish curiosity—I asked, almost timidly, whether

they would allow me to see the fakirs, those marvellous
Indian fakirs who have gifts and can work wonders.
Here at least I should see some proof of another
world, something superhuman, something beyond my
comprehension.

The Hindoo, who was seated opposite to me, raised
his eyes to the ceiling, and a frown contracted the cold
and refined Dantesque face, framed in a white turban.
" Fakirs ? " he repted—" fakirs ? There are no more
fakirs."

And it was thus that I heard from the mouth of one
who was fully qualified to speak, that I must renounce
all hope of ever seeing anything miraculous on earth.

" Not even at Benares ? " I ventured shyly. " I
had hoped that at Benares—I had been told——"

" Let us understand each other. There are plenty of
begging fakirs, posturers, and those who are dead to
pain, and you will not need our help to find them.
But the ' seers,' the fakirs who could work miracles—
the last of these men was known to me. As to this,
you may believe us, such men did exist. But the
century which has just ended saw the last of them.
The old fakir spirit of India is dead ; we are a decaying
race, and the materialism of the West has hastened this
decay. We must, however, resign ourselves ; it is
fate, and the turn of the Western races will come too.
. . . Yes, we have had our fakirs. You can read the
records of them on those shelves. . . ."

The dead symbols of human faiths in the window-
panes were becoming faint and indistinct ; night fell,
and the library was wrapped in mournful darkness. I
had come to Madras with the intention of staying
some time with these Theosophists, and on the morrow
I was to have taken up my abode in their house, but
now I resolved to leave them, never to return. What
was there for me to do, shut up in that house of barren
emptiness ? Surely it was better to do as I had always
done, to feast my eyes on the things of this world,
which, if they be transitory, are at least, for an instant,
real. And then what of their proofs, the proofs of an

immortality such as they foresee ?   Is not the thought
of the perishing of the flesh torture enough to those
who have really loved ?   And what should we do, I
and mine, with the immortality which satisfied these
people ?   No, give me the Christian dream, that dream
of an immortality where I shall live a conscious, distinct, and *individual* self, where I may love and find
again those whom I loved on earth.   Without that
hope what would faith be to me ?

As I returned towards the town, it was the hour
when the crows intone their noisy hymn to Death
before settling themselves to sleep on the branches of
the trees.   The doctrines of the people I had just left
seemed to me as empty and as vain as the statues of
the little elephant-headed gods which I could dimly see
along the road under the palms and banyans.

The same evening I sent a grateful letter of disap-
pointed refusal to the Theosophists, telling them that
I should come to see them again in the morning, but
that it would be to bid them farewell, for that I had
made up my mind to leave Madras at once.

And that night, amongst the ruins of the old homes
of my childhood, I saw the pale, distorted faces of
those I had loved best, and knew that they were dead
for ever ; and, as in that other night in Jerusalem
when my first beliefs fell from me, dreams of unspeakable horror and of a sadness without surcease followed
on each other till the morning came, when I was
awakened by the harsh voice of a crow, which sang
the song of death to the rising sun.

When I returned in the afternoon to say farewell,
the leader of the Theosophists, who had read and had
understood my letter, met me with a sweetness that
I had little expected.

" Christian ! " he cried, clasping my hand in a long
embrace, " I had thought that you were an unbeliever.
I was wrong in offering you the matter-of-fact explanations of the principles which Buddha left us, the
explanations which we usually give first. . . . A mind
like yours needs the esoteric faith, and our friends at

Benares understand that better than we do, and there you will find prayer and recommunion under another form.   But prayer alone will not suffice, and they will teach you how to deserve. . . . *Seek and you will find.* I have searched for forty years, so take courage and seek further.   Indeed, I do not think that we would wish to keep you with us, for the teaching of our house is not suited to you, and, besides," he added smilingly, " your time is not come yet, the world still holds you in its clutches."

" Perhaps."

" You seek, but you are afraid to find."

" That may be."

" We speak to you of renouncing all things, and you, you wish to live.   Go your way, go to Delhi and to Agra, go where you wish and to all that calls and attracts you.   Only promise me that before you leave India you will go to Benares to our friends.   We shall have announced your visit, and *they will be expecting you.*"

The Hindoo whom I saw the day before entered silently and looked at me with a smile of sweet compassion.   All at once these two men seemed to be transfigured, to become greater, more subtle and impenetrable, but the same expression of peace and goodness radiated from the eyes of these strange ascetics, and though I could not understand this sudden transformation, I inclined my head before them in trustful thankfulness.

To stay a while with their friends at Benares before leaving India.   Ah ! yes ! I consented gladly, feeling a vague presentiment that there I should find a different environment where I might find peace.

But that I would reserve till the eve of my departure from India.   I would defer that last test as long as possible, for I still hesitated like a coward whom a double fear assails.   It might be that all my hopes would be taken away from me for ever, or I might *find.*   Then perhaps the new way would open out before me and an end would come to all these earthly joys, mere illusions doubtless, but still so delightful.

II

TWILIGHT AT JUGGERNAUT

The gigantic temple of Juggernaut stands in the centre of an old Brahmin town far away from everywhere among the sands and dunes of the Gulf of Bengal.

I arrived at sunset on my way from the interior. Suddenly my carriage glided along noiselessly, as if we were running on velvet. We were on the sands, and the long, blue line of the sea lay before us.

First we pass some fishermen's huts, scattered amongst the cactus hedges that grow on the dunes. Then Juggernaut appears, rising above myriads of gray, palm-thatched roofs. The aspect of the temple on this sea-girt shore is particularly strange, and the pyramid is so tall that all the objects lying at its feet seem dwarfed. It has the elongated and swollen appearance of a crocodile's egg, a huge egg placed upright on its end. Rose-coloured veins wander over a white surface that is without other ornamentation, and it is two hundred feet high without counting its bronze disc or the upright darts that bristle on its summit. It can easily be seen, standing on the flat sea-level shore, by ships which are making for the mouth of the Ganges, and nautical maps mark its site. The coast in this region, however, offers no favourable anchorage, so that seamen only know the old sanctuary from its dim outlines.

A large, wide road leads straight to the temple, that central point and lode-star of Juggernaut, and on my arrival there this road is thronged with people. This part of India is not so civilized, the natives view strangers with astonishment, and children turn back to follow one. The sea wind has deepened the colour of the nude men, and the women, who are wrapped in muslins, have so many rings round their ankles that they can hardly walk, and such a profusion of bracelets covers the space between their wrists and shoulders that their beautiful arms seem sheathed in metal. The little houses are more completely covered by paintings than I have seen elsewhere, and on their whitewashed fronts cruel-faced gods and goddesses are outlined in blue and red, after the style of the frescoes of Thebes and Memphis. The houses, too, with their columns, buttresses, and walls that slope inwards in such an exaggerated manner recall those of ancient Egypt.

The temple is a large and sullen fortress inclosed in a square of crested walls, each frontage of which has a central door. The principal entrance faces the street down which I am now walking, and two monsters with lolling eyes, flattened noses, and fierce grins guard its portal. Through the open doorway I can see large, white steps crowded with people ascending to the temple.

I need not say that to me the sanctuary is closed, and the priests even ask me to go farther off, for I had ventured to place my feet on some part of the paving-stones of the temple which jutted out into the road. I have to withdraw to the sand of the street, the sand which is free to all, with which the streets of Juggernaut are felted.

But I may walk round the square fortress which I must not enter. The four walls are surrounded by an avenue of massive houses, built of baked earth—old dwellings whose thick walls slope inwards and are painted with the usual rows of gods or devils, in blue or red, on their frontages. Broken staircases lead to verandas which overhang the street, and there parties of Indian women are sitting in the evening air, looking around or dreaming, braceleted creatures, often fair to look upon in their transparent muslin veils.

A troop of little girls, whose curiosity seems insatiable, follow me in my walk around the temple. The eldest may be eight years old, and all are charming. They wear golden rings on their ankles and in their noses, and look frankly at me with eyes that are painted into an almond shape.

It is expected that a great pilgrimage will arrive

shortly before nightfall, so I walk slowly round the crested walls while awaiting it. The avenue behind the temples is more lonely, and were it not for my escort it would be dismal ; but the little girls follow closely behind me, stopping when I stop, and when I push forward the tinkling of their metal-encircled limbs tells me that they are hastening forward also.

The great, white, rose-veined temple is still far from me, as it is in the centre of the square, round which I am walking, but there are many smaller temples clustered round the outer walls which I can see better. All have the same pumpkin-like shape, but they are cracked and blackened, and show signs of extreme old age. The giant in the middle, however, seems quite young, for it is quite white. Its shape, though, is an unexpected one. The bronze disc crowned with gleaming points and the childishly barbaric shape might make one think that it had been built by the denizens of the moon, or of some other planet. As usual, flocks of birds are flying madly round before seeking their evening shelter in the temple.

The little girls and I reach the third side of the forbidden square. Here many beautiful dreamers are gathered on the verandas, and there is a market being held in the street where fruits, rice, flowers, and painted muslins are being displayed for sale.

The sun has set, and all the earth is in shadow, but the temple is still bathed in rosy hues. It is nearly time for the sacred monkeys to take their customary evening walk. I see one on the crest of the sacred wall, where he sits and scratches himself, but as he squats there he can hardly be distinguished from the little gods and other monsters that are sculptured on the ramparts. Soon another comes and perches on a neighbouring crest, a third, a fourth, and now the walls are all alive with monkeys.

The light is fast fading. Only the upper part of the pyramid has a luminous rosy tint, the rest of the huge temple looks gray and old. On the edge of the wall there are stone-coloured monkeys and stone monsters of the colour of monkeys, and there are vultures perched everywhere. In the air clouds of crows and pigeons fly in narrowing circles round the disc of bronze.

Now it is time for the monkeys to take their evening walk. First one lets go his hold, glides down the wall, jumps to the ground and boldly crosses the street, the groups of merchants respectfully standing aside ; then others, running on all fours, follow him in single file. Were it not for their long legs one might have said that they were dogs with odd and frisky manners, and tails carried high in the air. The first monkey steals a plum from a basket as he passes ; the others do likewise, all from the same basket. Now they clamber quickly up the sides of a house and the mysterious procession disappears among the roofs.

On the outer walls of the temple a horrible black and grinning idol of Pandavas, twice the height of a man, dwells in a sort of shelter made of branches and palm-matting. An old priest mounts on a stool and places a garland of yellow flowers round the idol's neck ; then, after lighting a tiny lamp, makes many obeisances and tinkles a little bell. This done, he draws the curtains for the night, and goes away, still bowing. Something flits stealthily past my face : a large bat of the kind called " vampires," which has come out before its usual time and now flies low and fearlessly among the crowd.

A faint rosy glimmer lingers on the point of the tower, and the hour sacred to Brahma is at hand. The temple resounds with music and outcries, which reach me in a confused hum. What can be happening within the forbidden temple ? What fearful idols receive the evening homage of the people ? and what form can prayer assume in these souls, as impenetrable to me as the temple itself ?

One monkey, meanwhile, has remained seated on the crest of the wall, with his back turned on the people standing in the street, and his tail hanging over the edge of the coping. He looks sadly at the light fading from the top of the pyramid, on whose summit whirling clouds of crows and pigeons are taking

up their night quarters, and at the veins and projections of the monstrous building, now black with birds
whose wings still flap. I can scarcely see more than
the outlines of the monkey's form, though the nearly
human back and the pensive head with its pricked
ears stand out plainly against the rosy pallor of the
enormous tower.

Again the sensation of noiseless fanning, as the bat
flits backwards and forwards without heeding me.

The monkey looks at the great pyramid, I look at the
monkey, and the little girls look at me. An equal want
of comprehension divides each of us from the other.

I have taken up my position once more near the
chief entrance to the temple, on that sandy stretch
where the main street of Juggernaut ends. The crowd,
assembled to await the arrival of the pilgrims, now, as
they tell me, close at hand, grows denser every minute.

The sacred cattle are there, too, wandering among
the crowd. There is one especially petted by the
children, huge, quite white, and doubtless very old.
There is also a small black cow with five legs, and a
gray one which has six. The extra legs, however, are
too short to reach the ground, and hang from their
sides like dead or withered limbs.

Far away, at the end of the street, I can at last see
the pilgrims. There are some two or three hundred,
and their flat, grass parasols are open, though it is full
dusk. Wallets and gourds hang from their waists, and
shells and charms are fastened all about them. Their
faces and chests are powdered with ashes, and they
walk with feverish haste, as if the sight of the sacred
edifice had kindled the fire of religion within them.

Now music comes from a balcony, which is placed
above the entrance to the temple; cries of human voices
mingle with the tom-toms; sacred horns howl dolefully.

The pilgrims hasten forward, and when they have
reached the open space, throw down their clothes, parasols, wallets, and rush tumultuously, and like a crowd
of maniacs, through the doors guarded by the monsters
up the stairways and into the yawning temple.

The night has come, and I must go to seek the " Travellers' Rest," which, as in most towns, will probably be far distant, and almost in the country.

I find it in a little sandy waste, where the rocking sound of the sea is heard; that sound which is the same on every shore. I can see neither Juggernaut nor its strange tower, for both are drowned in dark blue shades. The smell of the sea and of the little wild plants with which the sands are carpeted, takes my melancholy musings away from the Gulf of Bengal to the land of my childhood, to the shores of the Isle of Oleron.

Only those can know the charms and all the bitter sadness of far journeyings who have an unconquerable attachment for their native land grafted in their souls.

III

THE WHITE SPLENDOURS OF THE GREAT MOGULS

Express trains now make it possible to annihilate space in India, just as they do with us. So I return in forty-eight hours from Juggernaut on the shores of the Gulf of Bengal to the region where the dry wind of famine blows, travelling across the dreary northern plains and passing Benares, which I still dread and hesitate to visit, and now I am in the Mohammedan city of Agra.

To any one coming, as I do, from Brahmin India for the first time, the most striking feature is the absolute change in the character of the religious monuments. Mosques replace pagodas, and a sober, precise, and elegant art takes the place of wanton luxury. Instead of the orgy and promiscuity of gods and monsters, which characterize the temples of the Pourana divinities, we see that the places of worship of the land of Agra are decorated by pure geometrical lines which arabesque amidst white marbles, with here and there a few formal flowers traced on their polished surfaces.

The Great Moguls! Those words sound to-day like the title of some old Oriental fairy-story, like the name of some legend

16

Here they lived, those magnificent monarchs, masters of the vastest empire that the world has ever seen. The city of Agra is still commanded by one of their enormous palaces, and it still stands much as they left it, though there are traces of ruin and poverty which they never can have known.

Under the burning clouds of dust, and whirling flights of crows, vultures, and eagles, the city of Agra remains as of old.

A marriage procession, preceded by huge drums, sallies forth as I enter. The husband is a lad of sixteen, he is dressed in red and green velvet and is mounted on a white horse. The wife, who cannot be seen, follows in a palanquin which is shut in; then come attendants, carrying on their heads the wedding presents in gilt chests, and closing in are four men pompously bearing on their shoulders the gilded marriage bed.

The houses are old and very tall, widening out towards the top, with overhanging galleries and balconies. On the ground floor are merchants who sell a thousand gaudy things which quiver with silks and spangles. On the first floor bayadères and courtesans, black and heavy-browed, lean from the windows, and above, many humble people live, whose curtains are kept discreetly drawn. On the roofs I can always see perching vultures and sometimes troops of monkeys, who either muse, or else watch the folk below. It is centuries since the monkeys first invaded Agra and made their homes like parrots on the roofs, and certain ruined quarters are almost given over to them, where they live at their pleasure, pillaging the surrounding gardens and markets.

From the distance the palace of Agra seems almost like a mountain of red sandstone that bristles with fierce battlements. Looking at these blood-coloured and gloomy prison walls one wonders how the court of the magnificent emperors could have used this spot as the scene on which their fantastic luxury was displayed. If, however, we approach from the riverside, where the sacred Jumna runs beneath its shady walls, alhambras of white lace appear, looking like some dreamland palaces, which by chance had sprung from the flanks of a rugged fortress of Titans. It was up there that the great Moguls and their sultanas lived, overlooking everything, almost in the sky, inaccessible and secluded amidst the whiteness and transparence of pure marble.

We enter through arched doors, not unlike vaulted tunnels, piercing the triple ramparts, and then we mount imposing stairways of the same deep sandstone hue.

Suddenly a diaphanous pallor dawns upon us, great white and silent splendour, for we have reached the marble palaces. Everything is white—pavement, walls, pillars, ceilings, and the chiselled balustrades of terraces which face the far-off hills. Here and there a few flowers are graven on the spotless walls, flowers worked in mosaics of agate and of porphyry, but they are so fine, so rare, and yet so simply wrought, that the snowy look of the palace is in no way changed. Silence and abandonment are everywhere, but everything is as clear and sharp as on the day which saw the banishment of the last emperor. Time has only left the faintest trace on all this marble. These exquisite things, so fragile, and of an appearance so delicate, are, compared with us, almost eternal.

A melancholy garden also was perched up there, on this artificial mountain, in the very centre of the enormous, closely shut-in citadel. It is surrounded by large porches of marble, which look like the entrances to white grottos, from the vaults of which stalactites hang down. But these are no natural grottos, for the smallest carvings on their vaulted ceilings are wondrously exact ; the least facet of their complex arches is geometrically precise. A narrow black line, which looks as though it had been traced with the tip of a brush, edges all these arabesqued designs. This is the work of no painter's brush, but a very skilful inlay of onyx.

These halls of melancholy splendour are doorless and either open into one another or lead to terraces through great arched openings. This would convey a sense of trustfulness were it possible to forget how these palaces were guarded by terrible bastions underneath. There is even an open terrace on which audiences were given, decorated with the most refined simplicity ; just a few masterly carvings of the marble, nothing more. Then there is a black marble throne for the Great Mogul, and by the side of it a white marble stool for the Court buffoon, and that is all. In those days, it appears, political discussions were of such serious import that the presence of the fool was needed so as to give relief to the minds of the debaters. We all know that in political gatherings to-day there is no need to select any special fool for this purpose.

The Emperor's bathroom is white—that goes without saying—snowy white, with an inextricable tangle of lines, arches, and sculptured windows. The sonorous vaulted roofs are carved into facets and look as if they were powdered with frozen milk. A few graceful flower-sprays are engraved at random over the marble walls, the meanest of which is a marvel of gold and lapis lazuli mosaic.

On the extreme edge of the ramparts which support the whole building, on the side of the Jumna and the great open plains, there are many little buildings and tiny kiosks overlooking the country in which the sultanas and veiled beauties used to sit and taste the evening air. It is here that the lace-like traceries of the marble give the most wonderful effects. The walls are transparent, but only from within, and the single plaques, of which they are constructed, are so elaborately worked that at a distance they resemble costly embroideries, stretched between slender and charming columns. Yet these traceries, which look so perishable and delicate, embody the most lasting and most ruinously beautiful creations that man has ever made. In the lower parts of this monstrous building there are other chambers, some even in the solid rock, rooms that are half in shadow, and whose magnificence has a furtive look. Among others are the baths of the

Grand Sultana, a kind of vast enchanted cavern where one feels an earthly chill, and where the feeble light drops from the ceiling like a shower of rain which frost has turned to ice. The walls are covered with mosaics made of silvered glass, but their lustre has been tarnished by damp and age, and the myriad prisms only shimmer now with the delicate reflections of worked brocade. In the old days this hidden place was peopled by all the fairest and most beautiful that the Indian race could offer, and the still untarnished stones and benches where they lay and rested are yet haunted by their youthful amber forms.

A royal fortress was situated here long before the arrival of the conquering Moguls, who introduced these milk-white marbles and these geometrical ornamentations. There still are some rooms where the archaic carvings on the sandstone dates from the Jaïna kings. At the bottom of the gloomy staircase, hollowed from the solid rock, one comes to strange and fearsome places, dungeons where people were thrown to the cobras, the room in which sultanas met their fate, bottomless black holes and underground passages leading to charnel- or to treasure-houses which no one dares to explore. These are the deep and noxious roots of the lily-like splendour which blooms above.

After leaving these gloomy vaults I return to the kiosks, whose fine traceries advance to the edge of the ramparts, and whose balconies overhang the yawning depths below. I linger awhile in places where the beauties and sultanas of bygone times, secluded in this palace far above the wheeling flights of birds, have stood and gazed between the marble plaques and fluted columns. All the surroundings are of exquisite refinement. Mosaic flowers and minute carvings are scattered over the unvarying white background and everything here looks whiter than elsewhere, though a lingering sadness seems to hover round this spot. Doubtless, the view that the sultanas saw was less desolate than it is now ; the same plains extending to the horizon, the same wandering river, but the wind of famine did not blow nor did that death-like haze of dust hang over the land like some dreadful pall. Beneath the balconies and almost under their feet, the belles could overlook the arena where bloody fights between elephants and tigers were given for their sport ; but now the courtyard is overgrown with shrubs and trees whose leaves have been withered by the drought.

In no part of India are the birds so numerous or so troublesome as they are here. Their cries are the only sounds which reach me on the lonely terraces, and the pale marbles echo with their screams. As twilight comes on the winged crowd seems to segregate. One tree below me is black with crows ; another is so thronged with parrots that it looks as though its dead branches had once again put forth leaves. White-bosomed eagles and bald-headed vultures wander tamely round the abandoned circus.

Amongst the distant plains white cupolas, of that diaphanous pearliness that no artifice can ever imitate, are seen rising from the dusty haze that covers all the land, a haze which turns from blue to purple in the evening twilight. These are the resting-places of the princesses who once trod these lofty terraces, and, arrayed in gold-striped muslins and precious stones, displayed their naked loveliness. The largest dome is that of the Taj, Taj the incomparable, where the great sultana, Montaz-i-Mahal, sleeps since two hundred and seventy years ago. Everybody has seen and has described the Taj, which is known as one of the classic wonders of the world. Enamels and miniatures still preserve the features of the much-beloved Montaz-i-Mahal and of her husband, the sultan, who created the place, wishing to enshroud his dead wife with unheard-of splendour. Standing in a park-like cemetery that is walled in like a fortress, the Taj is the largest and most stainless mass of marble that the world has seen. The walls of this park and the high cupolas rising over the four outer gates are of red sandstone encrusted with alabaster, but the artificial lakes, shady groves, and boskages of palm and cypress that lie within display a cold formality of tracing. Out of these the incomparable monument towers forth in a whiteness which the surrounding sombre greenery seems to enhance. An immense cupola and four minarets, lofty as towers, stand on a white pediment, and everywhere the same restful purity of outline and the same calm and supremely simple harmony of tone pervade a colossal edifice entirely built of white marble, diapered by almost imperceptible lines of a pale gray.

On coming nearer, delicate arabesques of thin black marble inlay are observed, which damascene the walls and underline the cornices, twining round the doors and minarets.[1]

Under the central cupola, which is seventy-five feet high, the sultana sleeps. Here there is nothing but the most superb simplicity, only a great white splendour. It should be dark here, but it is as light as if these whitenesses were self-illuminating, as if this great carved sky of marble had a vague transparence. There is nothing on the walls but veins of pearly gray and a few faintly outlined arches, and on the dome's white firmament nothing but those facets traced as with a compass, which imitate the crystal pendants of some stalactite cave. Around the pediment, however, there is a bordering of great lilies sculptured in bold relief. Their stalks seem to spring out of the ground, and the marble flowers look as if their petals were about to fall. This decoration, which flourished in India in the seventeenth century, has now been more or less indifferently imitated by our modern Western art.

The wonder of wonders is the white grille that stands in the centre of the translucent hall and incloses the tomb of the sultana. It is made of plaques of marble placed upright, so finely worked that it might be thought that they were carved in ivory. On each marble upright and each stud with which these fretted marble plaques are surrounded little garlands of tulips, fuchsias, and immortelles are worked in mosaics of

---

[1] The Taj formerly had doors of solid silver. These were taken away when Agra was sacked by Suraj-Mall.

turquoise, topaz, porphyry, or lapis lazuli. The
sonority of this white mausoleum is almost terrifying,
for the echoes never seem to cease. If the name of
Allah is intoned the exaggerated echo lasts for several
seconds and then lingers in the air like the faint breath
of an organ.

Behind the formidable ramparts of Delhi, about
sixty leagues farther north, the Great Moguls had
another enchanted palace even more magnificent than
the one at Agra.

The great pointed arches of the Delhi palace look
on to a garden shut in by high and crested walls.
The splendour of the delicate structure has never been
exceeded, but it is a prison if only for fairies and genii.
What need to say that it is of the whitest marble, or
that the ceilings rain their frosted icicles upon the
matchless carvings ? But here masses of gold mingle
with the whiteness of the marble, and their colours
blend into a new harmony. The thousand wondrously
chiselled arabesques lining the walls and roof appear
in a setting of sparkling gold.

No other light but that which comes through the
arches opening on to the garden enters the palace, so
that the columns and indented arches which succeed
each other in a diminishing perspective appear to fade
into a thin blue haze, yet all the roofs and walls seem
to have the transparency of alabaster.

The throne-room, which contained the famous peacock throne of emeralds and gold, is entirely white and
gold. In some of the rooms the tall marble walls are
strewn with bouquets of roses, roses like the roses of
a Chinese embroidery, with tints varying from bright
to pale pink, and whose every petal is faintly edged
with gold. In other rooms there are blue flowers of
lapis and of turquoise. Each room generally opens
into the adjoining one, only being separated from it
by one of those lace-like marble plaques which replace
the hangings of our uncouth abodes.

The famine-bearing wind harries the thickets of the
lonely garden and scatters their last leaves like an

autumn tempest ; whirlwinds of dead leaves invade the silent palace and the white pavement where the precious throne once stood.

IV

AMONG THE RUINS

The land in which the Mogul emperors lived is now but a winding-sheet for ruined towns and palaces. Egypt herself cannot boast so many ruins on her sands as this decaying region. There, on the banks of the Nile, is the land of monstrous granite temples ; here, chiselled marbles and fretted stones lie like lost souls scattered about these sad wastes.

India, cauldron in which the first human intelligence seethed, is filled with innumerable wrecks of bygone days, whose beauty and profusion plunge us into bewilderment. Besides the towns which fell into decay through wars and massacres, there are others whose magnificence rose into being at the whim of some sovereign, but never was completed. There are palaces, too, raised by a myriad workmen to gratify the longing of some sultana which have never known an occupant.

Between Delhi and that capital of olden times where the great tower of Kuth stands, built of pink granite, the road is lined with ruined fortresses and phantom towns, great crested walls with moats and drawbridges. Within, no living soul. The silence is only broken by monkeys rushing through the bushes or clambering up the heaps of fallen stones.

There are cemeteries, too, almost boundless in extent. For miles the earth has been filled with the dead, and funeral pavilions and tombs of all ages are heaped together in a bewildering labyrinth of crumbling ruins.

Some tombs, hidden among the myriad trees whose wreckage strews the ground, are still kept up in a spirit of splendid piety, but it would be impossible to find the paths which lead up to them through the heaps of stone and holes and yawning pits were they not mapped out by swarms of maimed and leprous

beggars who solicit alms from the passing pilgrims,
It is strange, indeed, to one who follows these dusty
tracks to come upon some marvellous mausoleum with
walls of fretted marble hung with red silks and decked
with carpets, over which bunches of fresh gardenias
and tuberoses are strewn.   The most splendid of these
are the tombs of the fakirs and the dervishes of the
olden days, who lived lives of purposed wretchedness and
complete renunciation, and to whose memory sultans
of long ago paid such madly extravagant honours.

The rose-coloured granite tower was visible on the
horizon of this famine-stricken land long before the
ramparts and the chiselled palaces could be descried.
These nestle at its feet hidden amidst the undulations
of a stony land, where only goats and shepherds dwell.

It is almost the oppressive hour of noon as I pass
through double gates which lead into this phantom
town.   A vast and melancholy space, so vast that its
extent cannot be gauged, extends before me.   All
around are trees dying of drought, whose yellow leaves
are scattered by the parching wind, and shapeless
heaps of stones, domes, and towers, so worn as to resemble rocks.   By the foot of the tower there are those
remains of pompous magnificence which mark that this
was once royal ground.

All styles are mingled in these glorious relics.   So
many wars and invasions have passed over the place,
so many buildings have been razed to the ground, and
have sprung up anew, phoenix-like from their ruins,
that it is no longer possible to retrace the history of
this land of shades.

I take refuge from the midday heat in the shadow of
a palace which belonged to a king whose name is now
but a legend, and I occupy the corner of a high gallery,
a sort of loggia overlooking a hall filled with great
square columns which are emblazoned with archaic
sculptures.   Here for some hours I may sleep or muse
alone, or seek to penetrate the spirit that once animated
these ruins, or if not that the thoughts of the animals
which now inhabit it.   Outside, the torrid sun parches

the desert lands : the grasshoppers are still, and the flies no longer busy. Only from time to time the screech of a parrot retur ing to its shady nest among the carvings, or the rustling of dry leaves chased past the pillars by the famine wind.   Nothing else is to be heard.

The ceiling is made of long superposed granite blocks, placed in pyramids like the beams of our old timber-work.   This kind of roofing denotes a period when men knew nothing about building vaults or domes, or if they did know of them, mistrusted such work.   Under me lies a forest of superb monolithic blocks whose squared frontages carry the mind back to the earliest Hindoo period.   From the dim corner where I sit I can look out through the large bayed openings, and I see the red sandstones, the fiery granites and the porphyries below, enkindled in the blazing sun.   Wonderful porticoes rear their many-pointed arches inscribed with Kufic characters into the clear transparent air.   An obelisk of black iron, covered with Sanskrit writing, and dating from an unknown age, rises out from among the tombs from a paved place which was the central court of a most sacred mosque, once said to be the most beautiful in the world.

I hear a light trotting on the pavement below. Three goats, followed by their kids, enter the palace and without any hesitation clamber up to the high gallery where I am standing.   Here, full of unconcern, they lie down to take their midday nap.   Crows and turtle-doves also come to the cool shade and settle down and sleep.

Then all is silence, unbroken even by the sound of the dead leaves, for the wind slumbers now like all else.

At the back of my loggia there is a little window, from which I ought to see the sky, but I only see a white embroidery on a rosy background, which seems to be suspended in the air at an uncertain distance from me.   It is the great tower whose marble incrustations gleam in the rosy granite.

This is the last halting-place before I reach Benares, the town which I so dread.   I shall be there in two days, for it has been impossible for me to dally longer, and I must face the supreme disenchantment which I feel sure awaits me. The peace that hovers about these ruins steals over me, and I think of the House of the Masters, whose strange and frugal hospitality I am soon to share.

The burning hazes beckon me to sleep and dreams, but my mind is still occupied with the great tower which rises near at hand. A king built it, so the legend tells, to satisfy the whim of his daughter, who wished to see the wanderings of a far-distant river. As I draw nearer the window, the tower comes into full view, and I see its rosy shaft rising into the sky implacably pure. The eye is bewildered by its height and slimness, which surpass those of all known towers or minarets, and the swelling of the base gives it an oddly curved appearance. It is astonishing to see a monument so splendid and so marvellously preserved rising from this desert strewn with ruins.

The stone is of so fine a grain and such a polish that centuries have never tarnished its perfection, and its fresh colour is matchlessly preserved. The flutings which traverse the entire length of the column look like folds in a fabric, or tucks in some lady's silken gown, and the whole tower is pleated with them like a closed parasol. One thinks also of a stack of organ pipes, or of a bundle of huge palm trunks, knotted at intervals with embroidered bands, which are the granite galleries loaded with Islamite inscriptions in white mosaic. Drowsiness comes over me. Suddenly there are footsteps beneath me, hasty footsteps unexpectedly breaking the long silence. Some twelve men appear, glowing with crude colours, whose blues and whites and golds break the monotony of the great ruddy stones. They are Mussulmans from the north, Afghans with pointed caps which fall over their faces, so that only their hooked noses and jet-black beards are visible. They walk quickly and have a false and cruel look. Concealed in my unsuspected hiding-place I can watch them at my leisure, and it is soon evident that they are only pilgrims who have come on some pious errand. They pause reverently before the porticoes of the ruined mosques or stop to kiss the tombs, and then, always with the same haste, move farther off, and at last disappear among the ruins.

It is now three o'clock and life's pulses stir once more. The green parrots peer from their holes, and with beaks hooked into the carvings look downwards. Then they fly off with the fierce cry of newly-wakened life. The three goats awaken too, and take their kids to pasture amid the short and burnt-up grass. I also descend and wander in the phantom town.

Ruined houses, ruined temples, ruins of mausoleums and of palaces ; and, here and there, lean flocks that nibble among the stones, and spread out over this vast, melancholy, and walled-in plain.

The shepherds play on muted pipes, as if saddened by the presence of the crumbling temples ; and in the midst of all this desolation the rose tower seems to keep a sleepless vigil.

There are still balconies overlooking open spaces which once were avenues, loggias jutting from the crumbling walls from which beauties of bygone ages could see elephants passing in purple pomp, processions of mailed warriors, and the moving crowds of the wondrous olden days.

Oh ! the sadness of these balconies and these deserted streets.

V

THE FUNERAL PYRES

A gray winter's evening on the Ganges. The night-mists rise from the sacred river and dull the rays of the declining sun. The dark outlines of the crumbling palaces and temples of Benares rear their black shadows against the still luminous Western sky.

Amongst the slumbering boats mine is the only one that is in motion. We drift slowly, at the foot of the sacred town, amidst the shadows of monstrous temples

and of frowning palaces. Three rainless famine years
have so lowered the water's level that the height of
the buildings above it seems increased, and the very
foundations of Benares are uncovered. Fragments of
palaces which have been submerged for centuries rear
their heads among the motionless barques, and ruins
of temples that have been swallowed up and forgotten
come to light. The old Ganges bares its bed of mystery
and desolation.

The ravaged banks attest the mad rages of a sacred
river that is both life-giver and life-destroyer, and that,
like the god Siva, begets but to destroy. Nothing can
resist the terrible force of its floods during the rainy
season ; stately walls of granite and whole embankments have slipped in a solid mass into the stream,
where, fantastic forms, they rest, as though hurled
there by an earthquake. Security is felt only some
thirty or forty feet away from highwater mark, and it
is there that the first windows, balconies, and miradors
are to be seen. Below that the Ganges is the master,
and everything is every year submerged. All buildings are constructed with that fact kept in mind by the
builders ; kiosks, massive as casemates, sheltering
heavy and thick-set gods, cyclopean embankments and
monstrous blocks that seem unmovable, but which
sometimes totter in the fury of the waters.

The pyramids of countless temples rise into the
evening air, high above the houses and palaces, and,
like those of Rajput, resemble carved stone yew trees,
but there is red, dull red, mingled with a dying gold.
These are so frequent as to cover all Benares. Along
the whole length of the town, which follows the bend
of the river in a matchless crescent, granite steps, like
those of a pedestal, descend from the habitations to the
very edge of the sacred stream. To-day the lowest
steps are visible, portent of famine and death, for they
are only uncovered in tears of drought. The majestic
stairways are now deserted ; up to noon they were
thronged by crowds of merchants selling fruits and
grasses for the sacred cattle, or flower-sellers whose

stalls were heaped with the garlands and bouquets which worshippers offer to the river in token of respect. The parasols of dried grass, under which everybody shelters, are still there, open and resting on their handles, parasols without folds which resemble metal discs. The terraces and stairways are so thickly covered with these as to look like a battle-field with the bucklers planted in limitless array. A dull twilight comes on and the air grows chill. I had not thought to see this wintry aspect and such gray skies here. My boat drifts at the current's will, sometimes grazing the shores, whose edges are overhung by gloomy palaces.

We come to a sinister-looking spot situated amid the ruins of overthrown palaces. On the blackened soil there are little heaps of sticks which ragged men of evil look are trying to light, and these little heaps, which smoke but will not burn, are of a peculiar long and narrow shape—funeral piles for the dead.

A dead body is laid on each of them with feet pointing towards the river, and, on drawing nigh, I can see the toes projecting among the sticks. How small the heaps are and how little wood it must take to burn a corpse! My Hindoo boatman explains to me that these are the pyres of the poor and that the wood is damp; that they had no money to buy any more.

Now the hour of Brahma is at hand and evening worship begins all along the stream. Brahmins draped in thin veils descend from all the stairways, hastening to fetch the sacred water for their rites and ablutions such as their rank prescribes. Multitudes throng the granite steps, just now so deserted, and the thousand little rafts anchored in the shadow of the temples or the palaces, and the thousand bamboo resting-places made for the hour of prayer, are crowded with dreamers who sit motionless in the posture which time has consecrated. The thoughts of the praying multitudes are soon lost in the unfathomable depths of the world beyond, that mysterious beyond into which our ephemeral personalities must shortly melt.

In the quarter of the dead and near the smoking

pyres two other human forms are, each resting on a frail litter. They are wrapped in muslin, and their bodies are half plunged into the river. These, like the living, are taking their bath in the sacred stream, their one last supreme bath before being placed on the piles of wood which are now being prepared.

The mists of evening settle on the opposite shore, a flat plain of mud and grass annually inundated by the Ganges. Gradually these vapours take shape, as may be seen in rainy skies, and the river banks are blotted out. I look upon the crescent of the sacred city, rising into the air, and it seems to me that its buildings have ranged themselves like the spectators of a theatre to watch the clouds that assembled at their feet.

A young fakir, whose long hair falls upon his shoulders, stands by the abode of the dead in a rigid attitude, with his head turned towards the smoking heaps of wood and their gruesome burdens. Though covered with white dust he is still beautiful and muscular. His chest is decked with a garland of marigolds, such a garland as the people here cast upon the river's breast.

A little way above the funeral heaps some five or six persons crouch upon the frieze of an old palace, which fell into the river long ago. Their heads are wrapped in veils, and, like the fakir, they stare fixedly at their kinsman who is being burned.

Two people especially, who seem to have the crouching attitude that betokens old age, look anxiously at the smallest of the pyres. It is only a little boy of ten years old, as my Hindoo boatman tells me after inquiring from people standing on the shore, but all the same they have brought too little wood for the purpose of burning his body. The smoke mounts up to the motionless pair, the smoke of their little one who now begins to burn, for the attendant has fanned the flame with his coarse loin-cloth. Temples and palaces look calmly on this blackened resting-place, and in the hazy air their magnificence seems to mock these slow cremations of the poor whose misery accompanies them even in death. A new occupant for the funeral pyres is seen at the top of the great staircase. A fifth body emerges from a dark passage and journeys to the Ganges where its ashes will be cast. On a litter of bamboo branches six half-nude and ragged men of lowly caste carry the corpse, feet foremost, down the steep incline. No one follows, no one weeps ; and children on their way to bathe skip merrily round as if they saw nothing. It is only the soul that counts at Benares, and when that has fled the rest is hastily disposed of. It is only the poor who accompany the dead, fearing lest there may not be wood enough or that the attendants may throw unburnt remains into the river.

A rose-coloured muslin of gorgeous design covers this corpse, and white gardenias and red hibiscus flowers are knotted round its loins. It has the form of a woman, which the flowers also show, and admirable, too, in spite of the chill touch of death, does the form reveal itself. " The daughter of a rich house," my boatman says. " Look at the beautiful wood which they have brought."

To await her coming I tell my boatman to stop upon the yellow, troubled, and slimy waters of the Ganges, where filth and weeds are always cloaked by flowers. Countless tuberoses, Indian pinks, marigolds, and necklets of the yellow flower, which are daily offered to the sacred river, float down this foul-smelling water. Golden blossoms cover the scum that clings to the banks and mingle with the human ashes in the fellowship of decay.

Entrusted to the common men who bear her like a thing of no account, the body of the beautiful dead woman comes down.

When she has reached the edge of the water, close by my boat, the porters place her on the muddy shore, with half the body in the water for her final bath. One of the men bends over her, and with some trace of respect uncovers the face, that she may take a supreme last look at the river. Then, following the prescribed rites, stoops and fills the hollow of his hand with the Ganges waters, which he pours into her mouth. I can

17

now see her long closed eyes, with their dark fringes, and her straight and delicate nose and her full cheeks. Lips of an exquisite shape are half closed on her pearly teeth. She must have been very beautiful, and no doubt that some evil chance came to cut her off in the full bloom of youth, for she has changed so little. The pink muslin in which she is wrapped has become wet and clings transparently to her, clings to her bosom and loins and does not hide her matchless nudity. . . . To think that all this loveliness should have been given to common porters, and that fire will claim it soon ! It is now the turn of one of the other two waiting in the sacred stream, a man huddled in a white muslin wrap, whom they carry to the pyre. He has not stiffened, and his head rolls from side to side before it settles on the wooden pillow. Now they cover him with branches, and now set fire to the bottom of the pile. As for the little boy, he is still burning badly, and his black smoke enfolds the motionless pair who stand watching.

It will soon be time for the birds to rest, but it even seems to me that they are more plentiful in Benares than in other parts of India. Swarms of crows, uttering hoarse cries, and clouds of pigeons wheel round and round, and each temple tower has its particular crowd, flying in circles like stones hurled from a sling. The deepening river-mists grow colder, and the odour of decay is ranker in the evening air.

I should like to stay longer to see them place the young goddess on her pyre, but that will not be for a long while yet, and the damp, transparent muslin almost makes it embarrassing to look further at her. It seems sacrilege to look at her since she is dead. No ! Let us away. I will return later when her time has come.

What a tireless destroyer, the Ganges ! So many palaces have fallen into its waters, whole frontages have slipped away without breaking, and lie there half submerged ; and so many temples ! Those that are built too near the water have their towers twisted like the leaning tower of Pisa and are irremediably undermined. Only those which are situated higher up and whose basements have been protected by heaps of granite or by old substructures have kept their red or golden towers erect, but what a strange aspect these towers have ! Seeking a comparison, I might have said, " a churchyard yew tree," but the aspect of these towers is stranger than that, for there are bundles of little steeples, and myriads of tiny spires, all resembling each other, and of the unvarying traditional form for which no parallel can be found in the range of Western architecture.

All Brahma's people are now gathered by the deep water, and the thousand little rafts bend under the weight of the praying multitudes. Gray staircases, foundations, and mud-coloured walls, which seem the bared roots of the sacred city, tower above the people, whose hands are joined in prayer, or who throw offerings of flowers into the river.

My barque leisurely ascends the stream and passes a spot where lonely old palaces congregate, and where there are no rafts moored to the shore. (All the rajahs of the surrounding country have a palace on the Ganges where they seek a retreat from time to time.)

The massive walls rear straight into the air without interruption ; the windows, the balconies, and the life of these impenetrable buildings only showing themselves at a higher level.

There is music within, this evening, a stifled, groaning breath of music, and bagpipes, which have a hautbois note, wail forth thin melancholy sound. Sometimes it is but a single phrase, a lamentation which rises and falls ; then there is silence, perhaps broken by the croak of a raven, and from a neighbouring palace an answering plaint is heard. Tom-toms resound with measured blows, like the slow tolling of a passing bell. Oh ! the mystery, the unspeakable sadness of these sounds, which float over my head as my boat glides on these death-tainted waters. To me it sounds like the death-wail for the young girl whose image is still before my eyes ; the swan-song of so many other beings and things that are no more.

I had not foreseen the gray skies and the wintry aspect of this sacred city, nor had I thought that I should find the old self of former days reviving in me, ever a prey to the allurements of the new and strange, and the seductions of the outer world. I had hoped to find peace and deliverance at the house of the Masters in the hallowed air of Benares, this city that is as the heart of a sacred land. My promised initiation commences to-morrow, but in spite of this I feel more than ever enthralled by all that is beautiful and transitory, and by the things of the kingdom which owns Death as lord.

It is quite dark as I return to the pyres, and the birds no longer fly in circles, but have settled in long rows on the cornices of the palaces and temples, forming black cordons which still tremble with the last fluttering of their wings. The towers of the Brahmin temples lose their sharpness of outline and look like black cypress trees rearing their heads into the pale sky.

My boat, with its train of yellow flowers and grasses, has come back to the still waters, which now reek more strongly with a deathly and insipid odour. In order to reach the place where the black smoke from the funeral pyres ascends, I have to pass the praying crowds, and to thread my way among rafts laden with motionless Brahmins. Yet, as my boat floats down the river, these men, in ecstatic attitudes, with their burning eyes fixed on vacancy, never see me as I brush past them. Their dust-coloured faces only seem to me like some far-distant vision.

I reach the quarter of the dead too late. A great pyre is flaming, and whirling sparks and tongues of fire ascend into the air. The young girl is in the midst of it, and nothing can be seen of her but one ghastly foot, whose extended toes seem to tell of agonies of suffering, standing out blackly on a red background of fire.

Four more persons have gathered on the walls which overlook the burning ghat, too closely veiled for their features to be recognized. They sit and look with tranquillity that almost seems indifference : relatives, no

doubt, perhaps even the parents from whom she in-
herited her matchless beauty.

How much must these beliefs (into which I am to be
initiated to-morrow) change these people's views of life
and death! A soul has passed away, a soul that scarce
knew itself, and which, moreover, was not akin to
theirs, a soul, maybe, that had been conscious for
centuries and centuries, and had but taken fleeting
shape in this daughter of their flesh. Later, no doubt,
they will meet again, but much later, when ages shall
have run their appointed course.

One of the two poor people who were crouching on
the wall to watch the burning of their little boy rises,
and, unveiling his face so as better to see, approaches
the little heap. The glare from the young girl's funeral
pyre lights up the features of an emaciated old woman.
Is he quite burnt? she seems to ask. She is very old,
a grandmother rather than a mother, for mysterious
sympathies and tendernesses are often seen between
grandparents and grandchildren. But is the body
totally consumed? Her poor eyes are tortured by the
thought that they did not have enough money to buy
the necessary wood, and that the pitiless attendants
might throw some tatters of unburnt flesh into the river.

She stoops again anxiously over the smouldering
heap, while the attendant moves the embers with a
stick to convince her that all has been duly consumed.
Then she makes a sign. " Yes, all is over. You can
throw the rest into the river." On her face, however,
I can see the eternal human agony that is just the same
here as it is with us, that agony which waits for us all
in spite of our courage or our nebulous beliefs. Doubtless this grandmother loved the small transitory form
which has just been destroyed, and doted on its face,
its expression, its smile. Her soul cannot have been
sufficiently detached, and her Brahmin insusceptibility
must have been at fault, for she is weeping.

Even the Christian faith, which is the kindest of all,
does not promise to give us back those childish
smiles and the kind eyes of white-haired grandams.

The attendant takes a wooden shovel, and scatters the embers of the pauper pyre into the river.

On the neighbouring heap the foot of the young girl falls at last into the ashes.

VI

THE HOUSE WHERE THE MASTERS DWELL

At the far end of an old garden stands a low and modest Indian house on which time has left few traces. The whitewashed walls and the green sunblinds remind me of the houses of my birthplace, but this roof slopes forward so as to form a veranda, and the white columns which support it tell of the land of eternal sunshine. But the garden, although neglected, is neither tropical nor strange, and the overhanging Bengal rose bushes shelter sweet old homely walks which resemble ours.

The masters of the house have grave and beautiful faces, the faces of a Christ with bronzed skin and black hair, and they welcome me with soft and radiant smiles and whispered words. Yet sometimes it seemed as if their thoughts were no longer with me, and that they had stolen away—into the other world to join their souls, that had already taken refuge there.

The House of the Masters is always open to those who care to come, and a kindly welcome awaits all.

And yet with what deep and unspeakable terror I knocked at their door, feeling that this was the supreme test, and that, if I found nothing here, I should never find anything anywhere else.

The Masters spend their time in work and meditation, but, like all Hindoos, share their houses with birds and beasts, putting up with gentle resignation with their importunities. Squirrels come in through the windows, sparrows build their nests in the ceilings, and the whole house is full of birds.

In an inner room there is a platform covered by a white cloth for the numerous guests, who sit upon it in Indian fashion while searching for the hidden things. Brahmins are crouching there, whose brows bear the

seals of Vishnu or of Siva, thinkers who wander bare-
foot and with no garment but a coarse cloth wrapped
round their loins, but who have looked on everything,
and for whom the world has no more snares, learned
men who, in their contempt of earthly things, look
like beggars or labourers of the fields, but who have
mastered the latest and most transcendental philosophies of Europe, and who say with tranquil assur-
ance : "Our philosophy begins where yours ends."

The Masters work or meditate the whole day, together or alone. The plain tables before them are
loaded with those Sanskrit books containing the secrets
of that Brahminism which preceded all our religions
and philosophies by so many thousand years.

In these unfathomable books the old thinkers, those
sages who had clearer vision than any men of our race
or age, have inscribed the sum of all human knowledge.
To them the inconceivable was almost clear, and their
long-forgotten works now pass our degenerate under-
standing; and so, to-day, years of initiation are required merely to see, hidden dimly amidst the obscurity
of the words, the unfathomable depths beyond.

If there be any people who can understand, it must
be these sages of Benares, for they are the descendants
of the wondrous philosophers who wrote these books.
Their blood is the same, the blood of men who never
slew and whose bodies were never nourished on the
flesh of other creatures.

Surely their bodies must be less earthly and more
ethereal than ours, and by their long heredity of meditation and prayer they must have reached subtleties
of perception and a delicacy of intuition impossible to
us. But they simply say : " We know nothing and
simply seek to learn."

One high amongst them is a European woman, who
has come here to seek shelter from the turmoil of the
world.

Her face is still beautiful, though crowned with silver
hair, and she lives here, barefooted and detached from
earthly strife, the thrifty and austere life of an ascetic.

It is on her goodwill that I have fixed my hopes, trusting that she may throw open to me the formidable gates of knowledge, for she was once of my race and understands my native tongue.

And yet I am filled with doubts and misgivings, and as if to entrap her in a snare I begin to speak of that other woman who lived here so long among the Masters, whose tarnished fame had caused me to doubt, for it was asserted of her that she was a juggling impostor.

" Do you not think that she is to be excused perhaps ?   Her intentions were good, and perhaps she only practised deceit in order to bring others to believe."

" No, it is never right to cheat.   Nothing can come from falsehood," replied the woman with a frank look. I feel a new and sudden confidence in my teacher.

" Our principles," she said to me a little later, " our dogmas ! We have none.   Amongst the Theosophists (such is the name by which they call us) you will find Buddhists, Brahmins, Mussulmans, Protestants, Catholics, and orthodox people, and even folks like you."

" But what must I do to join you ? "

" Swear to regard all men as your brothers and your equals, and meet them with the same love whether they be beggars or princes.   Swear to seek spiritual truth by all the means in your power.   That is all. Those whom you have lately left at Madras are tinged with Buddhism, from whose cold tenets your mystic temperament has recoiled.   It is in esoteric Brahminism in its oldest form that we find our light and peace.   To us it seems to offer the purest form of truth which men may know.   And we would wish you to journey on our road.   But you know the allegory of ' The Guardians of the Threshold,' those monsters which lurk outside the temples and seek to terrorize the neophyte in his initiation.   Their true meaning is that all knowledge is born with the pangs of labour.   You know that we say that personal individuality is but a faint and ephemeral spark, and for one so personal as you, this, I know, will be hard to learn.   We believe so much that is opposed to all the faiths in which you have been trained. But do not hate us if we pluck out those slumbering hopes which perhaps unconsciously still sustain you."

" No, my hopes are dead. I have none to lose."

" Then come to us. . . ."

VII

IN THE MORNING GLORY

The sun has just risen from the plain through which old Ganges wanders, a plain of mud and vegetation still overshadowed by the mists of night; and waiting there for the first red rays of dawn lie the granite temples of Benares, the rosy pyramids, the golden shafts, and all the sacred city, extended in terraces, as if to catch the first light and deck itself in the glory of the morning.

This is the hour which, since the Brahmin faith began, has been sacred to prayer and to religious ecstasy, and it is now that Benares pours forth all its people, all its flowers, all its garlands, all its birds, and all its living things on to the banks of the Ganges. Awakened by the kiss of the sun, all that have received souls from Brahma rush joyously down the granite steps. The men, whose faces beam with calm serenity, are garbed in Kashmir shawls, some pink, some yellow, and some in the colours of the dawn. The women, veiled with muslins in the antique style, form white groups along the road, and the reflections from their copper ewers and drinking-vessels shimmer amongst the silvery glints of their many bracelets, necklets, and the rings which they wear round their ankles. Nobly beautiful both of face and gait, they walk like goddesses, while the metal rings on their arms and feet murmur musically.

And to the river, already encumbered with garlands, each one comes to offer a new wreath. Some have twisted ropes of jasmine flowers which look like white necklets, others garlands of Indian pinks whose flowers of golden yellow and pale sulphur gleam in contrast, resembling the changing colours of an Indian veil.

And the birds who had been sleeping all along the friezes of the houses and the palaces awake too and fill the air with chirpings and with song in the mad joy of dawn.

Turtle-doves and singing birds hasten to bathe and drink with all these Brahmins and to sport amongst these men who never slay.

In all the temples the gods have their morning serenades, and the angry roar of the tom-toms, the wail of the bagpipes, and the howling of the sacred trumpets are heard from every side.

And up above all the festooned and sculptured windows, from which the east may be seen, are thronged with aged heads, those who from sickness or by reason of old age cannot come down, but who here invoke the morning light. And the sun bathes them in his warm rays.

Naked children holding each other by the hand come in gay throngs ; yoghis and slowly-moving fakirs descend the steps ; the sacred cattle advance with deliberate steps, while people stand respectfully aside offering them fresh wreaths of reeds and flowers. They, too, seem to look on the splendours of the sun, and in their harmless fashion appear to understand and pray.

Next come the sheep and goats ; then dogs and monkeys hurry down the steps.

Now the sun pours streams of warmth into the air which the night dews have chilled. All the granite temples scattered on the steps that serve as niches and altars, some for Vishnu, some for the many-armed Ganesa, protrude into the sunlight their squat little gods—gods which are gray with mud, for they have slept many months under the troubled waters of the river to which the ashes of the dead are consigned.

Now that the rays of the sun are fierce the people shelter under the large umbrellas whose shade awaits them. For these huge parasols, which resemble gigantic mushrooms clustering under the walls of the city, are always left open.

Above me the old palaces seem to have grown

young, and the rosy pyramids, the golden arrows, and all the shining weathercocks glitter in the morning air.

The many rafts and the lower steps are thronged with Brahmins, who, after setting down their flowers and ewers, hasten to disrobe. Pink and white muslins and cashmeres of all colours lie mingled on the ground, or are hung over bamboo canes, and now the matchless nude forms appear, some of pale bronze, others of a deeper shade.

The men, slim and of athletic build, plunge to their waists into the sacred waters. The women, still wearing a veil of muslin round their shoulders and waists, merely plunge their many-ringed arms and ankles into the Ganges ; then they kneel at the extremest edge and let fall their long unknotted coils of hair into the water. Then, raising their heads once more, they allow the water dripping from their drenched hair to fall upon their necks and bosoms. And now with their tightly-clinging draperies they look like some statue of a " winged Victory," more beautiful and more voluptuous than if they had been nude.

From all sides the bowing people shower their garlands and their flowers into the Ganges ; all fill their ewers and jars and then, stooping, fill their hollowed hands and drink. Here religious feeling reigns supreme, and no sensual thought ever seems to assail these beauteous mingled forms. They come into unconscious contact with each other, but only heed the river, the sun, and the splendour of the morning in a dream of ecstasy.

And when the long ritual is ended, the women retire to their homes, while the men, seated on the rafts amid their garlands, dispose themselves for prayer.

Oh ! the joyful awakenings of this primeval race, praying in daily unison to God, where the poorest may find room amongst the splendours of the sun, the waters, and the flowers.

And to think of the awakening of our sordid human ant-heaps, of the men who are a smoke and iron age, where, under our old and cloudy sky, the mob, poisoned with alcohol and blasphemy, hasten towards the murderous mills.

The white groups of women mount the stairs on their homeward way, and keeping closely under the shadow of the stone walls look like some bas-relief from the antique. The water still drips from their hair, which falls in heavy masses on the muslin draperies, and a bare arm supports a polished drinking vessel on each woman's shoulder.

The men still remain by the banks of the Ganges, and, seated in the prescribed fashion, complete their preparations before sinking into ecstasy. In honour of Siva they trace lines of dust on their newly laved chests and on their foreheads paint in red the dreadful seal.

There is no burning now in the quarter of the dead, and the walls that surround it look black in the morning light. Two muffled shapes wrapped in shrouds are there, but no one is busied with them. One is already stretched on his funeral pyre, but the other is still taking his last bath in the waters of the Ganges, there amongst so many human beings in the full strength and beauty of life. The hour of prayer is at its full on all the rafts and on the steps leading to the water, and there is no one to light the funeral fires, so the dead must wait.

On every face there is a strange vacant look. I notice eyes which do not see and features that are fixed and rigid. Through the closed fingers of a young man, sunken in mystic contemplation, one can only see the gleaming eyes staring into the other world. There are fakirs covered with beads, whose souls have fled from their heedless bodies, and old men whose limbs are covered with dust.

By the side of the water there is one who prays with upturned eyes. He is seated on the skin of a gazelle, crouching there motionless like a statue of Cakya-Mouni, with crossed legs and knees that touch the ground, the long, bony right hand clasping his right foot. He is old, and the colour of the wet garment glued to his emaciated form tells that he is a yoghi.

Wrapped in a cloth of pale rosy orange, he prays silently : his glassy eyes and livid face on which the seal of Siva has been newly traced stare fixedly at the sun with an expression of ineffable happiness.

By his side stands a young man, who from time to time bends forward to fill his hollowed hands that he may refresh the many flowers strewn round the holy man, or that he may drench the ascetic's flame-coloured robe. That he may dream more sweetly, two smiling boys are posted on the stones above him to play him music. One breathes into a sea-shell, which sighs " hou, hou," like the sound of a far-off horn, the other softly beats a little tom-tom. There are many crows around gazing with interest at the old fakir seated on his gazelle skin, the head and horns of which dip to the river's edge.

Women and children who are going home approach to offer him their greetings and pass with an affectionate smile or a murmured prayer, and then move noiselessly on as though they feared to distract his attention or to disturb his meditations.

I now ascend the river and reach the region of the mysterious palaces. On my return the old man is still there, still holding his bony foot in his emaciated hand. The direction of his gaze has never changed, and the burning rays of the sun cannot dazzle those dimmed eyes which stare into heaven with an expression of beatitude.

" How calm he is ! " I remark.

My boatman looks at me, and smiled as one smiles at a child who has made a foolish remark.

" That man ! Why, he is dead ! "

Oh ! he is dead ! I had not seen the leathern thong which passed under his chin and held his head to a cushion.

I had not observed the crow which flew so near his face, nor had I noticed that the young attendant, stationed there to freshen the jasmine garlands and the flame-coloured robe, often waved a cloth to scare the bird away.

He died yesterday afternoon, and after having bathed him they have piously placed him there in that praying posture, the posture which had always been his in life, so that he may view the full glory of the morning. The head was tied back so tightly in order that he might better see the sun and sky.

He will not be burned, for they never burn the yoghis, their holy lives having freed their bodies from all grossness ! This evening they will place his remains in an earthern vase and then consign them to the Ganges. So these were congratulations that each smiling passer-by offered to the happy saint whose virtues and ethereal nature proclaim that he is for ever freed from reincarnation, and that life and death shall know him no more.

A dog comes near and sniffs, and then slinks away with drooping tail. Three red birds come to look too. A monkey clambers down, just touches the hem of his garment, and then rushes up the stairway, and the young guardian suffers them all to come, only showing impatience towards the crow, whose obstinate return tells of approaching putrefaction. Yet the crow keeps coming back, almost brushing with its black wings the saintly face that is wrapped in the ecstasy of death.

VIII

AT THE BRAHMIN'S HOUSE, CLOSE BY THE GOLDEN TEMPLE

" The Supernatural ? It is quite possible that we have had fakirs who have been able to perform supernatural acts, and there may be such even to-day. But our sages do not favour such methods. No ! We reach our bourne by the road of profound meditation. *It is the only certain way.*"

The man who speaks to me thus is an old man, a Brahmin he is, entitled to be called a Pundit, for he is learned in the Sanskrit tongue and the Sanskrit philosophies, but I see that he has the same disdain for the miraculous as the Masters of the House of Silence.

We are seated on the terrace of the house, round which Benares stretches, and as we talk the growing twilight settles down upon us. The little terrace, which is reached by a stairway leading from the narrow street, is gloomy and secluded. My interpreter, who is a pariah by birth, may not set foot here, so he remains on the topmost step, where his outlines appear in the dusky background. His voice, when he translates, seems to come from afar in the still evening air. Sometimes in the eagerness of explanation he forgets and places his foot on the threshold, whereupon my host, who is neither a Theosophist nor a believer in equality, calls his attention to this breach of the decencies established by a thousand years of practice, and the pariah draws back complacently.

From the terrace little is seen but mouldering walls and myriads of flying crows, save only the one marvel, which rises close at hand from the surrounding ruin and decay, a jewelled dome glittering in the rays of the evening sun. It is the Golden Temple whose pinnacles now swarm with countless parrots.

I often come to visit this venerable Pundit whose house is rich in ancient books and manuscripts, and his dwelling stands in the oldest and most sacred quarter of Benares, far distant from the new districts which have been rendered commonplace by that great leveller, the railway.

The quiet surroundings inspire one's mind as in the olden times. Here is the mystic atmosphere which tells of meditation, and which ever turns the mind to thoughts of death and all that is beyond. The Masters of the still-white house grant that these are sacred, prayer-steeped places : Benares, Mecca, Lhasa, and Jerusalem, where, notwithstanding modern doubt, the carnal bonds are loosened and one is nearer heaven.

Even stately ceremonials and rich temples influence, so they tell us, the soul. Everything has its use. None of these things is indifferent.

IX

AT HAPHAZARD IN BENARES

As I leave the House of the Masters, where, in the silence only broken by the cries of the birds, such strange and new doctrines of eternity have been imparted to me, I am filled with whirling thoughts about the infinite, and cannot call back my mind to earthly scenes.

Yet the Oriental fairyland is ever waiting at the door of the humble dwelling, though it somehow seems to have lost all charm for me.   It may be that an air of mystery and meditation floats through this atmosphere of Benares and strangely alters and dims the fascination of the East.

The labyrinths of little Indian streets and the sculptured or painted houses resemble those of other cities, and everywhere women, lovely as those of Tanagra, pass lightly veiled along the shady narrow streets. Sometimes a sunbeam falls on their metal rings and bracelets, or on their many-hued robes, patterned in silver on a green or golden ground, making them shine luminously.   Then the women resemble the houris of a dream, and should you meet their glance it is as if that look contained all that may be of earthly bliss.

But the fakirs crouched in delirium at the street corners call back the thoughts of prayer and death, and there are innumerable shapeless sacred stones whose age and use have been forgotten, but which may not be touched by hands profane, but only by those of some caste who may touch them or wreathe them with flowers.   In the thicknesses of the walls dismal recesses are hollowed out where, behind iron gratings, the imaged gods are seated, and on every side the stone pyramids of the temples rise into the air.   Herds of gentle sacred cattle wander from morn till night, generally choosing the market-places, and where the crowd stand thickest.   Monkeys, pigeons, crows, and all the birds of the sky sport amidst the people entering their houses and eating with them, and this alone proclaims that this is a foreign land very far removed from ours.

We meet many bridal processions with their accompaniment of plaintive music and bell-hung dancers ; the faces of the bridal pair are hidden by veils of jasmine flowers, which rain down from their hair powdered with gold. Sometimes it is a marriage of the babes, the husband looking not older than five years, and the wife, two or three perhaps. Both are seated in the same litter, and their staid gravity is delightfully droll. Where the husband is older, fifteen or sixteen, he rides a horse, but his face is always hidden behind trailing flowers.

In worldly affairs this Brahmin people have retained their graceful and almost childlike simplicity, but in abstract conception and all the kingdoms of the soul, the meanest Brahmin, garbed in nothing but a loin-cloth, stands far above our pretentious wiseacres, who, passing him, merely deign to puff the smoke of their cigars into his face.

As the Masters of the Sacred House declare, the very atmosphere of Benares seems to contain some essence that lifts us out of ourselves and even those who have only stayed here a little while seem transformed. And yet in all the world there is no pageant so glorious, and matchless forms ever appeal to our bewildered senses, and in no other place does the flesh so loudly summon one from his celestial dreams.

The fearsome goddess Kali, too, has her temple in the sacred city, a dark red temple, red as the colour of the blood for which she is athirst, a temple with stones dabbled with blood and reeking of some recent sacrifice. A noxious smell of monkeys mingles with the odours from the carnage, and blinking eyes look at you from every corner. The monkeys spring upon your shoulders as you enter and thrust their cold, nimble fingers into your pockets, or gently pull your hair. A single family came from the forests long ago to make their home with Kali, but no one dared to drive them forth, so now the temple and the gardens

18

are full of them, and the old intruders have become
the masters, fed with grain and treated with religious
respect by all.

The Golden Temple stands in the very heart of
Benares, carefully hidden amid a maze of narrow
streets.   It is very small and so surrounded that it is
difficult to get a view of it.   Only the dreamers of the
neighbouring terraces and the flying swarms of birds
can see its fabulous domes which are wrought in pure
gold.   As we approach, the labyrinthine streets grow
closer and more tortuous, and idols are scattered everywhere.   I see ruins and filth of all sorts, gold in little
dens, rotting garlands of flowers, carved Lingams of
agate mounted on pedestals and sacred stones that one
dares not touch.

The idol-sellers offer their gods of bronze and marble,
sanctified by being made here, and fakirs, with strange
wild eyes and ghostly features dabbled over with secret
signs, crouch at the street corners.   As you pass they
look up from their fires of crackling wood, and with
hesitating gesture give you their blessing.

An inclosed space, overhung with ruined walls,
serves as a court to the Golden Temple, although it
does not join on to it, and one must plunge into a
dark, narrow lane to find an entrance.

This sacred courtyard is always filled with fakirs,
and it is sacrilege for a stranger to touch anything
here.   Niches closed with gates of fretted bronze are
hollowed out around the walls and in them are rows of
precious polished agates, sacred stones by which the
mysteries of life and death are prefigured.

Cages, as for wild beasts, are filled with fierce divinities, and in the corners, decked with flowers and
fineries, are horrible Ganesas, worn and besmirched
by all the fingerings of the faithful.   Necklaces of faded
flowers strew the ground, mingled with the dust of
centuries and the dung of the sacred cattle, who, having
wandered through the crowds all day, make this their
sleeping-place at night.   Here, too, the pilgrims coming
to the temple congregate, pious hermits from the

surrounding wastes, radiant-faced yoghis in flame-coloured robes, and men crowned with shells and beads, all clustering together under an old granite kiosk. Round them are seated the usual crowd of begging or epileptic fakirs, those loathsome skeletons in which alone the eyes seem to live, and lepers who stretch out fingerless hands for alms. A vague feeling of horror which I am unable to repress comes over me when I see these rigid forms, these faces plastered with cinders or with yellow powder, and I can never forget the look of one old fakir, whose straggling hairs were knotted high above his head.

No unbeliever may ever cross the threshold of the Golden Temple, but there is an ancient house of prayer just opposite the doors across a narrow lane, from which the mad richness of the Golden House is visible, and at sunset and sunrise players of horns and tom-toms sit on the balcony here and serenade the god of death. There are three domes, one of which is of black marble, covered with images of the gods, but the two others are hammered and sculptured from sheets of purest gold. No gilding or other artifice could convey such an impression as these thickly wrought sheets which time cannot tarnish.

Whole flocks of green parrots have built their nests undisturbed amongst the golden leaves and flowers, and, as they flutter by, their colours seem to catch an unnatural lustre from the priceless background.

Nearly all the streets lead to the Ganges, where they grow wider and become less gloomy. Here, suddenly, the magnificent palaces and all the brightness of the day dawn upon us.

These massive tiers of steps, which stretch along the banks and reach to the water's edge even in these times of drought, where fallen temples emerge from their slimy bed, were made in honour of the Ganges, and on each landing there are little granite altars, shaped like niches, in which diminutive gods are placed. These images are like those of the temples, but they are of more massive construction, so as to withstand the swirl of the waters which cover them during the annual rains.

All the life of Benares centres round the river. People come from palaces and jungles to die on its sacred banks, and the old and the sick are brought here by their families to await the end. The relatives never return to their homes in the country after the death has taken place, and so Benares, which already contains three hundred thousand inhabitants, increases rapidly in size. For those who feel their end approaching this is the spot so eagerly desired.

Oh ! to die at Benares. To die on the banks of the Ganges ! To have one's body bathed for the last time, and then to have one's ashes strewn into the river !

X

HESITATION

" *Manas*, soul : in Sanskrit, a radiant matter diffused around us, to which it is impossible to assign those definite limits which pertain to a separate and distinct individuality, irreductibly and for ever distinct."

The sound of these words penetrates through the calm air of the little house, where I am seated on the linen-covered bench in front of my instructress. Her task is to banish from my mind all thoughts of a distinct existence, and to this she returns unrelenting, though with kindness, again and again. Those whom I have loved, my friends, my relatives, myself, all atoms separated but for one instant from the great whole, atoms which when years have run their course will melt into an Eternal and Ineffable Unity. What a clear, sad interpretation of the sweet, vague Gospel words : " One day we shall be returned to the bosom of God."

So it is a delusion that the individuality of those we have loved persists. Their smiles, the expression of their faces, and all the things which distinguish them from others, and which seem the ethereal reflection of their souls, all that we would wish to be imperishable and unchangeable, is but of the passing moment.

For a long time I clung, almost with despair, to our Christian faith, and refused to consider even a doctrine which seemed so pitiless. Lately, at Madras, I once more rejected it in its hard old Buddhist form, but now, the pure faiths which have been taught almost from the beginning of time grow on me day by day, and after passing through realms of terror, which I neither can nor will describe, I feel that here at last I can find peace and consolation.

As the masters had foretold, a growing sense of distance seems to separate me from this world and the memories of my lost ones. I no longer invoke with agony those who have left me. Doubtless they still exist, freed from the earthly trammels of their personality. Yet I accept the idea of that far-distant meeting, that melting into them which will not be to-morrow, but after centuries—the length of which our ephemeral nature cannot conceive.

I know that this mood is but a passing one, and that when I have left this place the world will claim me once more, but never again in the old way, for the seed sown in my soul will grow, and Benares will call me back.

How empty, pitiable, and vain my past in life has been ; I, who doted on the world's array of changing forms and colours, and but sought to pass the things that pass away.

It grows dusk as I leave the Masters' House, and all the charm of the East awaits me with its lures. In aimless wanderings I happen to light upon the quarter of the bayadères and courtesans. Lights kindle in all the upper floors of the houses, where by day muslin-sellers display their rich gold-spangled wares. A whole street is occupied by these creatures of night and shade, now appearing at the windows or on the balconies, adorned for the evening. Their rooms, decorated with mirrors and many childish baubles, are brilliantly lighted up, and on the whitewashed walls images of Ganesa, Hanouman, and the bloody Kali may be seen. Rings and gems shine from their ears and naked arms, and necklaces of heavy-scented flowers fall in rows upon their breasts. They have the same velvety eyes as those daughters of Brahma who unveil themselves each morning by the Ganges, and it may be the same flesh of bronze and amber.

XI

A BENCH ON WHICH BUDDHA SAT

To-day my friend the Pundit takes me into the country to see a bench on which Buddha used to sit, and on our way there we converse about the hidden things.

Barley and corn grow in the peaceful and lonely country round Benares, and were it not that ripe harvests and green trees are to be seen here in February, I might fancy that this was France. Shepherds watching their zebus, bulls, and goats, play on pipe and reed. By the woodside there are the sacred stones on which pious peasants have placed yellow wreaths, stones which long ago may have represented Ganesa or Vishnu, for some resemblance is still visible. Birds of gorgeous colours, some turquoise blue, some emerald green with scarlet crests, hop near us, fearless of the men who never slay. A tranquil calm seems to hover over all this land. Heaps of ruins and tombs almost buried under trees and roots of trees lie scattered around, and over them lowly villages have been built, whose roofs are those of the old cemeteries or temples. Monasteries built when Buddhism was at its height, which were transformed into mosques when Islam swept the land and then abandoned when the Brahmin faith resumed its sway, and tombs of fakirs, warriors, or dervishes, all lie in confused masses under the bluish shade of banyan or of mango trees. Some large stones bear on their several sides the signs of diverse faiths; here Buddha's lotus, there some verses from the Koran.

The occupants of the little huts built upon the ruins follow the ancient trade, weaving sashes, whose silken threads are stretched over old graveyards, or dyeing muslins, which they spread out to dry over the doorways of the ancient temples in sunny places where the lizards sport.

The spot which forms the object of our pilgrimage is still far distant. On our way we pass a cart drawn by zebus. It is filled with children, and is led by an old wizard of a man, who reminds me of the bogey of the fairy-tale.

There are at least twenty boys and girls, some five or six years old. Their heads are to be seen everywhere ; some peep through the open sides, and others stick out under the awning which they have raised. All these children are decked with jewels, necklaces, and nose-rings, and wear their best clothes and tall, spangle-covered caps. Their eyelids have been rimmed with black, not, I am told, out of vanity, but to avert the glance which some evil witch might cast on them. The good-natured old bogey who leads the team has a long white beard like a river god, and his naked breast is covered with gray hairs like the fur of a polar bear. Where is he taking these babies to ? Doubtless to some childish festival, for they look so happy and gay in their holiday finery.

Now that we are in the heart of the country our carriage is useless, so we must cross the sunny plains afoot. At last we reach the goal of our journey, and see that it stands in the centre of a stony dell, over-hung with grayish rocks that look like ruins. Here goats nibble the short grass, while shepherds make music with their pipes.

An old bench of blackened stone stands under a shady tree, which might be mistaken for our oaks, and the Pundit and I seat ourselves reverently, for this is the place where Buddha sat more than two thousand years ago, the place where he preached his first sermon. The Buddhist faith, which is still the creed of the far East, has long departed from these lands, and Indians no longer come to this once hallowed spot. In spite of its forlorn appearance, this old bench is still the spot round which millions of human thoughts revolve, and the unfathomable intellects of countless yellow men, living either in the heart of China, the islands of Japan, or the dark forests of Siam, dream of the holy place, and sometimes pilgrims cross the many intervening miles merely to kneel and kiss this ancient bench. Here in the exquisite silence of this pastoral spot the Pundit and I talk of the tenets of the Brahmin faith.

Close by the seat from which Buddha preached his doctrine of cold wisdom a huge rounded granite tower rises. It, in its day, was much covered with sculpturings, but the two thousand years which have passed over its head have worn away the carvings, and filled the chinks with grass and weeds. These are the remains of the first Buddhist temple. This is the place where Benares once stood. At about a man's height from the ground the rough stones and projections are gilded, and this gives a strange and unexpected appearance to so old a monument. It appears that whenever Chinese, Annamites, or Burmese pilgrims realize their dream, and at last journey to the seat and tower, they bring these gold leaves with them from their far-off lands and nail them up as tokens of respect—one might almost say in guise of visiting cards—to the forsaken sanctuary.

As we return to Benares, at the close of the day, my companion stops our carriage at the country house of one of his friends, a noble Brahmin, learned like himself in philosophy and Sanskrit. They offer me fruits and fresh water, but, I need not say, do not eat of the food rendered impure by my presence. The old dwelling is exquisite. The garden, too, has straight walks, edged with a plant which resembles box, and water-basins with fountains in the old French style. Our marguerites, nasturtiums, and roses grow here too, and, although the winter has robbed some trees of their foliage, the flowers, the warm air, and the yellowy leaves give the impression of a lingering summer, or maybe of a dying autumn, an autumn whose end has been hastened on by too much sun and drought too long.

XII

WHAT THE MASTERS AT BENARES THINK OF CHRISTIANITY

" If you are a Christian," say the sages of Benares, " cling fast to the faith you have, and do not seek further. Christianity is a beautiful symbol, marvellously adapted to the Western mode of thought, and the germs of truth are hidden in it. You have in Christ a divine and ever-living master, for there is no death: only the life here and the life eternal, and the expectation of those who die in Him will not be unfulfilled.

" But if your reason cannot accept the teachings of Christ and ' the letter which kills,' then, and then only, come to us. If the path of prayer and devotion is closed to you, we will show you the more difficult way of abstract knowledge. Yet, after countless ages, both roads meet, and end at the same bourne."

" Prayer," they say on another occasion, " cannot perhaps influence the daily events of our lives, but for the development and consolation of our souls it is supreme."

" We cannot think that the great God, ' the One whose Name may not be spoken,' listens to the prayers of men."

" But the astral sphere is peopled by beneficent beings, individualized particles of Him, who watch us from afar. Christians ! call on Jesus, and never doubt He and those who live in Him are there, and that you will be heard."

XIII

ANOTHER MORNING

The morning air of Benares is fresh and dewy. They call it winter here, but it is a winter which resembles one of our fine October days.

At daybreak I make my way to the river from the far-off suburb where I live, and on the road I pass country market-folk hastening to the town, wrapped to the eyes in muslins and cashmeres as though the cold were great. They carry jars of cream and baskets of rice cakes suspended from sticks which are slung over their shoulders ; flowers too, whole hampers of flowers, always the same jasmine garlands and yellow marigolds, offerings to old Ganges, whither the people flock each morning.

I reach the top of the steps, but before descending pause by an old kiosk where a fakir has lived for more than thirty years, tending a little fire lit on the ground by his fakir predecessors more than a thousand years ago. He is old and fleshless, and his long hair is knotted into a roll upon his head, and his naked body is covered with ashes. After throwing a jasmine collar round my neck he glances at me for an instant with eyes that have a far-off look. Then, with a gesture which gently bids me sit and meditate, he smiles and sinks gently back into the land of dreams.

Before us, framed in by the ancient columns of the little shelter, lies the Ganges, the opposite shore and the still flat plains yet wrapped in the mists of night, out of which the great enchanter, the sun, slowly rises.

From a neighbouring kiosk, which also overhangs the river, the morning serenade to the Ganges and all the gods of Benares commences. I can see the long horns pointing towards the east through the sculptured pillars, and can distinguish their howls, which are those of a monster at bay, and the sullen and hollow roar of the tom-toms that are being beaten inside.

Following the general custom, I go each morning to the river where my boat awaits me. First we pass the place of the funeral pyres, and as it is several days since the plague broke out, there is only one corpse there. It is lying on the shore, plunged half into the water, taking its last bath. Many must have been cremated in the night, however, for smoking embers fill the burning ghat, and under the flowers the water is all blackened by the human embers that float past mingled with filth and rubbish. The young fakir who watches the dead stands motionless, with crossed arms and sunken head powdered with dust ; he resembles some Grecian bronze newly unearthed, save that his long hair is dyed, and that he wears a jasmine crown. Carcasses of drowned cattle and dead dogs float amongst the flowers, and the Ganges diffuses a faint sickly smell into the limpid air, speaking of death even in the rosy hues of the enchanted morning.

I feel that spring is near and even the traces of winter which I had noticed at first seem to have vanished. I feel a languor in the morning air, and it may be that the river has felt it too, for the long-haired bathers, whose breasts are hidden in fine muslins, seem to tarry longer. The winged bathers come in crowds, and sparrows, pigeons, and birds of all colours swarm among the praying Brahmins, alighting on their shining drinking-vessels or amongst the flowers. Some cling to the boat ropes and sing at the top of their voices. The sacred cattle are more indolent, and lie sunning themselves at the foot of the steps, where children come and caress them, bringing bunches of fresh-cut grass and handfuls of green and juicy reeds.

All the worshippers of Benares are assembled on the banks, and as ever nude, bronze forms of Indians, nobly born, throng the huge steps lining the shore or seek the shelter of the strange expanded umbrellas ; and even the niches of granite, in which six-armed gods dwell, and the rafts that lie in the full glare of the sun, teem with men.

I am the only man by the riverside who does not pray. All the others at least perform the sacred rites, ablutions, obeisances, and offerings of white and yellow flowers.

The morning prayer ascends from all the rafts and landing-places ; but I have no place among the faithful, who look scornfully at me or feign to ignore my presence, taking me to be one of the tourists who, now that the journey has been made so easy, flock here in great numbers.

But I am no longer the same as I used to be, and the hours spent in the House of the Masters have left an impression on me which I think will never fade. I have crossed the terrors of the threshold and can see what place awaits me. Everything around me has changed : life and even death in the new and different light which the Masters have thrown on the Life Eternal.

And yet " the illusions of this world," as the sages call them, have a hold upon me still. Those feelings of supreme detachment and renunciation of all that is earthly and transitory, which they have instilled into me, grow in my soul ; but I know no place where the spiritual and the fleshly so mingle as at Benares. Here people think of prayer and death, yet the lights, the colours, the young women, whose damp veils but half conceal their charms, and the incomparable displays of Indian beauty, lurk on every side to trap the senses.

My boatmen, needing no instructions, row up the river to the lonely quarter of the old palaces. I am to return this afternoon to the Masters' House, not indeed without dread, though their teachings, which at first shocked me, gain hourly upon my attention. I am no more what I used to be, and it seems as if they had taken possession of my inmost soul, that they might fuse it into that soul which is the Essence of the Universe.

" You can only desire," the sages say, " that which is different from yourself, that which you have not ; and did you but know that the things you seek are within you, for the Essence of all things is within you, then desire would melt away."

" You are a part of a Godlike spirit, from which all truth and beauty radiates, and could you but engrave this truth upon your heart, those narrow and mistaken views from which suffering and sadness and the desire to be a separate entity arise would of themselves fall from you."

We pass by old mysterious palaces, but there are no women by the river's edge, wringing the water from their dripping hair, nor is there any one on the stairs, or at the foot of the high and dismal walls. Suddenly, however, the heavily barred door in the basement of one of the princely dwellings—a door which must be submerged in the rainy season—is thrown open and a young woman appears in the bright sunshine, in radiant contrast to the sombre granite background. She is covered after the fashion of the Roman woman, with two veils which fall from her head—one of violet edged with silver, the other of an orange hue. She looks across at the barren plain on the opposite bank of the river, and her bare arm is raised so that she may shade her large eyes, those Indian eyes, whose charm is undescribable. The violet and yellow muslins serve to accentuate the matchless lines and harmonious curves of her young body.

She is I and I am She, and we are part of one God-like Whole, the sages tell me, and it feels as if already I felt their serenity growing upon me.

I look for a while at the woman standing there without regret or troubled feelings, resting my eyes upon her as on a young sister of whose beauty I am proud. A feeling of brotherhood links us together, and the splendour of the morning seems to unite us. We are the sun, the ever-changing fantasy of nature, the Universal Soul.

Can it be that the delusion from which the desire to be a separate entity springs has already fallen from me ?

XIV

TO MY UNKNOWN BROTHERS

I have taken the simple oath required of me, and the Masters of the little House of Silence have made me one of their disciples.

I shall not attempt to repeat what they have commenced to teach me, for I am not sure that any one would care to follow me so far out of my usual course.

I know well that it is only expected of me that I

should speak of the trifling events of my journey, and catch the glint of passing things.

And how, too, after but a few days of initiation, could I think myself capable of teaching ? The little that I could tell might unbalance or even lead to the terrors of the threshold, but no further.

And I do not claim to have discovered the Vedas any more than I claim to have discovered India. Imperfect translations of these wonderful works have long been amongst us.

I only wish to tell my unknown brothers, and in this present age I have many, that more consolation resides in the Vedic doctrines than they might at first suppose, and the consolation offered there cannot be destroyed by reasoning like that of the revealed religions.

This collection of the Vedas is not the work of one man, but of a whole race ; and one finds contradictions, obscurities, and even childish inanities by the side of passages that are supremely marvellous. The Masters at Benares, who study these writings, inextricable as a jungle and bottomless as the sea, are, I think, the only men who can explain their meaning. None else had disclosed such abysmal depths, and I have never heard such words on life and death. They alone can give answers which will satisfy the burning questionings of the human mind, and such evidence is brought before you that it is impossible to doubt the continuance of life beyond the terrestrial sphere.

But the lonely little whitewashed house, standing in its rose garden, must not be approached too lightly, for here renunciation and death have their abode. Peace reigns within, but should it touch you for a single moment, you can never be your old self again, and it is a fearful ordeal to see, even dimly and from afar, Brahm the Absolute—He Who dwells afar, Who sits apart from earthly strife ; Brahm, the ineffable— He of Whom we cannot even think, and of Whom no words may ever be spoken, and Whose nature may only be expressed by Silence.

INDEX

19